The Koran
with decorations by
Valenti Angelo

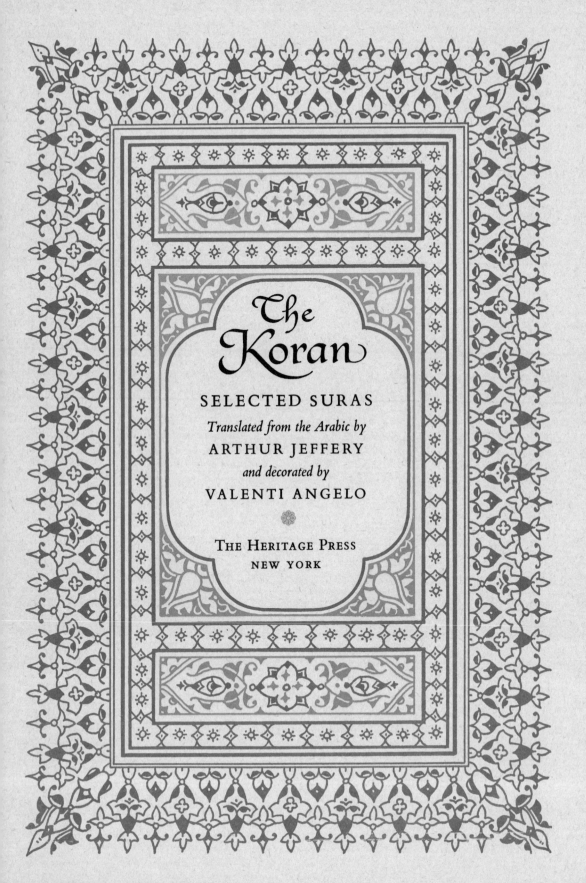

The Koran

SELECTED SURAS

Translated from the Arabic by

ARTHUR JEFFERY

and decorated by

VALENTI ANGELO

❋

THE HERITAGE PRESS

NEW YORK

Table of Contents

Middle Meccan Suras

Late Meccan Suras

Medinan Suras

The Closers

Al-Mu'awwidhatan: The Two Refuge Charms

Index of Suras

Introduction

THE KORAN (or, to use a more exact transliteration, Qur'an) is the sacred Scripture of the religion of Islam. It consists of material given out as revelation by Mohammed, the Prophet of Islam, during the years of his mission among his people in seventh-century Arabia, and gathered together for publication by his followers not long after his death.

Mohammed (properly Muhammad) was the child of humble and poor though honourable citizens of Mecca, and lived most of his life in that pagan city which was ruled by the merchant aristocracy of the Koreish tribe. The date of his birth is not known. It seems that his father died before Mohammed was born and his weakly mother not long thereafter, so that he was brought up by an uncle. The latter's son Ali became one of the Prophet's earliest converts, the husband of Mohammed's daughter Fatima, and a prominent figure in early Islam, coming ultimately to be regarded as the first of the Shi'ite Imams as opposed to the Caliphs of orthodox Sunnite Islam.

In his youth Mohammed seems to have worked, at least for a time, as a herdsman, and he may have gone as an attendant on some of his uncle's caravan journeys with merchandise to the market towns in the northwest of Arabia. Most of the stories that have come down to us about his early years, however, belong to the realm of legend, not to that of fact.

Mecca's wealth came from its caravans, which moved annually to the north and to the south along the great Spice Road that had been travelled from antiquity. But Mecca possessed also a famous shrine of the old Arabian Mother Goddess, which made it a centre of pilgrimage where worshippers congregated annually from all parts of the country. Its shrine, the Kaaba, was said to contain idols reverenced by all the various tribes of Arabia. It was in the midst of this merchant activity and pagan idolatry that the future Prophet grew up.

In his early manhood Mohammed was recommended to a wealthy widow among the Koreish (Quraish, to be precise) as a trusty man to direct her interests in the caravans to the north, and his success in this enterprise led to her meeting him and marrying him. This widow, Khadija, many years the Prophet's senior, was the mother of all his children save the son, Ibrahim, whom he had by the Coptic slave-girl Miriam. It was only after Khadija's death that Mohammed began to expand his harem. All his sons died in childhood, but daughters survived him.

Apparently Mohammed had been religiously inclined from youth. There is no reason to doubt his interest in the various seekers for monotheism in his contemporary Arab world, the men whom later tradition calls the Hanifs. Nor is there any question that he was greatly impressed by what he saw, within and without Mecca, of the religion of the Jews and Christians, the People of the Book.

Somewhere around his fortieth year he went through a crisis of religious experience. From the vague references to it in the Koran and the confused accounts we have in tradition we can gain no clear idea of the nature of this experience save that it included a vision of, or from, his Lord. From it, however, he emerged with a tremendous conviction of the truth of the monotheism being preached all around him, and of his own call to preach to his people what he considered to be the essential message of the Scripture of these monotheistic People of the Book. From then on till his death, Mohammed's life was dedicated to the fulfilment of this mission.

At first the Meccans were only mildly amused by his preaching. His early pronouncements in rhymed prose were so like those of their own soothsayers that they called him a soothsayer (kahin), a crazed poet, one ensorcelled or jinn-possessed. His early converts were from his own domestic circle and friends, and then from certain of the poorer elements in the city. Mohammed seems to have had great hopes that the Jews and Christians would recognize him and accept him, and was bitterly disappointed at their persistent rejection of his claim to be in the prophetic succession. As his following grew and the Meccan leaders became more conscious of the threat to their position involved in his attacks on the idolatrous worship at their sanctuary and his championship of the underprivileged, they took steps to silence him. Pious legend later exaggerated greatly this "persecution" of the Prophet and his followers, but there undoubtedly was some persecution, as a consequence of which he urged certain of his followers to emigrate and seek refuge with the Christian ruler of Abyssinia, where they were kindly received.

Rumour that Mohammed had weakened and made a compromise with the Meccan leaders, brought many of these emigrants back home. The Prophet was conscious, however, that his position in Mecca was becoming impossible, and he seems to have made unsuccessful attempts to find a more promising locale for his mission at Ta'if and other places. Some citizens of Yathrib, a place on the Spice Road some miles north of Mecca, who had come to the city for the annual pilgrimage ceremonies at the Kaaba, took notice of him, and on their return home suggested to various leaders there that Mohammed might be the solution for their local problem.

Yathrib was a city with a large and important Jewish population, where the people were fairly well acquainted with the kind of Biblical doctrine Mohammed was preaching. They were, however, plagued by a long-standing community conflict between their two main Arab groups, a conflict which had reached an impasse. It is clear that the visitors from Yathrib must have discerned the political sagacity of the Prophet, a sagacity which showed up remarkably in later years, and at the next pilgrimage season a group from Yathrib extended to him an invitation to come and make their city the centre of his mission. As the opposition in Mecca became sharper, Mohammed in 622 made his famous "Flight," or Hegira (more accurately hijra), *from Mecca to Yathrib, which thus became "the Prophet's city"* (Madinat an-Nabi), *familiar to us as Medina.*

In Medina there were from then on three main parties: the Ansar, or helpers, who had invited the Prophet and pledged themselves to stand by him; the Arabs who had to accept his position as leader there but more or less resented it, and whom he calls the Munafiqun, or hypocrites; and the People of the Book, who in this city were mainly Jews. Numbers of his followers now emigrated from Mecca to join him in Medina, and these emigrants (Muhajirun) took their place alongside the Ansar.

From now on, Mohammed's mission reflects his growing concern with elaborating his religion and developing his community, and with maintaining his claims against those—among both the pagans and the People of the Book—who rejected his prophetic pretensions. To provide for his impoverished followers, and also to weaken his Meccan enemies, he organized from Medina raids on their caravans. This led to the famous battle of Badr in 624 (or 2 A.H.; A.H.=Anno Hegirae), which he won; the battle of Uhud in 3 A.H., which he lost; the battle of the Ditch in 5 A.H., when the Meccans vainly attempted to besiege Medina; the Truce of Hudaibiyya in 6 A.H., and the battle of Hunain in 8 A.H.

At Hudaibiyya he had secured a truce with the Meccans, but it quickly became apparent to Mohammed that he must be master of Mecca. In the first place his alliances with various surrounding Arab tribes, and even his position in Medina, were insecure so long as the Koreish held that key city. That was the political factor. Secondly, his failure to win acceptance by the Jews and Christians had led him to outmanoeuvre their position by claiming to be the restorer of the religion of Abraham from which both Judaism and Christianity had sprung. Centuries earlier than his time the idea had spread in Arabia that the Arabs were descended from Ishmael. Mohammed now therefore claimed Abraham as a Hanif, and linked the Abraham and Ishmael story with the Kaaba at Mecca, which made it religiously necessary for him to be master of that city. A technical breach of the treaty was the pretext for attack, and in 8 A.H. Mecca had to submit.

Once he was master of Mecca the Prophet's major concern was legislation for his growing community. There were still expeditions to be organized and sent, there was still controversy with his opponents, but he was more and more occupied with problems of organizing the cult, regulating prayer, almsgiving, fasting, pilgrimage, issuing rules for guidance on questions of marriage, divorce, inheritance, and similar matters of importance for a community which looked to him for instruction. He continued to live in Medina, where he finally succeeded in crushing and then expelling the Jews, and where he received delegations from the Arab tribes now coming in to acknowledge the undoubted master of Arabia. The chieftains in the north, however, many of whom were Christianized and under Byzantine influence, remained obdurate. Mohammed was busy with plans for subduing them when he sickened and died in the house of his girl-wife Ayesha (A'ishah) in 10 A.H. = 632 A.D.

In Mohammed's preaching his early utterances were apparently hardly to be distinguished from those of the local Arabian soothsayers. They were delivered in a rhythmical, rhymed prose, in short and at times obscure sentences, with a fondness for strange words. What distinguished them was their subject matter, which was concerned with the power and wonder of God in His creation, the wickedness and perversity of man, and the imminence of the dreadful Day of Doom. As his mission progresses the ethical content of the Prophet's message increases; but though he knows about and is interested in the religion of the People of the Book, he knows but little of their Scripture, and is mostly impressed by the stories of past peoples who rejected the messengers sent to them and on whom fell awful disaster.

His acquaintance with the content of Scripture increased gradually, so that material therefrom comes to be woven more and more into his discourses, though he cannot distinguish genuine Scriptural material from that of Midrash and apocryphal legend, and he feels able to claim that he is setting forth in plain Arabic the essential message of the older religions. This is why the Western reader meets in the Koran so many familiar figures—Adam and Noah, Abraham, Isaac, and Jacob, Joseph and Job, Moses and Aaron, David and Solomon, Jesus and John the Baptist—and finds so much there about familiar religious concepts, about God and man, about angels and demons, about sin and salvation, about Paradise and Hell.

Mohammed called his messages Qur'an, which is an adaptation of the Syriac word for a Scripture lesson. Sura, as he uses it, means practically the same thing. In his later years he was engaged in preparing much of this material to be used as a Book (Kitab) which would be for his community what the Old Testament (which he called the Torah) was for the Jews, and the New Testament (which he called the Injil) was for the Christians. On the basis of Sura 7, where he refers to himself as an ummi Prophet, Moslem orthodoxy has insisted that Mohammed could neither read nor write. Western scholarship has always doubted this, there being too many little indications in the Koran itself that he could write, and in recent years both Bell of Edinburgh and Torrey of Yale have independently seen that by the application of the principles of "Higher Criticism" to the Koran it becomes quite evident that Mohammed had been gathering, recasting, and revising in written form the material he planned to issue as his Book. Early tradition says that the Prophet's public utterances were for the most part quite short, seldom more than five to ten verses, and it is remarkable how this "Higher Criticism," as may be seen in Bell's translation, shows that the material being worked up for the Book consisted for the most part of small pieces fitted together.

The Prophet, however, died before he had issued the Book. The early community does not seem at first to have felt the need of it, but as those who knew by heart much of what they had learned thereof from the Prophet began to die off, the need for collecting the material became urgent. Several individuals made personal collections in codex form, but it was the Caliph Uthman (23-35 A.H.) who made the official recension of the material that has come down to us as the Koran.

The form in which we have it—comprising one hundred and eleven Suras arranged with the longest first and the shortest last, preceded by an opening prayer and concluded by two little charms—is that given it by the Committee to whom Uthman committed the task of making a recension. Doubtless they used the Prophet's own collection of material as a basis, though arranging it as they saw best, and adding other material that came to them where it seemed appropriate. That this recension contains all the pronouncements of the Prophet may be doubted, for many passages are obviously but fragments whose context is now lost. That all it contains is genuinely from the Prophet is fairly certain, for very few passages are of doubtful authenticity. That it contains a good deal that the Prophet himself would not have included had he lived to issue his Book is also certain. We are thankful, however, that Uthman's Committee had such reverence for the Prophet's words that they omitted nothing they were sure came from him.

Mohammed's own theory of Scripture was derived from legendary ideas common among the Jews and Christians of those days, which held that there was a heavenly archetype of Scripture from which portions were delivered to various Prophets by angelic messengers. So we find him referring to the "Mother of the Book," to the sending down of revelation from Allah through the angel Gabriel, and to the idea that, since all Scripture is from the same heavenly original, his message will be found also in the Books of the Jews and the Christians. When Moslems later came to know the contents of the Old and New Testaments and found that they by no means agreed with Mohammed's message, this was proof to them that the Jews and the Christians had altered their Scriptures. The Prophet seems also to have learned, perhaps from some Gnostic source, the idea that there had been a regular succession of Prophets from Adam onwards, and so was able to think of himself, as Mani had done at an earlier time, as the promised successor to Jesus.

Moslem orthodoxy has developed its own doctrine of Scripture, according to which each Prophet in turn had revealed to him by Gabriel from the heavenly archetype such material as was necessary for his situation in his generation. When a new Prophet was sent, his revelation abrogated that of his predecessor, though all that was still relevant and useful in that previous revelation was continued in the new revelation of God's mind and will and purpose for mankind.

When Mohammed was called to his mission, Gabriel, over some twenty and more years, revealed to him piecemeal what was to be his Book. As soon as any portion was revealed, Mohammed had his amanuenses write it down, and once a year Gabriel would come and collate with him this written material, comparing it with the heavenly original to see that it was quite correct. On the last year of the Prophet's life they so collated it twice. Thus when the Prophet died the whole of the material was written out in its final form, properly collated, and ready for publication.

The first Caliph, Abu Bakr, made a first recension of this. Then the third Caliph, Uthman, made a second and final recension, and all that has been added to the text since then has been the pointing, vowelling, punctuation, and aids to reading, about which there are small differences among the Schools. This, naturally, is not a doctrine likely to find favour with critical scholarship, which can see clearly the growth of the material in Mohammed's mind, knows something about the various recensions which preceded Uthman's, and is conscious of the textual problems presented by the Koran as we have it. What is of the greatest importance, however, is that this orthodox theory, taking the material as literally the words of Allah, of which Mohammed was only the mouthpiece, has developed a doctrine of I'jaz, i.e. of the miraculous nature of the Koran, a doctrine which has influenced profoundly every branch of Islamic learning.

One consequence of this doctrine is the strongly entrenched notion that the Koran cannot be translated. Since it was dictated to the Prophet in Arabic it follows that Arabic must be the heavenly language, so the Book must always be recited in that language, and must inevitably lose something when translated into any other tongue. There has thus been very strong opposition in orthodox circles to the appearance of translations. Translations have been made by Moslems into Persian, Turkish, Urdu, and other eastern languages, and in more recent times also into some western languages, but almost always accompanied by the Arabic text, and frequently not called translations but rather paraphrases of the meaning. Even to these there has been vigorous opposition. Serious objection was raised to Mustafa Kemal Ataturk's official Turkish translation, and when an enlightened Rector of the Azhar in Egypt appointed a Committee to plan translations of the Koran into modern western languages he was met by a storm of bitter denunciation in the Arabic press. Translations by non-Moslems, it goes without saying, are anathema.

We hear of Latin translations being made as early as the twelfth century, and today translations are available in all the major European languages. The earliest English translation was made in 1649 by Alexander Ross from the French of André du Ryer, who had been French Consul in Alexandria and in 1647 produced his version at Paris. Ross's work, being an indifferent translation of an inadequate version, had little to recommend it, yet it went through several editions and was reprinted in America in 1806:

Printed by Henry Brewer,
for ISAIAH THOMAS, Jun.
Sold by him at his respective Stores in Springfield and
Worcester; by Thomas & Whipple, Newburyport,
and by Thomas & Tappan, Portsmouth.

Ross's attitude to his subject is evident from his "Needful Caveat" addressed by the translator to the Christian reader:

"Good Reader, the great Arabian Impostor now at last after a thousand years is by way of France arrived in England, and his *Alcoran* or Gallimaufry of Errors, (a brat as deformed as the parent, and as full of heresies as his scald head was full of scurffe), hath learned to speak English. I suppose this piece is exposed by the Translator to the publicke view no otherwise than some monster brought out of Africa, for people to gaze, not to dote upon; and, as the sight of a monster, or misshapen creature, should induce the beholder to praise God, Who hath not made him such; so should the reading of this *Alcoran* excite us both to bless God's goodness towards us in this land, who injoy the glorious light of the Gospell, and behold the truth in the beauty of holinesse, who suffers so many Countreyes to be blinded and inslaved with this misshapen issue of Mohamets braine; being brought forth by the help of no other midwifery than of a Jew and a Nestorian, making use of a tame pigeon (which he had taught to pick corn out of his ears) instead of the Holy Ghost, and causing silly people to believe that in his falling sickness (to which he was much subject) he had conference with the Angell Gabriel."

The most famous of all the English translations is that made by George Sale in 1734, which has gone through some thirty editions in England (the latest, edited by Sir Denison Ross, in 1929) and several in America, beginning with that printed by Thomas Wardle at Philadelphia in 1833. It was Sale's version which, with explanatory notes by Fred Myron Cooper, was issued in the Home Library at Boston in 1900. It was translated into German by Theodor Arnold (Lemgo, 1746), into Russian by Kolmakov (St.

Petersburg, 1792), and into Bulgarian by Litza (Philippopolis, 1902). Sale was largely dependent on the Latin version of Ludovico Marrucci (Patavii, 1698), and prefaced his translation by a "Preliminary Discourse" which still repays reading, and which, indeed, has been reprinted as a separate work, and translated into Dutch (Amsterdam, 1742), French (Geneva, 1751; Algiers, 1846), Swedish (Stockholm, 1814), and Arabic (Cairo, 1891). Rodwell's translation, so well known because of its issue in Everyman's Library, was first published in 1861. A new translation was made by E. H. Palmer in 1880 for Max Müller's Sacred Books of the East, and in 1928 this was reissued in the World's Classics. In some ways Palmer preserves better than his predecessors the flavour and the crudeness of the Arabic original, but his work was done in great haste and is disfigured by numerous oversights and omissions.

There have been many translations into English by Indian Moslems, notably by Abdul Hakim Khan (Patiala, 1905), Mirza Abu'l-Fazl (Allahabad, 1911), Muhammad Ali (Lahore, 1916), Ghulam Sarwar (Singapore, 1930), Yusuf Ali (Lahore, 1934), and by the English convert to Islam, Marmaduke Pickthall (London, 1930). This latter, unfortunately, has been reprinted in a cheap edition in this country and widely circulated. It, like the Indian translations, is a tendentious propaganda work which should be avoided. More recently have appeared The Qur'an Interpreted, (2 vols. London, 1955), by A. J. Arberry, and The Koran, a New Translation by N. J. Dawood (London, 1956) in the Penguin Classics. The most satisfactory translation in English, from the point of view of modern scholarship, is Richard Bell's The Qur'an, Translated with a Critical Rearrangement of the Surahs (2 vols., Edinburgh, 1937-39). For readers of French there is the even more up-to-date work of Régis Blachère, Le Coran, Traduction Nouvelle (2 vols., Paris, 1949-50).

Since the initiation of modern critical study of the Koran by

Gustav Weil's Historisch-kritische Einleitung in den Koran *(Bielefeld, 1844; 2nd ed., 1872), and Theodor Nöldeke's epoch-making* Geschichte des Qorans *(Göttingen, 1860), it has been customary to recognize four periods in the composition of the Koran, and to mark out passages which belong to the Early Meccan, Middle Meccan, Late Meccan, and Medinan periods. Nöldeke gave in detail the criteria by which it is possible to distinguish material coming from each of these periods, and gave a list of the Suras to be assigned to each. This chronological arrangement has been followed for the most part by Rodwell in his translation.*

The difficulty, however, is that almost all the Suras as we have them are composite. The Moslem exegetes themselves were well aware that both Meccan and Medinan material was included in many Suras, and note this fact. Recent investigation has shown that we must advance beyond the position of Nöldeke and recognize that much that had been classified as Meccan is really Medinan, and that a good deal of the Meccan material was worked over by the Prophet during the Medinan period.

In presenting this selection of material from the Koran for The Heritage Press, it seemed appropriate to select passages illustrating Mohammed's teaching as it developed from the rhapsodic style of his pronouncements in the Early Meccan period, when he was primarily a preacher, through the Middle and Late Meccan periods, where the poetic fire gradually dies down, to the prosaic legislative material of the Medinan period. Objections can, of course, always be brought against any selection that may be made, but it is hoped that the selections here offered present a fair sampling of the material and give the reader an adequate understanding of the message of the Book. To this end it has been necessary in translating to make at times a compromise between what critical scholarship would regard as the correct meaning of a passage, and what Moslem orthodoxy takes the passage to mean. As the translator worked over the whole of this material in detail with Dr. Bell in Edinburgh in the 1920s, it was inevitable that this work should be in many places influenced by that fine scholar's interpretation and renderings. As for English style, it has seemed wiser to sacrifice it in an attempt to convey some feeling of the Prophet's awkwardness of expression.

The notes to the translation have been reduced to the barest minimum, and are perhaps too few, for to readers unacquainted with the background of Oriental religions the bare rendering of a text into English is often quite inadequate. Words have been added to the original where necessary to make readable English sentences. Explanatory additions within the text are marked off by square brackets: [   ]. Biblical names are given in their familiar forms; and the eighteenth-century spellings of the better-known Arabic names are retained, despite their inaccuracy, in order not to dismay the casual reader. Other Arabic names are transliterated.

Most renderings of the Koran preserve the original verse form, which grew out of the rhythm of the Arabic language but becomes meaningless in translation. In this edition, for the sake of ease in reading, the verse form has been dropped; we have, however, retained the capital letter which marked the beginning of each verse.

Arabic, being an Oriental language, has a phonetic system very different from ours, and for that reason scholarly works use diacritical marks to indicate as accurately as possible the pronunciation of the words. It is very important, for example, to distinguish between long and short vowels, and so we find $\bar{a}$, $\bar{i}$, $\bar{u}$, used beside a, i, u. Moreover Arabic has more consonants than we have in our language, and so ' and ' are used to represent the Hamza and the 'Ain, while a distinction is kept between s and ṣ, z and ẓ, t and ṭ, d and ḍ, h and ḥ. These diacritical marks have been omitted here, not as a slighting of scholarship, but to ease matters in a work intended for the general reader.

ARTHUR JEFFERY

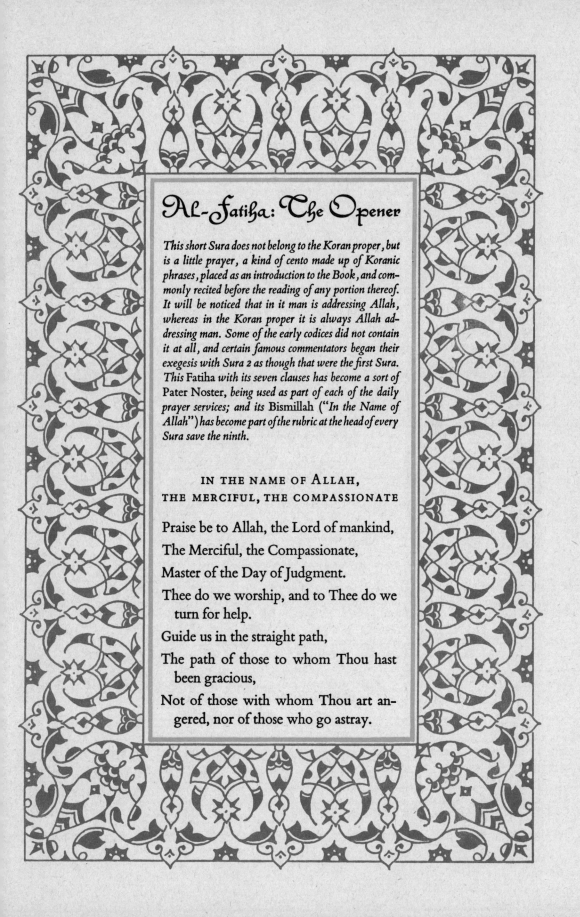

Al-Fatiha: The Opener

This short Sura does not belong to the Koran proper, but is a little prayer, a kind of cento made up of Koranic phrases, placed as an introduction to the Book, and commonly recited before the reading of any portion thereof. It will be noticed that in it man is addressing Allah, whereas in the Koran proper it is always Allah addressing man. Some of the early codices did not contain it at all, and certain famous commentators began their exegesis with Sura 2 as though that were the first Sura. This Fatiha with its seven clauses has become a sort of Pater Noster, being used as part of each of the daily prayer services; and its Bismillah ("In the Name of Allah") has become part of the rubric at the head of every Sura save the ninth.

IN THE NAME OF ALLAH,
THE MERCIFUL, THE COMPASSIONATE

Praise be to Allah, the Lord of mankind,

The Merciful, the Compassionate,

Master of the Day of Judgment.

Thee do we worship, and to Thee do we turn for help.

Guide us in the straight path,

The path of those to whom Thou hast been gracious,

Not of those with whom Thou art angered, nor of those who go astray.

Early Meccan
Suras

Surat al-Alaq: The Blood-Clots

Common tradition in Islam holds that the first five verses of this Sura comprise the earliest revelation given to Mohammed. The Masoretes, however, were by no means unanimous about this and suggest various other passages as having a claim to be considered the first to be revealed. Modern scholarship is inclined to agree that this is not the earliest, but was elected to that position after the notion of Gabriel's connection with revelation came to be emphasized. In any case it is early, and perhaps the first section is very early.

The second section comes from a later period when Mohammed had begun to organize regular prayer services for his followers. The commentators assert that it refers to Abu Jahl, who came to be pictured as the typical Meccan opponent of the Prophet and his early followers.

IN THE NAME OF ALLAH,
THE MERCIFUL, THE COMPASSIONATE

Recite! O Mohammed, in the name of thy Lord, who has created, Created man from blood-clots.[1] Recite! seeing that thy Lord is the most generous, Who has taught by the pen, Taught man what he did not know.[2] Nay, indeed, man assuredly acts insolently Because he considers himself self-sufficient. Verily, to thy Lord is the return.

Hast thou considered, O Mohammed, him who hinders A servant when he is saying prayers?[3] Hast thou considered if he is in the way of guidance, Or is commanding piety? Hast thou considered if he counted the message false and turned away? Did he not know that Allah sees? Nay, indeed, if he desist not We shall drag him by the forelock, A lying, sinful forelock. So let him summon his party, We shall summon the Zabaniyya.[4] Nay, indeed, obey him not, but do obeisance to Allah and draw near.

Surat al-Muddaththir: The Enwrapped

A composite Sura, the first six verses of which were considered by some authorities to be the earliest revelation given to the Prophet. Parts of the Sura are very early but others are certainly Medinan additions. The opening address is doubtless to Mohammed, though the stories which explain why he was wrapped in a mantle, or cloak, were composed by Divines who no longer understood the Semitic association of a mantle with the mantic art. The dithar (mantle) here is the equivalent of the khimar of the old Arabian soothsayers, and familiar to us from the famous mantle of Elijah which fell on Elisha (II Kings ii, 13, 14). The wrath he is to flee from is the wrath to come.

IN THE NAME OF ALLAH,
THE MERCIFUL, THE COMPASSIONATE

O thou who enwrappest thyself in a mantle, Arise! Warn! And thy Lord, magnify Him,[1] And thy garments, purify them, And the wrath, flee from it, And do not do favours in order to seek increase, But for thy Lord wait patiently.

So when there shall come a trump on the Trumpet,[2] That then will be a difficult Day, For the unbelievers it will be far from easy.

Leave Me alone with him whom I have created, Since I have appointed for him extensive wealth, And sons as witnesses, And I have smoothed out everything for him smoothly —Then is he covetous that I do more. Nay, indeed, he at Our signs was obstinate, But I shall overtake him with something grievously difficult.

He, indeed, thought and pondered. Death to him! how he pondered. Then, death to him! how he pondered. Then he looked; Then he frowned and looked crossly; Then he turned

Sura
74

his back and showed pride, And said: "This is naught but magic being employed; This is naught but human speech." I shall roast him at Saqar.[3] And what will teach thee what Saqar is? It lets nothing remain, and desists not, Scorching the skins.[4] Over it are nineteen.[5] We have not set as masters of the Fire any save angels, nor have We fixed their number save as a testing for those who disbelieve, that those who have been given the Book [the Jews and Christians] may be certain, and that those who believe [the Moslems] may increase in belief, that those who have been given the Book and the believers may not be in doubt, and that those in whose hearts is disease, and the unbelievers, may say: "What does Allah mean by such a similitude as this?"

❊·Thus does Allah lead astray whom He will and guide whom He will. Yet no one knows the hosts of thy Lord save Him Himself, so this is naught but a reminder to humans.

❊·Nay, indeed, by the moon, By the night when it retreats, By the morning when it shines bright, It[6] is one of the great things, A warning to humans, To whosoever among you wishes to push forward or to lag behind. Every soul for what it has gained is a pledge, Except the Companions of the Right Hand [the Blessed]. In celestial gardens they will be asking one another About the sinners. They will ask them: "What led you into Saqar?" They [the sinners] will say: "We were not of those who prayed, Nor were we feeding the unfortunate, But we were engaging in dispute with those who so engaged, And we were treating as false the Day of Judgment, Until the certainty[7] came upon us." So the intercession of those who intercede will benefit them not.

❊·Now what is the matter with them that they are turning from the reminder? As though they were startled asses Who flee from a lion. Yet every man among them desires that he be given scrolls unfolded. Nay, indeed, but they do not fear the hereafter. Nay, indeed, it [Mohammed's message] is a reminder, And he who wills will remember it, But they will not remember save should Allah so will. He is worthy of your piety, and He is worthy to forgive.

Surat Quraish: The Koreish

The Koreish (Quraish) were the dominant tribe in Mecca during the lifetime of Mohammed, and to all intents and purposes the city was ruled by their merchant aristocracy, men who had grown wealthy from the success of their caravan ventures both to the north and to the south. The central shrine at Mecca, the Kaaba, had been there long before the days of the Koreish, who were relatively newcomers, and Mohammed is here suggesting that it was the Lord of the Kaaba who had guarded them and was the real source of their prosperity, so they should worship Him. This has all the appearance of being a fragment from a longer passage, and must be very early, perhaps from the period when Mohammed was only tentatively feeling out his mission as a preacher.

IN THE NAME OF ALLAH,
THE MERCIFUL, THE COMPASSIONATE

For the uniting together of Koreish, For their uniting for the winter and the summer caravan journey, So let them worship the Lord of this House,[1] Who has given them provision of food against hunger, And made them secure from fear.

Surat al-Kawthar: Abundance

A fragment that has survived from some originally longer revelation. It belongs to the very early period when Mohammed was still taking part in the sacrifices offered at the Meccan shrine, for the verb nahara, *which is normally used for sacrificing an animal ritually, is found only here in the Koran. The last verse suggests that the revelation was one of encouragement to Mohammed against his enemies.*

IN THE NAME OF ALLAH,
THE MERCIFUL, THE COMPASSIONATE

We, indeed, have given thee abundance,[1] So pray to thy Lord, and offer sacrifice. Truly the one who hates thee is the one who will be childless.[2]

Surat al-Humaza: The Backbiter

An early piece from the days when Mohammed's preaching was being scoffed at and he himself maligned by the rich merchants of Mecca. Bell thinks the first four verses are original, and that then, because people did not understand the strange word Hutama, the remainder was added as explanation. This word is obviously meant to be a name for Hell-fire, but it occurs only here in the Koran, and seems to have been a word invented by the Prophet.

IN THE NAME OF ALLAH,
THE MERCIFUL, THE COMPASSIONATE

Woe to every backbiter, maligner, Who gathers wealth and hoards it up. He thinks that his wealth has made him immortal. Nay, indeed, but he will assuredly be flung into

Sura 108

Sura 104

29

al-Hutama. And what will teach thee what al-Hutama is? It is Allah's kindled fire Which mounts up over the hearts. Verily it shall be a vault over them In outstretched columns of flame.

Surat al-Fil: The Elephant

It is customary to regard this short passage as an address to the Meccans, reminding them of how Allah had saved their city from an attack by Abraha's army of Abyssinians. The pronoun, however, is singular, and the piece is rather to be taken as an encouragement to the Prophet himself, reminding him of how Allah has ever been able to defeat the stratagems of the powerful and mighty. Abraha's expedition against Mecca is traditionally set at c. 570 A.D., and would seem to have failed because of an outbreak of smallpox among the troops, which may, of course, be what is referred to in the fourth verse. Since the Abyssinians did not use war elephants, Conti Rossini has suggested that the legend of Abraha's elephants arose from a misunderstanding of the name of Abraha's royal master, Alfilas, which, when the ending was dropped, sounded like al-Fil, "the elephant."

IN THE NAME OF ALLAH,
THE MERCIFUL, THE COMPASSIONATE

Hast thou not seen, O Mohammed, how thy Lord dealt with the companions of the elephant? Did He not set their scheming all astray? He sent against them birds in flocks,[1] Which pelted them with stones of hardened clay, And thus made them like grain stalks eaten down.

Sura
105

Surat al-Lail: The Night

This is a good example of Mohammed's early preaching at Mecca. He begins, with the swearing formula customary among the old Arabian soothsayers, by calling attention to the might of Allah as revealed in creation, then introduces the matter of the two ways of life, and goes on to emphasize this by bringing in the fear of Hell-fire. It is possible that the original message ended at the break near the middle of the Sura, and that the rest is a later, perhaps a Medinan, addition, in which Mohammed himself, and not Allah, is the speaker.

IN THE NAME OF ALLAH,
THE MERCIFUL, THE COMPASSIONATE

By the night when it spreads its veil, By the day when it brightly shines, By Him who created the male and the female, Your course,[1] indeed, is diverse. So as for him who gives in charity and acts piously And puts his trust in that which is best, His path to ease We shall facilitate. But as for him who is niggardly, yet boasts in his riches And treats the best as a lie, We shall facilitate his path to lack of ease, And not a whit will his wealth profit him when he falls. It is Ours to give guidance, For to Us, indeed, belong both the Last and the First.

So I give you warning of a Fire that blazes, None will be roasted thereat save the one, most wretched, Who has counted the message false and has turned away. But the one who is truly pious will avoid it, He who gives his wealth in charity to purify himself, And is under obligation to no one for a favour that is to be recompensed, Desiring only the face of his Lord, the Most High, So anon he will assuredly be well-pleased.

Sura
92

Sura
90

Surat al-Balad: The Land

The land here referred to may be the Hejaz area in which Mecca is situated, though some think that balad means "town" rather than "land" and take the reference to be to Mecca itself, of which Mohammed was a free citizen by birth. The swearing formula introduces again the doctrine of the Two Paths and the duties of religion, enforcing the lesson by the threat of Hell-fire. It is clearly an early Meccan passage in which the Prophet is preaching to his fellow-citizens, though it is possible that it was worked over during the Medinan period.

IN THE NAME OF ALLAH, THE MERCIFUL, THE COMPASSIONATE

I swear not[1] by this land, And thou art a free inhabitant in this land, Nor by a parent and what he has begotten. We, indeed, have created man in trouble. Does he think that no one will ever have power over him? He says; "I have squandered enormous wealth." Does he think that no one saw him? Did We not give him his two eyes, And a tongue, and two lips? And give him guidance to the two highways?[2] But he has made no attempt at the steep. And what will teach thee what the steep is? It is the setting free of someone in bondage, Or feeding someone in a day of famine, An orphan who is near of kin, Or some unfortunate person in destitution. Then to be, besides, one of those who believe, and who counsel one another to endure patiently, and counsel one another to compassionateness. These are the Companions of the Right Hand. But those who disbelieve in Our signs, they are the Companions of the Left Hand, Upon whom will come a fire that is closed in.

Surat Ash-Sharh: The Expanding

Mohammed is here given encouragement that he may not lose heart. This was a danger during those early years when there were so many things to discourage him. The Prophet is reminded of all that Allah has done for him, and he is encouraged to persevere, with a hint that difficulties are but preliminary to easier times. Since sharh may mean "opening up," the opening verse has provided a basis for the famous legend of the "Opening of the Breast," which tells how celestial beings came and opened up the breast of the youthful Mohammed and cleansed his heart in preparation for his mission.

IN THE NAME OF ALLAH,
THE MERCIFUL, THE COMPASSIONATE

Have We not expanded for thee, O Mohammed, thy breast? And removed from thee thy burden of guilt[1] Which was breaking thy back? And have We not raised for thee thy reputation? Now, verily, along with difficulty there comes ease, Verily along with difficulty there comes ease, So whenever thou art free, prosecute diligently thy task,[2] And to thy Lord make supplication.

Surat ad-Duha: The Bright Morn

This is another message of encouragement to the Prophet during the early days of his struggle to get his mission started, and at a time when he was so often despondent. Beginning with the soothsayer's swearing formula, it encourages the Prophet by reminding him of Allah's constant and continuing care, which will surely lead him to success, and it urges him to continue in the good way.

Sura
94

Sura
93

❋·By the bright morn, And by the night when all is still,
Thy Lord has not left thee, nor come to dislike thee. So the
latter situation will be better for thee than the former, And
thy Lord anon will assuredly give to thee that which thou
desirest, so that thou wilt be well content. Did He not find thee
an orphan and shelter thee? Did He not find thee erring and
guide thee? Did He not find thee poor and enrich thee? So
as for the orphan, treat him not harshly, And as for the beggar,
do not drive him away, And as for thy Lord's bounty, tell of it.

Surat al-Qadr: The Decree

*Qadr means "power" but is a technical Moslem word for the
Decree which predestines everything whether for good or for ill.
So in the title of the Sura it is rendered "the Decree," but in
the body of the Sura by the more commonly used "power," for
that Night of Power which is said to be the night towards the
close of the month Ramadan when the celestial powers descend
with all the "fates" that have been fixed and decreed for the
ensuing twelve months. The "it" in the opening verse is generally taken to mean the Koran, which was sent down during the
month of Ramadan. As this passage, however, is merely a fragment surviving from some longer revelation, the "it" would
refer to something previously mentioned, possibly the Record
of the decrees.*

IN THE NAME OF ALLAH,
THE MERCIFUL, THE COMPASSIONATE

❋·We, indeed, sent it down on the Night of Power. And
what will teach thee what the Night of Power is? The Night

Sura
97

of Power is better than a thousand months; The angels and the Spirit descend therein, by permission of their Lord, about every matter. Peace it is till the breaking of the dawn.

Surat at-Tariq: The Shining Star

A composite Sura, made up, as the rhyming endings show, of a number of small fragments put together. Parts of it are certainly early. Tariq means something which travels a known path, and apparently refers here to some star whose brightness served to make it the subject of the introductory swearing formula. This formula occurs again, however, in the second section. The orthodox commentators insist that the "guardian" or "watcher" in the fourth verse is Allah, but it is more likely that this is a reference to the guardian angel.

IN THE NAME OF ALLAH,
THE MERCIFUL, THE COMPASSIONATE

By the heaven, and by the Tariq. And what will teach thee what the Tariq is? It is the shining star.[1] Assuredly each soul has over it a guardian. Let man then look at that from which he was created. He was created from water[2] that pours forth, Which comes from between the loins and the ribs. He [Allah] is quite capable of bringing him back On the Day when the secrets will be tried, And he will have no strength and no helper.

By the heaven which has its return, And by the earth which has its splitting,[3] It [the Prophet's message] is indeed a saying, a statement, It is no piece of frivolity. It is they who are devising a stratagem, And I, Allah, shall devise a stratagem also. So do thou show forbearance to the unbelievers; grant them a little respite.

Surat Ash-Shams: The Sun

An early Meccan passage to which a later Meccan passage has been added using the same rhyme. The first section is in the characteristic soothsayer style, with an excellent series of swearing formulae leading up to the doctrine of the Two Ways. To this has been added, doubtless to illustrate the two ways, a passage giving briefly the ancient Arabian legend of Thamud, whose pious people by following Allah's messenger were saved, but whose wicked people, who rejected the messenger and the message, were destroyed.

IN THE NAME OF ALLAH,
THE MERCIFUL, THE COMPASSIONATE

By the sun and its morning brightness, By the moon when it follows along after, By the day when it reveals its [the sun's] splendour, By the night when it enshrouds it, By the heaven and Him who[1] built it, By the earth and Him who spread it forth, By a soul and Him who fashioned it And implanted within it its wickedness and its piety, He has prospered indeed who has kept it pure, And he has failed indeed who has corrupted it.

Thamud[2] in their presumptuousness counted the message false, When the most wretched of them was sent.[3] Allah's messenger said to them: "The she-camel of Allah and her drinking." But they counted him as false and hamstrung her, whereat their Lord destroyed them in their sin, treating all alike, Nor did He fear the outcome thereof.

Surat Abasa: He Frowned

The Sura as a whole is Meccan, some of it early Meccan, though it is obviously made up of five small pieces put together. The Sura gets its name from the opening verse, which is said to be a rebuke to Mohammed for discourtesy to a blind man named Abdallah b. Umm Maktum who annoyed him by interrupting his conversation with a wealthy and important Meccan. The Prophet is reminded that such attention to the rich and neglect of the poor is not the way of religion. The second section is supposed to refer to the celestial prototype of Scripture. Pieces three and four suggest lessons for men, and the final piece is a characteristic warning of the Final Judgment.

IN THE NAME OF ALLAH,
THE MERCIFUL, THE COMPASSIONATE

Sura 80

He frowned and turned his back, Because the blind man had come to him. And what will teach thee? Maybe he will purify himself, Or be reminded, so that the reminding will profit him. As for him who is rich,[1] Why to him thou didst give much attention; And what dost thou care that he does not purify himself? But as for him who comes to thee in earnest search, While he is in fear for his soul, Of him thou art neglectful.

Nay, indeed, it is a reminder,[2] So whoever wills remembers it. It is in honoured scrolls,[3] Exalted, purified, Written by the hands of scribes Honoured, pious.

Death to man! How ungrateful he is! From what thing did He create him? From a drop of semen He created him, and gave him his allotment.[4] Then the way He made easy; Then He caused him to die and had him buried; Then, when He wills, He will raise him up. Nay, indeed, not yet has he fulfilled what He commanded him.

❧·So let man have a look at his food. We it was who poured out the water copiously, Then We split the ground in cracks, So that therein We caused grain to grow up, Also grapes and nutritious plants, And olives and palms, And orchards thick with trees, And fruits and herbage, A provision for you and for your flocks.

❧·But when the crack⁵ of doom arrives, A Day when a man will flee from his brother, And his mother and his father, And his wife and his sons, Every man of them on that Day will have a concern to occupy him. Some faces on that Day will be radiant, Laughing, joyous. And there will be faces on that Day with dust upon them: Black dust will cover them; These are the unbelievers, the wicked.

Surat al-Qalam: The Pen

The beginning of the Sura, which some authorities claimed was the earliest piece to be revealed, is early Meccan. It encourages the Prophet by an assurance that even though he may use the style of the soothsayers he is not, as the Meccans said, a crazy fellow possessed by the jinn, but belongs to those to whom Scripture revelation was given, and therefore he must not compromise with the pagan Meccans. Toward the end the example of Jonah is brought in as an added encouragement.

Perhaps the chief interest to us in the Sura is the example of a parable it gives us in the second section. This parable at least suggests that the following verses may belong to the same piece, the blighted garden of the parable being contrasted with the garden of Paradise, though this, of course, may have been the reason why these verses were added on here.

IN THE NAME OF ALLAH,
THE MERCIFUL, THE COMPASSIONATE

❊Nun.[1] By the pen and by what they write, By the grace of thy Lord, O Mohammed, thou art not jinn-possessed,[2] But truly for thee there is a reward that will not be cut off, For thou art at a mighty undertaking. So thou wilt see and they will see Which of you it is that is demented. Verily thy Lord is the One who best knows who has gone astray from His path, and He knows best about those who have yielded to guidance, So obey thou not those who count the message false. They would love to have thee deal smoothly, whereat they would deal smoothly. And obey thou not any despicable swearer of oaths,[3] A backbiter who goes about with slander, A hinderer of the good, a transgressor, a guilty fellow, A man of violence, and beyond that a man of doubtful birth. What matters it that he has much wealth and many sons? When Our signs are recited to him he says: "Tales of the ancients." We shall brand him on the proboscis.[4]

❊Verily We have made trial of them as We made trial of the owners of a garden, when they swore that they would surely gather its fruits in the morning, And made no reserve.[5] So an encircler from thy Lord went around it while they were sleeping, And by morning it was as a garden whose fruits have been gathered. Then they called to one another in the morning, saying: "Go out early to your field if ye are going to be gatherers." So off they went, whispering to one another: "See to it that no poor man enter it today to your loss." Thus they went out early with their fixed purpose, But when they saw it they said: "We, indeed, are those astray; Nay, but we are the ones forbidden to gather any fruit." The worthiest one of them said: "Did I not say to you: 'Why give ye not glory'?" They said: "Glory be to our Lord, we, indeed, have

Sura
68

been wrongdoers." So they approached each other, blaming one another. They said: "Woe to us, we, indeed, have been presumptuous. Maybe our Lord will give us instead another garden better than it. Verily to our Lord are we making supplication." Such is the punishment; but the punishment of the Hereafter is worse, did they but know.

❋ Verily for the pious, with their Lord, are gardens of delight. Shall We then make those who have surrendered themselves[6] like the sinners? How think ye? How would ye judge? Or do ye have a Book of Scripture in which ye study?[7] Verily ye have in it that to which ye should give preference. Or do ye have oaths binding on Us which extend to the Day of Resurrection? Verily ye have that which ye judge. Ask them, O Mohammed, which of them will go surety for that. Or do they have associate-gods?[8] Then let them produce their associate-gods, if they are those who speak the truth, On the Day when the leg will be bared,[9] and they are summoned to do obeisance but will not be able, Downcast will be their looks; humiliation will cover them, because they had been summoned to do obeisance while they were sound in body. So leave Me with such as count this discourse false. We shall bring them along gradually from whence they know not. Yet I shall respite them. Verily, My stratagem is sure. Or art thou asking them for some recompense so that they are weighed down by debt? Or do they have the Unseen with them, so that it is they who write? Then wait with patience for the judgment of thy Lord, and be not like the fellow of the fish, [Jonah], when he called upon Allah while he was with sorrow oppressed. Had it not been that favour from his Lord reached him he would have been cast forth upon the naked shore disgraced. But his Lord chose him and set him among the righteous. Behold! those who disbelieve would well nigh cause thee to slip by their very looks, when they hear the reminder.

And they say: "Assuredly he is jinn-possessed," Yet it is nothing other than a reminder to mankind.

Surat al-A'la: The Most High

A very early Meccan Sura with Medinan insertions. The Prophet apparently has only just begun to recite publicly his "revelations," and is afraid of lapses of memory. He is encouraged by the promise that Allah, who had done such mighty things in nature, will aid him in his mission, which offers prosperity for those who accept the message, but the Fire for those who do not. The late addition of the last four verses suggests that this message is the same as that sent through Abraham and Moses.

IN THE NAME OF ALLAH,
THE MERCIFUL, THE COMPASSIONATE

❋Glorify, O Mohammed, the name of thy Lord, the Most High, Who created and then fashioned, Who determined and then guided, Who brought forth the pasture-land, Then made it blackened stubble. We shall cause thee to recite, and thou wilt not forget Except what Allah wills. He, indeed, knows what is published abroad and what one conceals. And We shall make it easy for thee, very easy, So remind, if the reminder profits anyone. Whoso fears Allah will receive the reminder, But the reprobate will turn aside from it, He who will roast in the great fire of Hell, Then therein will neither die nor live. Prospered, indeed, has he who has purified himself, And made mention of the name of his Lord, and said prayers. Nay, but ye prefer this present life, Though the Hereafter is better and more enduring. Truly, all this is in the former scrolls,[1] The scrolls of Abraham and Moses.

Sura 87

Sura
95

Sura
103

Surat at-Tin: The Fig

Probably this is only a fragment of a longer piece. It is very early, with perhaps the exception of the sixth verse, which looks like an insertion. The swearing formula introduces a reflection on the nature of man, which is itself an assurance to Mohammed that his expectation of a coming Judgment is correct.

IN THE NAME OF ALLAH, THE MERCIFUL, THE COMPASSIONATE

By the fig, and by the olive, By Mount Sinai, By this land so secure,[1] We have, indeed, created man in the goodliest form,[2] Then We brought him down to the lowliest of the low, Save those who believe and work righteous works, for there is for them a reward that will not be cut off. So what [or who] after this will declare thee false with regard to the Judgment? Is not Allah the justest of Judges?[3]

Surat al-Asr: The Afternoon

An early Meccan fragment to which the last verse was added in Medina.

IN THE NAME OF ALLAH, THE MERCIFUL, THE COMPASSIONATE

By the afternoon, Verily man is in loss. Save those who have believed and worked righteous works, and have enjoined on one another truth, and enjoined on one another patient endurance.

Surat al-Buruj: The Towers

On stylistic grounds this Sura breaks clearly into two parts, of which the second is quite probably earlier than the first. Bell considers both parts Medinan but they are more likely early Meccan, the first passage being a reference to the persecution of the Christians at Najran in 524 A.D., and the second using the apparently well-known stories of Pharaoh and Thamud to encourage the Prophet to maintain faith in his mission from Allah. It is a feeling that Mohammed could not have known a Pharaoh story so early that is the main ground for taking the passage to be Medinan.

IN THE NAME OF ALLAH, THE MERCIFUL, THE COMPASSIONATE

❊ By the heaven furnished with towers,[1] By the promised Day, By a witness and that which is witnessed, Death take the Masters of the Trench,[2] Of the fire fed with fuel. Lo! they were sitting around it, And they were witnesses to what they were doing to the believers. They were wreaking vengeance on them for no other reason than that they believed in Allah, the Sublime, the Praiseworthy, To Whom belongs the kingdom of the heavens and the earth. But Allah is a witness of everything. Verily, those who vexed the believing men and the believing women, and then did not repent, for them is the punishment of Gehenna, for them is the punishment of the burning. But those who have believed and worked works of righteousness, for them are the gardens beneath which rivers flow. That is the great success.

❊ Verily thy Lord's assault is terrible. He it is who originates and restores. And He is the Forgiving, the Loving One, Lord of the Throne, the Glorious One,[3] He who accomplishes that which He intends. Has there come to thee, O Mohammed, the story of the hosts Of Pharaoh, and of those of Thamud? Nay, but those who disbelieve are at their perverse way of counting false. But Allah from behind them is encompassing them. Nay, but it is a glorious lesson [qur'an] Inscribed on a preserved tablet.[4]

Surat al-Muzzammil: The Enwrapped

A Sura composed of three Meccan pieces to which a Medinan passage has been added. The first part apparently belongs to the same period as the opening verses of Sura 74 (same English title), and describes the Prophet as still struggling to formulate his message by night that he may preach it by day. He is encouraged by the thought that though the Meccans oppose him, Allah is well able to deal with them as He dealt with the people of Pharaoh, and in any case ahead of them lies Judgment. The Sura concludes with a Medinan passage which was probably added by some compiler who thought that verses 2-4 ("Rise up . . . the lesson") referred to night prayers.

IN THE NAME OF ALLAH,
THE MERCIFUL, THE COMPASSIONATE

O thou enwrapped one,[1] Rise up at night, save a little, Half of it—or shorten it somewhat, Or increase it—and prepare carefully the lesson [Qur'an],[2] For We are going to cast on thee a weighty discourse. Verily the early part of the night is the best for getting a strong impression and a just word. During the day thou hast, indeed, long hours of toil, So commemorate the name of thy Lord, and devote thyself to Him with complete devotion. Lord of the East and of the West, there is no other deity save Him, so take Him as thy guardian, And be patient under what they are saying, and make a graceful withdrawal from them.

❊·Leave Me alone with those comfortably living fellows who count the message false, and bear with them for a little. Truly, right here with Us are fetters and fire,[3] And food that chokes,[4] and painful torment, For a Day when the earth and the mountains will be quaking; indeed, the mountains will be soft sand-heaps.

❊·Truly, We have sent unto you a messenger, a witness against you, just as We sent a messenger to Pharaoh, But Pharaoh opposed the messenger, and We took painful hold on him, So how will ye, if ye disbelieve, protect yourselves on a Day which will make children grey-headed? By which the heavens will be rent asunder; of which the promise will be fulfilled? Lo! this message is a reminder, so let whosoever wills take a path to his Lord.

❊·Truly thy Lord well knows that thou dost rise for prayer, O Mohammed, almost two-thirds of the night, or a half, or a third thereof, as also do a group of those with thee. Allah measures the night and the day. He knows that ye do not keep count of it, so He has relented towards you. So recite as much of the Koran as is easy. He knows that some among you will be sick, and others will be going around in the land seeking Allah's bounty, and others fighting in the way of Allah, so recite as much thereof as is easy, and observe prayers, and pay the legal alms, and lend Allah a goodly loan. Whatever good ye send forward for yourselves you will find again with Allah. That is a good, indeed a very great reward. And ask Allah's forgiveness. Truly Allah is forgiving, compassionate.

Surat al-Qari'a: The Striker

This is only a fragment which doubtless was once part of a longer revelation. Its interest is as an example of how effectively Mohammed could use in his preaching the terrors of the coming Judgment. There has been much discussion of the word hawiya *toward the end of this Sura; it is obviously meant as a name for Hell-fire, but seems to be an invented word.*

IN THE NAME OF ALLAH,
THE MERCIFUL, THE COMPASSIONATE

The Striker! What is the Striker? And what will teach thee what the Striker is? On a Day when people will be like scattered moths, And the mountains will be like carded wool, As for him whose balance weighs heavy, He will be in a life well-pleasing. But as for him whose balance weighs light, Hawiya will be his mother. And what will teach thee what that is? It is a scorching fire.

Surat az-Zalzala: The Earthquake

A fragment concerned with the Last Day, on which men will be raised from the dead and assembled at Judgment to face the record of their deeds.

IN THE NAME OF ALLAH,
THE MERCIFUL, THE COMPASSIONATE

When the earth with her quaking will quake, And her burden the earth will cast forth, And man will say: "What is the matter with her?" On that Day she will tell forth her news,[1] Because thy Lord will have inspired her.[2] On that

Day the people will go forward individually, that they may be shown their works. Whosoever has done an atom's weight of good will see it, And whoso has done an atom's weight of evil will see it.

Surat al-Infitar: The Rending

A description of the celestial and terrestrial upheavals on the Last Day leads to a warning to men, all of whose deeds are being recorded, and who will assuredly have to face Judgment and its consequences.

Sura
82

IN THE NAME OF ALLAH,
THE MERCIFUL, THE COMPASSIONATE

When the heavens have been rent asunder, And when the stars have been dispersed, And when the seas have been commingled,[1] And when the graves have been upturned, A soul will know what it has sent forward and what it has kept back.

O man! what has led thee away from thy generous Lord, From him who created thee and formed thee and shaped thee rightly, Building thee up in such form as He willed? Nay, indeed, but ye count the Judgment[2] as something false, Yet over you, indeed, are guardians, Noble ones, those who write.[3] They know what ye do. Verily, the righteous will be in delight, While the wicked assuredly will be in Jahim,[4] Where, on the Judgment Day, they will roast, And may not be absent therefrom. What will teach thee what the Day of Judgment is? Again, what will teach thee what the Day of Judgment is? It is a Day when no soul will avail aught for another soul,[5] but the matter on that Day will be with Allah.

Surat at-Takwir: The Removal

*Again we have a Sura made up of two independent passages,
the second of which is probably of earlier date than the first.
This second passage uses the swearing formula of the soothsayers to introduce a denial of the charge that Mohammed's
message derives from jinn-possession, and to make a claim that
it is a true revelation from Allah. The passage which precedes
this is another description of the terrors that accompany the
arrival of the Last Day, and is interesting for the number of
points it has in common with Judaeo-Christian apocalyptic.*

IN THE NAME OF ALLAH,
THE MERCIFUL, THE COMPASSIONATE

When the sun has been removed,[1] And the stars have fallen
down, When the mountains have been moved away, And
the she-camels in their tenth month have been abandoned,[2]
And when the wild beasts have been gathered together, And
the seas have been set boiling, And when the souls have been
paired again with their bodies,[3] And when the female infant
who was buried alive has been asked For what sin she was
put to death, And when the scrolls have been opened out,
When the heaven has been stripped away, And al-Jahim[4] has
been set blazing, And the garden of Paradise has been brought
near, Each soul will know what it has got ready.

So I swear not[5] by the planets[6] Which swiftly move and
conceal themselves, By the night when it draws on, By the
morn when it comes in. It is, indeed, the speech of a noble
messenger,[7] One possessed of power, established beside the
Lord of the Throne, Obeyed there, faithful. And your companion [Mohammed] is not jinn-possessed, For, indeed, he
saw him [the angel Gabriel] on the clear horizon,[8] Nor was
he niggardly concerning the Unseen. It is not the speech of a

stoned Satan. So where are ye going?[9] It is naught but a reminder to mankind, To such among you as are willing to go straight, But ye will not so will, save if Allah, Lord of mankind, wills.

Surat an-Najm: The Star

This is a composite Sura, the first section of which gives an account of Mohammed's vision. In this passage he again denies that he is crazy and tells how revelation first came to him. The passage following it contains the famous "altered verses," in the original form of which the Prophet acknowledged the Meccan goddesses al-Lat, al-Uzza, and Manat, thereby ending much of the enmity of the Meccan leaders. This acknowledgment, however, he later said had been Satan's suggestion, and so the passage was altered to state that these goddesses are naught but empty names. The second part of this passage (from "Except") is later, as is the entire third section, the latter having a special interest in that it shows us the Prophet linking his message to that of previous revelations. The concluding verses are quite different in style and are apparently an odd fragment which the compilers added.

IN THE NAME OF ALLAH,
THE MERCIFUL, THE COMPASSIONATE

By the star when it falls, Your companion [Mohammed] has not gone astray, nor has he been misled, Nor is he speaking out of his own inclination. It is naught but a revelation that has been revealed to him. One mighty in power[1] taught him, One possessed of strength, who stood erect When He was at the highest point of the horizon. Then He drew near and descended, So that He was two bows' length off, or nearer, And He revealed to His servant what He revealed.

His heart [i.e., his mind] did not falsify what he saw. So will ye now dispute with him about what he saw? Why, indeed, he saw Him coming down another time, At the sidra-tree of the boundary,[2] Beside which is the garden of resort, When the sidra tree was covered with what covers it. His gaze neither turned aside nor did it go beyond, For, indeed, he was seeing one of the greatest signs of his Lord.

❊·Is it that ye have considered al-Lat and al-Uzza, And Manat,[3] the other, third one? Do ye have males while He has only females? That would, indeed, be an unfair partition. These are nothing but names. Ye and your fathers named them so, but Allah has sent down no authority for them. They [the Meccans] follow naught but opinion and what their souls desire, even when there has come to them guidance from their Lord. Or shall man have what he has longed for? To Allah belong both the last and the first, And how many an angel there is in the heavens whose intercession will avail not at all, Except after Allah gives permission to whom He wills and is well-pleased. Verily it is those who do not believe in the Hereafter who give female names to the angels. They have no knowledge about the matter, merely following opinion, but opinion avails not at all against the truth. So turn thou aside from those who turn their backs on Our reminder, and who desire naught but the life of this world. That is as far as their knowledge reaches. Truly thy Lord knows best about who has gone astray from His way, and knows best about who has accepted guidance. Allah's is whatever is in the heavens and whatever is on earth, that He may recompense those who have done evil in accordance with what they have done, and recompense those who have done good with what is best, Those who avoid the greater sins and shameful crimes save inadvertently. Truly thy Lord's forgiveness is wide. He knows very well about you, when He produced you from the earth, and when ye were embryos in your mothers' wombs, so seek not to justify yourselves. He knows very well who it is shows piety.

❧·Hast thou, O Mohammed, considered him who has turned his back,[4] Who has given but little in charity, and is niggardly? Does he have knowledge of the Unseen so that he sees? Or has he not been told about what is in the scrolls of Moses And of Abraham, who carried out what he was bidden?[5] How no burdened soul may bear the burden of another, And that there is nothing for man save that for which he has striven? And that the object of his striving will one day be seen? Then will he be recompensed the fullest recompense. And has he not learned that to thy Lord is the final coming? That He is the One who causes laughter and weeping, Just as He is the One who causes to die and causes to live? That He created the couples, the male and the female, Creating them from a drop of semen when it is emitted, And that upon Him lies the task of the other producing,[6] That He is the One who grants riches and possessions, And that He is the Lord of the Dog Star,[7] That He destroyed Ad, the former people,[8] And Thamud, leaving no survivors, And earlier still the people of Noah, because they had been wrongdoers and had transgressed, And the overturned cities [Sodom and Gomorrah] He overthrew, So that there covered them what covered them? Which then of the benefits of thy Lord wilt thou make matter of doubt?

❧·This warner [Mohammed] is one of the warners of old. That which draws on [Judgment Day] is drawing on, But there is no one save Allah who can reveal it. Can it be that ye consider this discourse strange? And laugh and do not weep? But are spending your time on vanities? Rather do obeisance to Allah and worship Him.

Surat al-Inshiqaq: The Rending

A sermon on the Day of Judgment. From the breaks in the rhyme it is apparent that it has been composed of five pieces of various dates, but most of them are quite early and have been worked up into an impressive Sura.

IN THE NAME OF ALLAH,
THE MERCIFUL, THE COMPASSIONATE

When the heaven has been rent, And has given ear to its Lord and become worthy.[1] And when the earth has been stretched out flat, And has cast forth what was in it and become empty, And has given ear to its Lord and become worthy. Then, O man, thou wilt be toiling painfully unto thy Lord, for thou art going to meet Him. Then as for him who is given his record book in his right hand, He will be reckoned with by an easy reckoning, And he will turn back happily to his kindred. But as for him who is given his record book behind his back, He will invoke destruction, But will roast in Sa'ir.[2] He, indeed, had been happy amongst his kindred; He, indeed, thought that he would never be brought back to a reckoning. Aye! but his Lord was watching him. So I swear not[3] by the twilight glow, Nor by the night and what it gathers, Nor by the moon when it is full, Assuredly ye shall ride on stage after stage. So what is the matter with them that they do not believe? And when the lesson [*Qur'an*] is recited to them they do not do obeisance? Nay, those who have disbelieved count the message false. Allah, however, knows well what they have in mind, So give thou to them good tidings of a painful punishment,[4] Which awaits all save those who have believed and worked works of righteousness. For them there is a reward that will not be cut off.

Sura
84

Surat al-Adiyat: The Chargers

An early passage in the soothsayer style, the meaning of whose opening verses is quite obscure. It is generally taken to be a description of tribal horsemen dashing off in the early morning on a raiding expedition. This is then used to suggest to the hearers that man's heart is set on the wrong things, as he will find out on the Day of Judgment.

IN THE NAME OF ALLAH, THE MERCIFUL, THE COMPASSIONATE

By the chargers as they breathe heavily, And those who with their hooves strike sparks of fire, And those who dash forth in the early morn, Thereby trailing a cloud of dust, In the midst of which they move as a troop.[1] Truly man is ungrateful to his Lord. And, indeed, he himself is witness to that. And, truly, he is vehement in love of this world's good. Does he not know that when that which is in the graves is dragged forth, And that which is in the breasts is made manifest, Their Lord will indeed on that Day be well informed about them?[2]

Surat an-Nazi'at:

Those Who Draw Forth

The opening verses of this Sura closely resemble those of Sura 100, being a series of verses in the swearing formula leading to a warning of the Resurrection Day. On the ground of this reference to the Day the feminine plurals in these early verses are generally taken to refer to the celestial assistants of the Angel of Death who draw out souls from bodies. The real reference,

Sura
100

Sura
79

53

however, is quite unknown, and Bell takes them as referring to the commercial operations of the Meccan merchants. The next section, which gives the story of Moses' call to his mission, is in quite a different rhyme and style. Section 3 is a separate little piece illustrating the wonder of Allah's creative work. The last section is in the same rhyme but is an answer to some who questioned Mohammed about the coming of the Hour. Section 4 is in the rhyme of the passage about the call of Moses, but is probably a later passage from a description of the Last Judgment.

IN THE NAME OF ALLAH,
THE MERCIFUL, THE COMPASSIONATE

By those who violently draw forth, And those who draw out gently,[1] By those who move swimmingly along, By those who, making an effort, get ahead, By those who arrange affairs, One day the quaker will start everything quaking,[2] And the follower will follow right after. Hearts on that Day will be beating fast And looks will be downcast. Men will say: "Are we really to be returned to our original estate? Can such a thing be when we have become rotten bones?" They will say: "That then will be a losing turn." Yet it will be only one single blast, And lo! there they are looking around.[3]

Has there come to thee, O Mohammed, the story of Moses? When his Lord called to him at the holy vale Tuwa:[4] "Go to Pharaoh. He has, indeed, become overweening, So say to him: 'Hast thou any desire to purify thyself? And that I might guide thee to thy Lord, that thou mightest fear Him?'" So Moses showed him a very great sign, But he counted it false and rebelled. Then he turned his back in haste, Assembling his people and making proclamation. He said: "I am your Lord, the Most High." So Allah took hold of him for punishment in the Hereafter as well as in this first life. Truly, in that there is a lesson for such as fear Allah.

❧ Are ye the more difficult to create, or the heaven? He built it, Raising high its vault and fashioning it orderly, Making dark its night, and drawing forth its morning brightness. And the earth, after that, He spread out, Producing from it its water and its pasture land, And the mountains He set firm, All this as a provision for you and for your cattle.

❧ But when the great calamity[5] has come, A Day when man will be reminded of that for which he has been striving, When al-Jahim will have been set clearly in view for everyone to see, Then as for him who has transgressed, And made choice of this world's life, al-Jahim will assuredly be his abiding-place. But as for him who feared the Judgment-seat of his Lord, and kept his soul from desire, The garden of Paradise will assuredly be his abiding-place.

❧ They will question thee, O Mohammed, about the Hour, saying: "When is the time fixed for it?" And: "What hast thou to do with the mentioning thereof?" Its arrival is the concern of thy Lord. Thou art only a warner of such as may fear it. The day they see it they will seem not to have tarried more than an evening and its morn.[6]

Surat al-Mursilat: Those Sent

As we have it, this Sura is a unity, though it seems to have been made such by using a refrain to bind together a number of small pieces so as to constitute a description of the Last Day and the state of the unbelievers. As in Suras 100 and 79, the opening verses use the swearing formula, employing a number of nouns in the feminine plural to introduce a threat of coming Judgment. What these nouns originally meant is quite unknown, but they are commonly taken to refer to various groups of

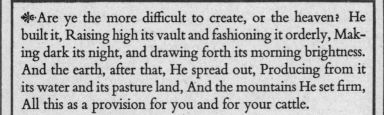

Sura
77

angels who are busy with their ministrations. Others have taken them to refer to various types of winds by whose activities the Prophet, like a soothsayer, swears.

IN THE NAME OF ALLAH,
THE MERCIFUL, THE COMPASSIONATE

By those sent forth one after the other, By those that blow in violent gusts, By those that scatter scatterings, By those that divide up into parts, By those that cast down reminders, Whether as excuse or as warning, Verily, that which ye are promised is about to happen. So when the stars are blotted out, And when the sky is rent asunder, When the mountains are crumbled, And when the messengers have a time set:[1] For what Day is all this being arranged? For the Day of Severance.[2] And what will teach thee what the Day of Severance is?

Woe on that Day to those who count it false! Did We not destroy those of former times? Then We shall cause those of later times to follow them, For thus do We deal with sinners.

Woe on that Day to those who count it false! Did We not create you from contemptible water? Which We placed in a repository secure Until a known measure of time. We determined it, and what excellent determiners are We.

Woe on that Day to those who count it false! Did We not appoint the earth as a gathering place For the living and for the dead? And We placed upon it firmly fixed mountains rising lofty, and gave you water sweet[3] to drink.

Woe on that Day to those who count it false! Off with you to that which ye were counting false. Off with you to a three-branched shadow,[4] Which gives no shade and protects not against the flame, That casts out sparks in size like castles, A shadow which is as though it were tawny camels.

✤ Woe on that Day to those who count it false! This is the Day on which they will not speak, Nor will permission be given them to make excuses.

✤ Woe on that Day to those who count it false! This is the Day of Severance. We have gathered you along with those of former times. So if you have any stratagem then try your stratagem on Me.

✤ Woe on that Day to those who count it false! Verily, the pious will be amidst shades and fountains, And fruits of whatsoever kind they may desire. We shall say: "Eat and drink with full enjoyment[5] because of what ye have been doing. Thus it is that We recompense those who do good."

✤ Woe on that Day to those who count it false! Eat and take your enjoyment for a little. Ye, indeed, are sinners. Woe on that Day to those who count it false! For when to them is said: "Bow down in worship," they do not bow down.

✤ Woe on that Day to those who count it false! For in what discourse after this will they believe?

Surat an-Naba: The Announcement

As in the previous selection, the main subject of this sermon is the Day of Severance, or Day of Distinction, which is described in the third section. To this is prefixed a short piece on the wonders of Allah's creation, and to the whole are added a little introduction and a conclusion which are both late material.

Sura
78

About what are they questioning one another? About the great announcement, With regard to which they are in disagreement. Nay, indeed! anon they will know. Then nay, indeed! anon they will know.

Did We not set out the earth a flat expanse, And set thereon the mountains as tent-pegs?[1] And We have created you as pairs, And have appointed your sleep for resting. Also We have appointed the night to be a covering, And have appointed the day as the time for gaining your livelihood. Above you We have built seven solid heavenly vaults,[2] And have placed therein a brightly-burning lamp. And from the rain clouds We have sent down water in abundance, That thereby We might bring forth grain and herbage, And gardens thickly planted.

Truly, the Day of Severance is a time already appointed, A Day when there will be a blast on the Trump[3] and ye will come in crowds, And the heavens will be opened up and become portals, And the mountains will be set moving and become a mirage. Hell truly has become a place of snares, For the presumptuous transgressors an abiding-place, In which they will remain for ages. Therein they will taste no coolness nor any drink Save scalding water and putrid pus.[4] A fitting recompense. They were, indeed, not expecting an accounting, So they counted Our signs as utterly false. Yet We have made an account of everything in a Book,[5] So We shall say to them: "Taste ye! never shall We give you increase in anything save punishment." But truly for the pious there is a place of bliss, Gardens enclosed and vineyards, And full-bosomed damsels of the same age, And a cup full to overflowing,

An abode in which they will hear no foolish talk nor any counting false, A recompense from thy Lord, a free gift, a reckoning.

❊ Lord of the heavens and the earth and what lies between them, the Merciful, from Whom they shall obtain no word of address, On the Day when the Spirit[6] and the angels will stand in due order arranged they will not speak, save him to whom the Merciful may give permission, and he will say only that which is correct. That is the real Day. So let whosoever wills take a path back to his Lord. Truly We have given you warning of a punishment that is near at hand. The Day when man will see what his hands have sent ahead, and the unbeliever will say: "O would that I were dust."

Surat al-Ghashiya: The Enveloper

"The Enveloper" is one of the many names of the Last Day, and this Sura is a pronouncement on the subject of the Day of Doom. It is made up of two pieces, of which the first describes the fate in store for both the wicked and the righteous, and the second justifies Mohammed's mission as a warner.

IN THE NAME OF ALLAH,
THE MERCIFUL, THE COMPASSIONATE

❊ Has there come to thee the account of the Enveloper? On that Day faces will be downcast. Travailing, worn out, They will roast at a scorching fire, Given to drink from a fountain fiercely boiling; No food will they have save that of thorny shrubs,[1] Which neither fattens nor avails against hunger. Other faces on that Day will be joyous, Well-pleased with the course they have run. They will be in a lofty garden, Wherein they will hear no foolish talk, A garden in which is a gushing fountain, In which also are high-raised couches, And drinking-goblets placed in readiness, And cushions laid out in rows, And luscious carpets spread.

❊ Will they not look at the camels,[2] how they have been created? And at the sky, how it has been raised aloft? And at the mountains, how they have been firmly fixed? And at the earth, how it has been spread out flat? So warn, O Mohammed! Thou art only a warner. Thou art no overseer over them, Save him who has turned his back and disbelieved, But him will Allah punish with the greater punishment. Truly to Us is their returning. Then, truly, with Us is their reckoning.

Surat al-Fajr: The Dawn

The main portion of this Sura consists of a reminder of the fate of the ancient peoples whom Allah destroyed in their sins (first half of second passage), leading up to a reflection on man's lack of true religion (balance of passage), and a description of the Judgment (last section). To this is prefixed a passage with the soothsayer type of swearing formula, but here this seems to be held up to ridicule, and so the passage would belong to the period when the Prophet was becoming anxious to distinguish his "revelations" from the utterances of contemporary soothsayers.

IN THE NAME OF ALLAH,
THE MERCIFUL, THE COMPASSIONATE

❊ By the dawn, And ten nights,[1] By the double and the single, By the night when it runs its course, Is there in that an oath for a man of intelligence?

❊ Hast thou not seen, O Mohammed, how thy Lord dealt with Ad At Iram, adorned with pillars,[2] The like of which had not been created in the land? And with Thamud, who hewed out the rocks in the valley for dwellings, And with Pharaoh, Lord of the stakes?[3] Who, all of them, acted presumptuously in the land, And increased corruption therein, So thy Lord poured out upon them the scourge of chastisement. Verily, thy Lord is assuredly lying in a place of snare. But as for man, whenever his Lord tries him, then honours him and is graciously bountiful to him, he says: "My Lord has honoured me," But whenever He tries him and sets a measure to His provision for him, he says: "My Lord has humiliated me." Nay, indeed, but ye do not honour the orphan, And do not urge one another to feed the unfortunate, But ye do devour heritages greedily, And ye love wealth with an ardent affection.

❧ Nay, indeed, when the earth is pounded to dust, pounding, pounding, And thy Lord comes along, and the angels, rank by rank, And Gehenna on that Day is brought in: Man, on that Day would fain be reminded, but whence shall the reminder come to him? He will say: "O would that I had sent ahead provision for my life." But on that Day no one will chastise with His chastisement, And no one will bind with His binding. Then will it be said: "O tranquil soul, Return to thy Lord approving and approved; And enter among My servants, And enter My garden."[4]

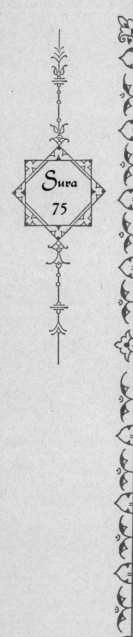

Surat al-Qiyama: The Resurrection

Here is a Sura composed of a number of short pieces concerned with the resurrection and Judgment, into which the compilers have inserted two quite foreign passages: Section 2, a very early piece in which the Prophet is being instructed how to prepare his proclamations, and Section 4, whose connection we cannot even guess.

IN THE NAME OF ALLAH,
THE MERCIFUL, THE COMPASSIONATE

I swear not[1] by the Day of Resurrection, Nor do I swear by the self-accusing soul. Does man think that We shall never reassemble his bones? Aye, We are quite well able to re-arrange even his fingers. But man desires to deny what is ahead of him. He asks: "When is the Day of Resurrection?" So when the sight is dazzled, And the moon is darkened in eclipse, And the sun and the moon are brought together,[2] On that Day man will say: "Where is a place to which to flee?" Nay, indeed, there is no refuge.[3] With thy Lord on that Day is the resting-place. On that Day man will have announced to him what he has sent forward and what he has held back. Nay, but man will be a clear demonstration against himself, Even though he put forward his excuses.

Move not thy tongue therein, O Mohammed, to hasten with it, The assembling of it and reciting it is Our affair, So when We recite it do thou follow its recitation. Then it is Our affair to make it clear.

Nay, indeed, but ye love this transitory world, And neglect the Hereafter. On that Day some faces will be beaming, Looking towards their Lord. But other faces on that Day will be dismal, So you would think they are being subjected to nose-slitting.[4] Nay, indeed, when it [the departing soul] reaches the collar-bones, And there is a cry: "Who can give a charm?" And he thinks that it is the parting, For leg is entwined with leg, On that day the on-driving will be to thy Lord. So he did not consider it true, and he did not say prayers, But counted it as false and turned away, Then he went to his folk walking haughtily.

❋ Near to thee, ever nearer is the Hour.[5] Then nearer to thee, still nearer.

❋ Does man think that he will be left forsaken? Was he not a drop of semen emitted? Then he was a blood-clot. So did He create and fashion, And make of him the two sexes, the male and the female. Is that One not powerful enough to bring to life the dead?

Surat al-Kafirun: The Unbelievers

A fragment from the early days of the Prophet's ministry in Mecca. It is unrhymed, and is probably complete in itself. Tradition says that the Meccan leaders had made a proposition that they would give Mohammed a certain recognition if he would acknowledge the deities worshipped at their shrine, and this is his rejection of their offer.

IN THE NAME OF ALLAH,
THE MERCIFUL, THE COMPASSIONATE

❋ Say: "O ye unbelievers, I worship not that which ye worship, Nor are ye worshipping that which I worship. Never shall I be a worshipper of what ye worship, Nor will ye be worshippers of that which I worship. Ye have your religion, and I have my religion."

Sura
109

Sura
112

Surat al-Ikhlas: The Keeping Pure

*This little passage is very commonly used in the daily prayers.
It is a pregnant statement of the doctrine of Allah's uniqueness.
The last two verses are commonly thought to be a rejection of
the Meccan notion that the deities at their shrine were daughters
of Allah. It is more likely, however, to be a rejection of Christian teaching, for it was the Christians who spoke of the
"only-begotten Son," and put Jesus on a level with God.*

IN THE NAME OF ALLAH,
THE MERCIFUL, THE COMPASSIONATE

Say: "The fact is, Allah is One, Allah is the Eternal. He did
not beget and He was not begotten, And no one has ever
been His peer."

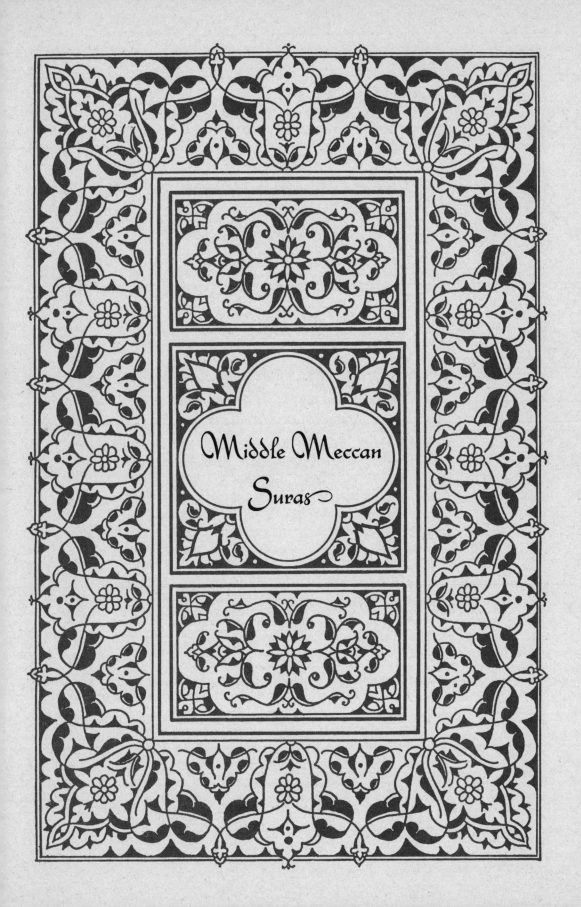

Middle Meccan
Suras

Surat al-Qamar: The Moon

The splitting of the moon mentioned in the opening line was taken by later piety as an actual event and counted as one of the miracles of Mohammed. The passage, however, is obviously eschatological, so some partial eclipse of the moon, visible at Mecca, was apparently taken as a sign pointing towards the Last Days. This reference to the Day then introduces a series of references to former peoples who were destroyed because of their refusal to heed the warning. Each of these passages save the last ends in a refrain. This was probably the case originally with the last also, but only the beginning of that story has survived and in its place we now have a number of unconnected fragments.

IN THE NAME OF ALLAH, THE MERCIFUL, THE COMPASSIONATE

❋ The Hour has drawn nigh. Indeed, the moon has been split. Yet if they see a sign they turn away, and say: "Passing magic." And they have counted the message false, and have followed their own desires, even though every matter is settled. Yet of the stories of former peoples there has, indeed, come to them that in which there is eloquent warning, Far-reaching wisdom, but the warners profit them not. So, O Mohammed, turn thou from them. On the Day when the Summoner[1] will summon to a difficult thing, With downcast looks will they emerge from their graves, as though they were scattered locusts. As they hurry along to the Summoner the unbelievers will be saying: "This will be a difficult day."

❋ Before them the people of Noah counted the message false. They counted the messenger false and said: "Jinn-possessed,"[2] and he was rejected. So Noah called upon his Lord, saying: "Truly I am overcome, so come to my help." Whereupon We opened the portals of the sky with water pouring down

Sura 54

in torrents. And We made the springs of the earth bubble up, so the waters met together in accordance with a determined decree. But him did We bear upon a vessel made of planks and nails, Which floated along under Our eyes—a recompense for him who had been disbelieved. And We have, indeed, left it[3] as a sign, but is there anyone who is reminded? So how was My punishment and My warning? Why, We have, indeed, made the lesson [qur'an] easy for a reminder, but is there anyone who is reminded?

❀ Ad counted the message false, and how was My punishment and My warning? We sent against them a roaring wind on a day of passing calamity, Which snatched men away as though they were uprooted palm-trunks. So how was My punishment and My warning? Why, We have, indeed, made the lesson easy for a reminder, but is there anyone who is reminded?

❀ Thamud counted the warning false, And they said: "Is it a man from among ourselves, a single fellow, that we are to follow? We should in that case most assuredly be in error and in foolishness. Has the reminder been sent to him alone amongst us? Nay, but he is a liar, an insolent fellow." On the morrow they will know who is the liar and the insolent fellow. We are going to send the she-camel as a testing for them, so keep watch on them, O Salih,[4] and be patient, And announce to them that the water is to be divided between them, each to drink by turn. But they summoned their companion, and he made himself ready and hamstrung her. So how was My punishment and My warning? Truly, We sent against them one single blast, and they were like dried stalks used by sheepfold builders. Why, We have, indeed, made the lesson easy for a reminder, but is there anyone who is reminded?

❀ The people of Lot counted the warning false, So We sent

against them a sandstorm, except the family of Lot whom We delivered at day-break As a favour from Us. Thus do we recompense whosoever is thankful. Lot had, indeed, given them warning of Our severity, but they had doubts about the warning, And had made lustful demands on him for his guests, so We put out their eyes, saying: "Taste ye then My punishment and My warning," And there came upon them in the morning a lasting punishment, While We said: "Taste ye My punishment and My warning." Why, We have, indeed, made the lesson easy for a reminder, but is there anyone who is reminded?

❧Just as truly did the warning come to the family of Pharaoh, But they counted all Our signs false, so We laid hold of them with the grip of One mighty, One endued with power.

❧Are the unbelievers among you Meccans any better than these? Or do ye have a promise of immunity in the Books?[5] Or are they saying: "We are a group who will lend one another aid?" Their group will be put to flight, and they will turn tail. Nay, but the Hour is their appointed time, and the Hour is more grievous and more bitter. Truly, the sinners are in error and in foolishness. On the Day when they are dragged on their faces into the Fire, We shall say: "Taste ye the touch of Saqar."[6] We have, indeed, created everything by a decree,[7] And Our command is naught but one word, swift as a glance with the eye, And We have already destroyed the likes of you,[8] but is there anyone who is reminded? Everything they do is in the Record Books, Where everything whether small or great is written down. Truly, the pious are in gardens and among rivers, In a seat secure, in the presence of a King endued with power.

Surat as-Saffat:
Those Who Set in Array

The introductory verses to this Sura may be early Meccan, but most of the pieces which have gone into its composition are middle Meccan. The core of the Sura is the group of passages telling of the previous messengers from Noah to Jonah, that about Abraham having been expanded in Medina by additional verses. To these "Prophet stories" have been prefixed certain characteristic passages vindicating Mohammed against Meccan sneers by descriptions of Allah's creation and of the Judgment and its consequences. These admirably introduce the "Prophet stories," which are then followed by passages which sharply criticize Meccan paganism and rebuke their negative attitude towards the Prophet's message. The precise references in the introductory swearing formulae are unknown, though they are commonly thought to refer to various classes of angels.

Sura
37

IN THE NAME OF ALLAH,
THE MERCIFUL, THE COMPASSIONATE

By those who set the ranks in array,[1] By those who scare away by a cry, By those who recite a warning, Verily your God is One, Lord of the heavens and of the earth and of what is between them, and Lord of the rising-places of the celestial lights,[2]

Truly We have adorned the lower heaven with an adornment of stars, And We have set a guard against every rebellious satan.[3] They [the satans] do not listen in at the Highest Council but are pelted away from every side. Banished are they, and for them is a continuing punishment. They learn naught save such an one as may snatch a chance phrase, but there follows him a gleaming flame.[4] So question thou them.[5] Are they a stronger creation, or those others whom We have created? Indeed, We created them [i.e., humans] of sticky clay.

❊ Nay, but thou art amazed at Allah's signs while they make mock, And when they are reminded they do not pay heed, And when they see a sign they set to making mock of it. And they say: "This is naught but manifest sorcery. Is it that when we have died and become dust and bones we are to be raised up? And also our sires, those of former times?" Say: "Yes! and ye will be abashed." For it is only a single blast, and behold! they are looking about them, And they say: "O woe to us! this is the Judgment Day." This is the Day of Severance which ye were counting false. Gather together those who have done wrong, and their consorts, and what they used to worship In place of Allah, and guide them to the path to al-Jahim.[6] And make them stand, for they are to be questioned by One who will ask: "How is it that ye do not help one another?"[7] Nay, but they are today seeking their own safety. They will approach one another making enquiry. Men will say: "Verily, ye used to come to us from the right hand."[8] They [the false gods] will say: "Nay, but ye were not believers. We had no authority over you. Nay, it was ye who were a people given to transgression. So the sentence of our Lord has come true upon us; we, indeed, are tasting it. We made you err because we were ourselves erring." So they, on that Day, are sharing in the punishment; Thus do We deal with sinners.

❊ They, when it was said to them: "There is no deity but Allah," were haughty, And were saying: "Shall we abandon our gods for a crazy poet?" Nay, but he came with the truth and confirmed the envoys.[9] It is ye who will be tasting the painful punishment, Nor will ye be receiving recompense save for the works ye have been doing: Save Allah's servants the single-hearted,[10] Those have a well-known provision, Fruits to eat while they are honoured, In gardens of delight,

Upon couches, facing one another. Borne around among them is a cup filled from a spring, White, a pleasure to those who drink, In which is no headache, nor from it will they be intoxicated. And beside them are wide-eyed damsels, restrained of glance, As though they were sheltered eggs. So they will approach one another, making enquiry. One of them will say: "I, indeed, had a close friend Who used to say: 'Are you of those who consider it true? Is it that when we have died and become dust and bones we are going to be judged?' " He will say: "Are you folk able to look down?" So he will look down and see him [his doubting friend] in the midst of al-Jahim. He will say to him: "By Allah, you came near to causing me to perish also: Had it not been for the favour of my Lord, I too should have been among those brought to torment. Is it then that we do not die Save our first death, and are we not to be punished? Truly this is the great success; For the like of this, then, let the workers work."

Is that a better repast, or the tree of Zaqqum?[11] Verily, We have appointed this tree as a trial for the wrongdoers. It is a tree which emerges from the bottom of al-Jahim, Its fruit[12] is as though it were satans' heads. Indeed they will be eating of it and from it filling their bellies, Then they shall have on top of it a drink of scalding water.[13] Then, indeed, the place to which they will return will be al-Jahim. Truly they found their fathers erring, Yet they in their footsteps are hastening along. Indeed, before them most of those of former times had erred, Even though We had sent among them warners. So see what the latter end was of those who were warned, Save Allah's servants, the single-hearted.

Verily, Noah called upon Us, and right good were those who responded.[14] We delivered him and his household out of the great distress, And We appointed his offspring to be the survivors, And We left for him with those of later times the saying: "Peace be upon Noah in the worlds." Thus, indeed, do We reward those who do well. Truly, he was among Our servants, the believers. Then We drowned the others.

❧Verily, of Noah's party was Abraham, When he came to his Lord with a sound heart. When he said to his father and his people: "What is this ye are worshipping? Is it some false devising ye prefer as gods instead of Allah? What is your thought then of the Lord of mankind?" Then he gave a look at the stars[15] And said: "In truth, I am sick," So they turned from him departing. Then he went in alone to their gods, and said: "Do ye not eat? What is the matter with you that ye speak not in reply to me?" Alone there among them he began striking them with his right hand. Then the people came towards him, moving hastily. He said: "Is it that ye worship that which ye carve, Though Allah created both you and what ye make?" They said: "Build for him a pyre and cast him into the blaze."[16] They wished to find some stratagem against him, but We made them the inferior ones. And he said: "I, indeed, am going to my Lord. He will guide me. O my Lord, give me one of the righteous as a son." So We gave him the good tidings of a meek-tempered youth.[17] Then when he [the son] had reached the age of working with him,[18] he said: "O my son, I see in a dream that I am to sacrifice thee. So look! what is it that thou dost see?" He said: "O my father, perform what thou art bidden. Thou wilt find me, if Allah wills, one of those who patiently endure." So when the two had thus resigned themselves, and he had laid him face downwards, We called to him: "O Abraham! Thou hast treated the vision as worthy of trust. Thus do We recompense those who do well; This, indeed, was the clear testing." So We redeemed the son by an excellent sacrifice, And We left for the father with those of later times the saying; "Peace be upon Abraham!" Thus, indeed, do We reward those who do good.

Truly, he was among Our servants, the believers, And We gave him the good news of Isaac, a Prophet, one of the righteous, And We bestowed Our blessing upon him and upon Isaac. Of the offspring of these two some were well-doers and some were doers of manifest wrong to themselves.

✽ We showed favours also to Moses and Aaron, And delivered them both, along with their people, out of the great distress. And We aided them so that it was they who were the conquerors. And We gave to both of them the Book that makes clear, And guided them both to the straight path, And We left for them both with those of later times the saying: "Peace be upon Moses and Aaron!" Thus do We reward those who do well. Truly, both of them were among Our servants, the believers.

✽ Verily, Elias was one of the envoys, When he said to his people: "Will ye not be pious? Do ye call upon Baal and leave the Best One of those who create, Allah, your Lord, and the Lord of your fathers, those of former times?" But they counted him false, so it is they who will be brought in to judgment, Save Allah's servants, the single-hearted. And We left for him with those of later times the saying: "Peace be upon Elias!" Thus do We reward those who do well. Truly, he was among Our servants, the believers.

✽ And, verily, Lot was one of the envoys, When We rescued him and his household, all of them Save an old woman among those who hung behind. Then We destroyed the others. Ye, indeed, pass by them as ye go in the morning,[19] And by night. Will ye not then understand?

✽ And, verily, Jonah was one of the envoys, When he fled to the laden ship. So he took part in the casting of lots but he was one of those condemned,[20] And so the fish swallowed him, for he was blameworthy, And had it not been that he was one of those who glorify Allah, He would have remained in its belly till the Day when they are raised. But We cast him up on the naked shore, and he was a sick man. But We caused to grow over him a plant of the gourd species,²¹ And We sent him to a hundred thousand, or maybe more; Then they believed, so We gave them enjoyment of life for a while.

❈So do thou consult them.²² Is it that thy Lord has daughters and they sons? Or did We create the angels females while they were watching? Is it not a fact that it is out of their own false devising that they say: "Allah has begotten?" They, indeed, are speaking lies. Did He give preference to daughters over sons? What is the matter with you? How are ye judging? Will ye not be reminded? Or do ye have some clear authority? Bring out your Book if ye are speaking the truth. Moreover they have made kinship between Him and the jinn, though the jinn already know that they are to be brought to judgment. Glory be to Allah! He is far removed from what they describe, Save Allah's servants, the single-hearted.

❈"Ye, indeed, and what ye worship²³ Will not tempt any to rebellion against Him, Save such a person as is destined to roast in al-Jahim. There is not one of us angels but has an appointed place. We are those who arrange the ranks in order,²⁴ We are those who give glory to Allah." And though the unbelievers were saying: "Had we with us a reminder from those of former times We should have been Allah's servants, the single-hearted," Yet they have disbelieved in it [Mohammed's message]; but anon they will know. Our word came of old to Our servants the envoys. They are the ones who should have been aided. And, indeed, it is Our armies that are the conquerors. So turn thou from them for a while, O Mohammed, And observe them. Anon it is they who will observe. Is it that they would hasten on Our punishment? When it descends at their courts an evil morning will it be for those who were warned. So turn thou from them for a while, And observe. Anon it is they who will observe. Glory be to thy Lord, Lord of the greatness. He is far removed from what they describe. Peace be upon the envoys, And praise be to Allah, Lord of mankind.

Surat ash-Shu'ara: The Poets

Again the core of the Sura is an account of previous messengers, the individual members of the account being linked by a refrain. These "Prophet stories" belong to much the same period as those of Sura 37, though here the order is less chronological and more detail is given. To these stories has been prefixed a passage which chides the Meccans for their slowness to believe and then introduces the stories. The stories are followed by passages defending Mohammed's own "revelations," then the famous condemnation of the poets, from which the Sura takes its title, and a concluding passage which seems very late.

IN THE NAME OF ALLAH,
THE MERCIFUL, THE COMPASSIONATE

T.S.M.[1] These are the signs of the Book that makes clear. Maybe, O Mohammed, thou art grieving thyself overmuch that they are not becoming believers. Did We so will We could send down upon them a sign from heaven to which their necks would become humble, Yet no renewed reminder from the Merciful comes to him [i.e., to Mohammed], but they are turning from it. Thus have they counted the message false, but there will anon come to them news of that of which they have been making mock. Is it that they have not looked at the earth, at how much We have caused to grow therein of every noble species? Truly in that is a sign, but the

Sura
26

75

majority of them are not believers, Yet thy Lord, indeed, He is the Sublime, the Compassionate.

❦·Now when his Lord summoned Moses, saying: "Go to the people, the wrongdoers, The people of Pharaoh; will they not show piety?" He said: "O my Lord, I fear, indeed, that they will count me false. Moreover my breast is straitened and my tongue moves not freely, so send to Aaron. Also they have a crime they are holding against me, so I am afraid they may kill me." He said; "Nay, not so! Go both of you with Our signs. We shall be with you hearkening. So go both of you to Pharaoh, and say: 'We are messengers from the Lord of mankind; Send forth with us the Children of Israel.' " Pharaoh said: "Did we not rear thee with us as a child? Indeed, thou hast passed years of thy life amongst us, And hast thou not done that deed of thine which thou didst? Thus thou art one of the ungrateful." Said he: "I did it at a time when I was one of the erring, So I fled from you Egyptians when I was afraid of you, but my Lord gave me wisdom and made me one of the envoys. And what a favour that is thou bestowest on me in that thou hast enslaved the Children of Israel!" Said Pharaoh: "And what is this title—Lord of mankind?" He said: "He is Lord of the heavens and the earth and what is between them both, if ye are those who form right judgment." Said Pharaoh to those who were around him: "Do ye not hearken?" Said Moses: "Your Lord and Lord of your fathers of former times." Said Pharaoh: "Assuredly your messenger who has been sent to you is jinn-possessed." Said Moses: "Lord of the East and of the West and what is between them both, if ye are intelligent." Said Pharaoh: "As sure as thou takest another deity instead of me I shall appoint thee to be among the imprisoned." Said Moses: "But what if I bring thee something which makes the matter clear?" Said Pharaoh: "Come along with it then, if thou art of those who speak the truth." So he cast down his staff, and behold! it was a manifest serpent, Also he drew forth his hand from his bosom, and behold! it was white to the beholders. Said Pharaoh to the Council around him: "This fellow is indeed a knowing sorcerer Who wants to drive you out from your land by his sorcery, so what orders would you give?" They said: "Put him and his brother off awhile, and send into the cities those who will assemble And bring to you every knowing expert in sorcery." So the sorcerers were gathered together for the appointment of a day that had been fixed. Also the people were asked: "Are ye going to assemble?" They answered: "Maybe we shall follow the sorcerers, if they are the ones who overcome." When the sorcerers came they said to Pharaoh: "Is it that we shall have a reward should we be those who overcome?" Said he: "Yea! and in that case ye shall be those who draw near to me." Moses said to them: "Cast down what ye are going to cast down." So they cast down their ropes and their staves, and they said: "By the greatness[2] of Pharaoh we shall be those who overcome." Then Moses cast down his staff, and behold! it swallowed up what they were falsely devising, So the sorcerers cast themselves down, doing obeisance. They said: "We believe in the Lord of mankind, The Lord of Moses and Aaron." Said Pharaoh: "Is it that ye have believed in Him[3] before I have given you permission? Verily, He is your chief who has taught you sorcery, so ere long ye will know, for I shall assuredly cut off your hands and your feet on opposite sides, and I shall crucify the lot of you." They said: "No harm! We are turning to our Lord, Indeed, we earnestly desire that our Lord will forgive us our sins now that we have become the first believers." Then We spoke by revelation to Moses, saying: "Go forth by night with My servants, for ye will surely be followed." Then Pharaoh sent unto the cities those who would assemble troops. They said: "Lo! these are but a small band, few in number,

Even though they are enraged at us, But we are quite a band, on our guard." Thus We brought them forth from the land of gardens and fountains, And pleasures and a noble estate. Thus it was; and We gave them as an inheritance to the Children of Israel. But the Egyptians followed them, getting up at sunrise, And when the two hosts saw one another, the companions of Moses said: "We are surely overtaken." Said he: "Nay, not so! Truly my Lord is with me. He will guide me." So We spoke by revelation to Moses, saying: "Smite the sea with thy staff," and it was split asunder, so that each part was like a great mountain, And there We brought along the others. We saved Moses and all those who were with him, Then We drowned the others. Truly, in that there is a sign for the Meccans, but the major part of them have not become believers. Yet thy Lord, indeed, He is the Sublime, the Compassionate.

❀ So recite to them, O Mohammed, the story of Abraham. When he said to his father and to his people: "What are ye worshipping?" They said: "We worship idols and we maintain constant devotion to them." Said he: "And do they hear you when ye call upon them? Or do they do you either benefit or harm?" They said: "Nay, but we found our fathers acting thus." Said he: "Have ye ever thought about what it is ye are worshipping, Ye and your fathers of earlier times? They, indeed, [i.e., the false gods] are an enemy to me, save the Lord of mankind Who created me, for it is He who guides me, And He it is who gives me food and drink, And when I am sick then He heals me. And He it is who will cause me to die and then bring me to life, And Who, I earnestly desire, may forgive me my sins on the Day of Judgment. O my Lord, grant me wisdom, and join me up with the righteous, And appoint for me a tongue of truth[4] among the latter peoples, And appoint me among those who inherit the Garden of Delight. And forgive my father, for he was one of those who went astray, And put me not to shame on the Day men are raised, A Day when wealth will not profit one, nor children, Save such as come to Allah with a sound heart, A Day when the Garden has been brought near to the pious, While al-Jahim has been made visible to those who have been beguiled." Then to them it will be said: "Where is that which ye were worshipping Instead of Allah? Are they giving you any aid, or are they aiding themselves?" Then into it they will be thrown headlong, they and those who have been beguiled. And all the hosts of Iblis.[5] Men will say while they are therein wrangling with one another: "By Allah! we were indeed in manifest error When we put you on an equality with the Lord of mankind. It was none but the sinners led us astray, So now we have no intercessors, Nor any warm friend. Would that we might have another chance, so that we might be among the believers!" Truly, in that there is a sign for the Meccans, but the major part of them have not become believers, Yet thy Lord, He is the Sublime, the Compassionate.

The people of Noah counted the envoys false, When their brother Noah said to them: "Will ye not be pious? I, indeed, am a faithful messenger to you, So shew piety towards Allah, and obey me.[6] I am asking of you no reward for it. My reward depends solely on the Lord of mankind, So shew piety towards Allah, and obey me." Said they: "Are we to believe in thee when only the vilest folk follow thee?" Said he: "But what knowledge do I have of what they were doing? Their accounting is with none but my Lord. Would that ye could perceive this, For I am not going to turn believers away.[7] I am nothing but a warner who makes clear." They said: "If thou dost not put an end to this, O Noah, thou wilt assuredly be one of the stoned." He said: "O my Lord, my people have counted me false, So open Thou an opening[8] between me and them, and rescue me, and with me those who believe." So We did rescue him, and those with him, in the fully-laden ark, Then, afterwards, We drowned those who remained. Truly in that there is a sign for the Meccans, but the major part of them have not become believers, Yet thy Lord, indeed, He is the Sublime, the Compassionate.

❊Ad counted the envoys false, When their brother Hud said to them: "Will ye not be pious? I, indeed, am a faithful messenger to you, So shew piety towards Allah, and obey me. I am asking of you no reward for it. My reward depends solely on the Lord of mankind. Do ye build on every height a landmark, amusing yourselves? And do ye take for yourselves huge structures wherein maybe ye may long abide? And whenever ye make an onslaught ye make onslaught as though ye were giants? Shew piety towards Allah and obey me, And shew piety towards Him who caused you to abound in that whereof ye know. He caused you to abound in cattle and in children, And gardens and fountains. Truly I fear for you the punishment of a mighty day." Said they: "It is the same to us whether thou hast preached or hast not been one of the preachers; This is naught but some creation of the ancients, And we are not those who will be punished." Thus they counted him false and We destroyed them. Truly in that there is a sign for the Meccans, but the major part of them have not become believers, Yet thy Lord, indeed, He is the Sublime, the Compassionate.

❊Thamud counted the envoys false, When their brother Salih said to them: "Will ye not be pious? I, indeed, am a faithful messenger to you, So shew piety towards Allah, and obey me. I am asking you no reward for it. My reward depends solely on the Lord of mankind. Will ye be left in the midst of what is here secure? Amidst gardens and fountains, And cultivated fields and palm trees whose spathes are thinly smooth? And will ye hew out houses for yourselves from the mountains, working cleverly? Shew piety towards Allah, and obey me, And obey not the bidding of those who go to excess, Who cause corruption in the land instead of working reform." Said they: "Thou art only one of the ensorcelled, Thou art naught but a man like us, so produce a sign if thou art one of those who speak the truth." He said: "This is a she-camel I have produced. She shall have a drink and ye shall have a drink on a settled day,⁹ So touch her not with evil intent lest there overtake you the punishment of a mighty day." But they hamstrung her, and rose in the morning penitent, But the punishment overtook them. Truly in that there is a sign for the Meccans, but the major part of them have not become believers, Yet thy Lord, indeed, He is the Sublime, the Compassionate.

❋·The people of Lot counted the envoys false, When their brother Lot said to them: "Will ye not be pious? I, indeed, am a faithful messenger to you, So shew piety towards Allah, and obey me. I am asking you no reward for it. My reward depends solely on the Lord of mankind. Do ye come at the males among mankind, And leave what your Lord created for you, namely your spouses? Nay, but ye are a wicked people." Said they: "If thou dost not put an end to this, O Lot, thou wilt assuredly be one of the banished." He said: "Truly, I am one of those who abhor your doings. O my Lord, save me and my household from what they are doing." So We rescued him and his household, all of them Save an old woman among those who tarried. Then We destroyed the rest, For We rained upon them a rain, and evil was the rain for those who had been warned. Truly in that there is a sign for the Meccans, but the major part of them have not become believers, Yet thy Lord, indeed, He is the Sublime, the Compassionate.

✺The people of the Grove counted the envoys false, When Shu'aib[10] said to them: "Will ye not be pious? I, indeed, am a faithful messenger to you, So shew piety towards Allah, and obey me. I am asking you no reward for it. My reward depends solely on the Lord of mankind. Give full measure, and be not of those who cause loss to others, So do your weighing with a true balance, And defraud not men of their substance, and do not do evil in the land, causing corruption, But shew piety towards Him who created you and the multitudes of ancient times." Said they: "Thou art only one of the ensorcelled. Thou art only a man like us, and truly we think thee one of the liars, So make some segments of the sky fall down on us if thou art of those who speak the truth." He said: "My Lord knows best about what ye are doing." So they counted him false, and there overtook them the punishment of a day of the overshadowing cloud. Verily it was the punishment of a mighty day. Truly, in that there is a sign for the Meccans, but the major part of them have not become believers, Yet thy Lord, indeed, He is the Sublime, the Compassionate.

✺Now this message is indeed a revelation[11] from the Lord of mankind. The faithful spirit came down with it Upon thy heart, that thou mightest be one of those who warn. It has been sent down in clear Arabic speech, And indeed it is in the Books of the former peoples. Was it not a sign to them that the Divines[12] of the Children of Israel recognize it? Had We sent it down upon one of the foreigners And he had recited it to them, they would not have been believing in it. Thus have We made a way for it in the hearts of sinners. They will not believe in it until they see the painful punishment, For it will come on them suddenly while they are not aware, So that they will say: "Are we to be respited?" Is it that they are seeking to hasten Our punishment? Hast thou given thought? If We have given them enjoyment for years, And then there comes to them that which they were promised, What will what they have been enjoying avail them? We have not destroyed any city but it has had those who gave warning As a reminder, and We have not been wrongdoers.

❀ The satans did not come down with it. It was not befitting for them, nor were they able. They indeed are far removed from hearing it, So do not call on any other deity along with Allah, lest thou be among those to be punished, But warn thy kindred who are the nearest, And lower thy wing to whosoever of the believers may follow thee. Then, if they oppose thee, say: "I, indeed, am innocent of what ye do," And rely upon the Sublime, the Compassionate, Who sees thee when thou standest, And sees thee turning thyself among those who are prostrating themselves in obeisance. He, indeed, is the One who hears and knows.

❀ Shall I inform you Meccans upon whom the satans come down? They come down upon every wicked liar. They impart what they hear, but the majority of them are liars, And the poets, those who are beguiled, follow them. Dost thou not see that in every valley they wander love-distraught? And that they say what they do not do?

❀ Save those who believe and work righteous works, and make much mention of Allah, and who make their defence after they have been wronged. Also those who do wrong will know anon with what an upsetting they will be upset.

Surat Ta Ha: T. H.

*The main portion of this Sura was apparently constructed as a
unit to tell in some fullness the story of Moses. As such it has an
introduction and an epilogue. To this various odd bits, includ-
ing a piece with the Adam story, were added by the compilers;
these constitute the last two sections. Much of the material in
the Moses story is Middle Meccan but the whole would seem to
have been revised in Medina. The curiously mixed-up chro-
nology of the Moses story is due to the fact that the story has
been pieced together from a number of pieces of quite different
provenance. The Sura gets its name from the mysterious letters
with which it opens.*

IN THE NAME OF ALLAH,
THE MERCIFUL, THE COMPASSIONATE

T. H. We have not sent down the lesson [*qur'an*] upon
thee that thou shouldst be miserable, But as a reminder to him
who fears. It is a revelation from Him who created the earth
and the high heavens. The Merciful has taken His seat upon
the Throne. His is whatever is in the heavens, and whatever
is on earth, and what is between them both, and what is beneath the soil.[1] There is no need for thee to speak loudly, for
He knows the secrets and what is even more hidden. Allah,
there is no deity save Him; His are the most beautiful names.[2]

Has there come to thee, O Mohammed, the story of Moses?
When he saw a fire he said to his household: "Abide ye here.
I have caught sight of a fire; maybe I shall bring you a brand
from it, or maybe I shall find guidance at the fire." But when
he reached it there came a call to him: "O Moses! Verily, I
am thy Lord, so remove thy sandals. Truly thou art in the
holy vale Tuwa,[3] And I have chosen thee, so hearken to what
is revealed. It is I, indeed, who am Allah. There is no deity

save Me. So worship thou Me, and observe prayer as a remembrance of Me. Truly the Hour is coming—I can barely keep it hidden—that every soul may be recompensed for that after which it strives, So let not one who believes not in it, but follows his own desire, turn thee from it so that thou dost perish. And what is that in thy right hand, O Moses?" He said: "It is my staff on which I lean, and with which I beat down leaves for my flock, and for which I have also other uses." Said He: "Cast it down, O Moses!" So he cast it down, and behold! it was a serpent that moved along. Said He: "Take hold of it, and be not afraid: We shall make it return to its former state. Now put thy hand close into thine arm-pit;[4] it will come out white but unharmed, as another sign, That We may show thee some of Our greatest signs. Go to Pharaoh, for he has wickedly transgressed." He said: "O my Lord, expand for me my breast, And ease for me my affair, And loose a knot from my tongue,[5] So that they may understand my speech. And appoint for me a vizier from my own household, Aaron, my brother. By him strengthen my loins, And associate him with me in my affair, That we may give much glory to Thee, And make frequent mention of Thee. Thou hast, indeed, been regarding us." Said He: "Thou hast been granted what thou hast requested, O Moses, Though We had already bestowed favour on thee at another time, When We revealed to thy mother that which was revealed, Saying: 'Cast him into the ark[6] and cast it into the sea, and let the sea cast it on the shore. One who is an enemy to Me and an enemy to him will take him up.' And I threw upon thee a token of love from Myself, and all this was that thou mightest be fashioned according to My eye. So when thy sister was walking she said: 'Shall I point out to you someone who will nurse him?' Thus did We return thee to thy mother, that her eye might be cheered and that she grieve not. Then thou didst slay a person, but We rescued thee from that trouble, and We tried thee with trials, so thou didst tarry for years with the people of Midian, and then thou didst come in accordance with a decree, O Moses. And I fashioned thee for Myself. Go thou and thy brother with My signs, and be not slack in remembrance of Me. Go ye to Pharaoh! He, indeed, has wickedly transgressed, But speak ye to him with gentle speech, so that maybe he will be reminded, or will fear." They said: "O our Lord, truly we are afraid lest he break out in anger against us, or wickedly transgress." Said He: "Be ye not afraid, for I am with you. I hear and I see." So they came to him and they said: "We are two messengers from thy Lord, so send forth with us the Children of Israel, and do not punish them. We have now come to thee with a sign from thy Lord, and peace be upon him who follows the guidance! We, indeed, have had it revealed to us that the punishment will be upon him who counts the message false and turns away." He said: "And who is the Lord of you two, O Moses?" He said: "Our Lord, Who gave to everything its nature, then guided it the way it should go." Pharaoh said: "Then what about the former generations?" Moses said: "Knowledge about them is with my Lord in a Book. My Lord does not err nor does He forget, He who appointed the earth to be for you a cradle, and laid out paths thereon for you, and sent down rain from the skies, whereby We have brought forth various species of plants, Saying: 'Eat ye, and pasture your flocks.' Verily in that surely there are signs for those possessed of understanding. From the earth did We create you, and into it shall We return you, and from it bring you forth once more." Then We showed him all Our signs but he counted them false and disdained to believe. He said: "Hast thou come to drive us out of our land by thy sorcery, O Moses? We shall assuredly produce for thee sorcery like it, so appoint a time of meeting between us and thee, which neither we nor thou will fail to keep at some halfway place." Moses said: "Your appointed time will be the decoration day,[7] that the people may assemble in the forenoon." So Pharaoh turned away and prepared his stratagem. Then he came. Moses said to them: "Woe to you! devise not a lie against Allah lest He exterminate you by a punishment. He who devises devices against Allah has already failed." So the Egyptian sorcerers discussed their affair among themselves and kept their conference secret. They said: "These two are sorcerers who desire to drive you from your land by their sorcery, and take away your most excellent way of life, So prepare your stratagem, then come along in orderly ranks. He who today gets the upper hand will have prospered." They said: "O Moses, either thou wilt cast or we shall be the first to cast." Said he: "Nay, but do ye cast," and lo! their ropes and their staves appeared to him, because of their sorcery, as though they were running, Whereat Moses felt within himself a fearfulness. We said: "Fear not! it is thou who art the superior, So cast what is in thy right hand; it will swallow up what they have produced. They have produced only a sorcerer's stratagem, and no sorcerer will prosper, wherever it be he may come." Then the sorcerers fell down doing obeisance. They said: "We believe in the Lord of Aaron and Moses." Pharaoh said: "Have ye believed in Him before I gave you permission? He, indeed, is your chief who has taught you sorcery. I shall assuredly cut off your hands and feet on opposite sides, and just as assuredly shall I crucify you on palm-tree trunks,[8] so ye will surely know which of us is the severer and more enduring in punishment." They said: "Never shall we give thee preference over the clear evidences that have come to us, and over Him who created us. Decide what thou art going to decide concerning us, for thy deciding affects only this worldly life. We have believed in Our Lord, that He may forgive us our sins and the sorcery to which thou didst compel us, for Allah is better and is more enduring. The fact is that he who comes to his Lord a sinner, for him is

Gehenna, in which he neither dies nor lives, But he who comes to Him a believer who has done righteous works, for such as these are the highest ranks in Paradise, Gardens of Eden, beneath which rivers flow, in which they will be for ever. That is the recompense of him who has made an effort to be pure."

❧ Then We spoke to Moses by revelation, saying: "Go forth by night with My servants, and smite for them a way by dry land in the sea. Have no fear of being overtaken, and be not afraid." Then Pharaoh had them followed by his armies, so there covered them, of the sea, what covered them. Thus Pharaoh led his people astray instead of guiding them. O Children of Israel, We certainly rescued you from your enemy, and We made an appointment with you at the right-hand side of at-Tur,[9] and We sent down for you the manna and the quail. Eat of the good things which We have given you as a provision, but go not to excess therein lest My anger light upon you, for whosoever has My anger light upon him has already perished. Yet am I, indeed, forgiving to whosoever repents and believes and acts righteously, then submits to guidance.

❧ But what has made thee hasten away from thy people, O Moses? He said: "They are those following after me,[10] but I hastened on to Thee, O my Lord, that Thou mightest be well-pleased." Said He: "Now, indeed, have We tested thy people after thy leaving them, and the Samaritan has led them astray."[11] Then Moses returned to his people angered and chagrined. He said: "O my people, did not your Lord make you an excellent promise? Did the covenant then seem to last too long for you, or did ye desire that anger from your Lord light upon you, that ye failed my appointment?" They said: "We did not of our own accord fail thy appointment, but we were made to carry loads of the people's ornaments, so we threw them down." Thus also did the Samaritan cast,

And he produced for them a calf, a body which lowed. And they said: "This is your god, and the god of Moses, but he has forgotten." But do they not see that it returns no word to them, and that it possesses no power either to harm or to benefit them? Aaron had already said to them beforehand: "O my people, ye are only being put to the test by it. Your Lord is the Merciful, so follow me and be obedient to my command." They said: "We shall not cease being devoted to it till Moses returns to us." Said Moses: "O Aaron, what hindered thee when thou sawest them going astray, That thou didst not follow me? Hast thou disobeyed my command?" Said Aaron: "O mother's son, seize me not by my beard or by my head. I, indeed, was afraid thou wouldst say: 'Thou hast caused a schism among the Children of Israel, and didst not observe what I said.'" Moses said: "And what is thy statement, O Samaritan?" Said he: "I saw what they saw not, so I took a handful from the track of the messenger and threw it, for thus did my soul suggest to me."[12] Moses said: "Begone, then; and truly it shall be thine throughout life to say: 'No touching!' Thine also is an appointment thou wilt not fail to keep. So look at thy god to which thou didst continue so devoted. Most assuredly we shall burn it, then grind it to powder and cast it into the sea. Allah alone is your God, He than Whom there is no other deity, Whose knowledge embraces all things."

❋·Thus do We recount to thee, O Mohammed, some of the stories of what happened of old, and We have, indeed, given thee from Ourselves a reminder. Whosoever turns aside from it, he, truly, on the Day of Resurrection will carry a burden. Such will continue under it, and an evil load will it be for them on the Day of Resurrection—A Day when there will be a blast on the Trump [Sur], and We shall assemble the sinners, on that Day, blue.[13] Among themselves they will be softly saying: "Ye have tarried no more than ten days in the grave." We know right well what they will say, when the one of them whose way of life has been the most exemplary will say: "Ye have tarried no more than a day."[14] And they will question thee about the mountains. Say: "My Lord will grind them to powder, And leave them a levelled-off plain, In which thou wilt see no crookedness and no curve [i.e., there will be no hills or valleys]. On that Day they will follow the Summoner, who knows no crookedness, and voices will be lowered before the Merciful, so that thou wilt hear nothing but a shuffling of feet. On that Day no intercession will avail save that of him to whom the Merciful gives permission and is pleased to let speak. He knows what is before them and what is behind them, though their knowledge compasses not Him. Faces will be humbled before the Living One, the Self-subsistent, and whosoever is carrying his burden of wrong-doing will indeed have failed; But whosoever has done right-eous works, and is a believer, he will fear neither wrong nor defrauding.

❊ And thus We have sent it down an Arabic *Qur'an*, and in it We have set forth clearly some threats, that maybe they will shew piety, or that it may be again to them a reminder. So, exalted be Allah, the King, the True One. Be not thou hasty with the lesson [*qur'an*] before its being revealed to thee is finished, and say: "O my Lord, increase me in knowledge."

❊ Truly, of old We made a covenant with Adam, but he was forgetful, and We found in him no constancy. And when We said to the angels: "Do obeisance to Adam," they did obeisance, save Iblis, who disdainfully refused. So We said: "O Adam, truly this one is an enemy to thee and to thy wife, so let him not drive you both from the garden, that thou shouldst become wretched. Verily it is thine not to hunger therein nor be naked, And that thou shouldst not thirst therein nor suffer from the sun's heat." But Satan whispered to him. He said: "O Adam, shall I direct thee to the Tree of Eternity and a possession that grows not old?" So they both ate thereof, whereat their pudenda became noticeable to them, so they set about sewing for themselves garments from some leaves of the garden. Thus Adam disobeyed his Lord and went astray. Then his Lord chose him, so that He turned to him and gave guidance. He said: "Get ye down from Paradise, both together, the one of you an enemy to the other, but should guidance from Me come to you, then whosoever follows My guidance will not err, nor will he be wretched, But whosoever turns away from remembrance of Me, for him, truly, there is a narrow life, and We shall assemble him blind on Resurrection Day." He will say: "O my Lord, why hast Thou assembled me blind, though I used to be one who sees?" Allah will say: "Thus is it to be. Our signs came to thee, but thou wast forgetful of them and so today thou art forgotten." Thus do We recompense him who has transgressed and who did not believe in the signs of his Lord. Truly, the punishment of the Hereafter is more severe and more lasting.

✶·Has there been no guidance for them in the number of generations We have destroyed before them, through whose dwelling-places they walk? Truly, in that there are signs for those possessed of understanding. Had it not been for a word from thy Lord which preceded, the Judgment would have been right here, but it is a time fixed. So, O Mohammed, endure with patience what they are saying about thee, and glorify thy Lord with praise before the rising of the sun and before its setting, and at the night watches, and give glory also at the ends of the day; maybe thou wilt be well-pleasing to Him. And let not thine eyes look with longing at what We have given divers of them to enjoy, the splendour of this present world, that thereby We may put them to the test, for the provision of thy Lord is better and more lasting. Enjoin prayer on thy household, and continue steadfastly therein. We ask thee for no provision, rather do We provide for thee, and the final outcome depends on piety.[15] They say: "Why does he not bring to us a sign from his Lord?" Has there not come to them the clear evidence of what is in the former scrolls? Had We destroyed them by a punishment before it[16] came to them they would have said: "O our Lord, hadst Thou sent to us a messenger we would have followed Thy signs before we were humiliated and disgraced." Say: "Everyone is waiting expectantly for the Hour, so wait ye expectantly, and ye shall know who are the people of the even path, and who has accepted guidance."

Surat al-Hijr: Al Hijr

The Sura derives its name from the settlement in the northern Hejaz, the Hegra of the Nabataean inscriptions, which was a stopping place on the caravan route to the north, and which is mentioned toward the end of the Sura as a place to which one of Allah's envoys was sent. The passages about Iblis, about al-Hijr, and about Abraham and Lot are Middle Meccan, though as the Abraham and Lot stories are here connected, and it is obvious that two originally distinct stories have been combined, this must be later than those Suras in which they are still independent. The creation piece (second section) which leads up to the Iblis story is even earlier, but the introduction and the concluding verses are almost certainly Medinan.

IN THE NAME OF ALLAH,
THE MERCIFUL, THE COMPASSIONATE

❊ A.L.R. These are the signs of the Book, and of a lesson [*qur'an*] that makes clear. Often will those who have disbelieved wish that they had become submissive. Let them eat and enjoy themselves, and let hope beguile them, for anon they will know. Yet We have not destroyed any town save when there was for it a known decree.[1] There is no people that anticipates its term, and none can retard it.

❊ Now, they said: "O thou to whom the reminder has been sent down, thou art, indeed, one jinn-possessed. Why dost thou not bring us the angels, if thou art of those who tell the truth?" We do not send the angels down save with the truth, and these folk then would not be granted respite. We it is, indeed, Who have sent down the reminder, and it is We who will keep watch for it. We, indeed, have sent messengers before thee among the sects of former peoples, And never would a messenger come to them but they would be making jest of him. Likewise We make a way for it in the hearts of sinners. They do not believe in it, though, indeed, the customary rule of life of the former peoples has come to an end. Were We to open for them one of the gates of heaven so that they could mount up continually into it, They would say: "Our sight has been made drunken, Nay, but we are a people who have been ensorcelled."

❊ Truly, We have set constellations[2] in the sky, and have beautified them for those who behold, And have guarded them from every stoned satan, Save such as may stealthily hearken, but such are followed by a clear flame.[3] And the earth We have spread out, and cast mountains upon it, and in it have caused to grow everything that is measured. Also in it We have appointed for you means of livelihood, and for those for whom ye cannot make provision. And there is not a thing but with Us are its storehouses, and We do not send it down save by fixed measure. Also We have sent forth the winds as fertilizers, and from the skies have We sent down water, so that We may give you drink thereby. It is not ye

who are the storers of it. Also it is We, indeed, Who cause to
live and cause to die, and We are the ultimate inheritors.[4]
Truly We know those of you who seek to press forward, and
just as truly We know those who seek to hang back. Verily
thy Lord is He Who will assemble them for Judgment. He,
indeed, is wise, knowing. And We created man from potter's
clay, of moulded mud, But the jinn We created earlier from
the fire of the simoon.[5]

❧ And when thy Lord said to the angels: "Behold! I am
about to create a man from potter's clay, of moulded mud;
So when I have fashioned him and breathed into him of My
spirit, then fall down before him doing obeisance," Then the
angels, all of them together, did obeisance, Save Iblis, who
disdainfully refused to be among those doing obeisance. Said
Allah: "O Iblis, what is the matter with thee that thou art not
among those doing obeisance?" Said he: "I am not one who
would do obeisance to a man whom Thou hast created from
potter's clay, of moulded mud." Said Allah: "Then get out
from the garden, for thou art stoned, And, truly, on thee shall
be the curse till the Day of Judgment." Said he: "O my Lord,
grant me respite till the Day when they are raised." Said He:
"Verily thou art one of those respited Till the day of the set
time." He said: "O my Lord, inasmuch as Thou hast turned
me away I shall make things look fine to them on earth and
turn them away altogether, Save Thy servants among them
who are single-hearted." Said Allah: "This is the straight path
for Me. Truly, over My servants thou hast no authority, save
over those perverse ones who follow thee, And Gehenna, indeed, is the place appointed for all of them." It has seven gates
and to each gate is one section of them assigned. Those, however, who show piety are amidst gardens and fountains. To
them it is said: "Enter ye in peace, fully secure," And We
shall have removed any rancour there may have been in their

breasts, so that as brethren they may sit facing one another on couches. Therein no weariness will touch them, nor will they ever be turned out of it.

❧ Announce, O Mohammed, to My servants that I am, indeed, the Forgiving, the Compassionate, But that My punishment is the painful punishment. Tell them also about Abraham's guests, When they entered to him, and said: "Peace." He said: "Truly we are afeared of you." They said: "Have no fear. We are bringing you good tidings of a knowing youth." Said he: "Do ye give me such tidings in spite of the fact that old age hath touched me? So what is this good tidings ye give?" They said: "We have given you good tidings in very truth, so do not be among those who despond." Said he: "What then is your message, O ye envoys?" They said: "Truly, we have been sent to a people who are sinners, Save the family of Lot, all of whom we are going to rescue," Except his wife,[6] for We had decreed that she be one of those who tarried. Then, when the envoys came to Lot's family, He said: "Ye are people unknown to me." They said: "Nay, but we have brought that about which they are in doubt, So set off with thy household in one of the night watches, and do thou follow behind them, saying: 'Let not one of you turn around, but pass along whither ye are bidden.'" We delivered to him this command to depart because these Sodomites were to be cut off to the last man as they arose in the morning. Now the people of the city came to Lot's house rejoicing. Said he: "But these are my guests, so do not disgrace me, But show piety towards Allah, and put me not to shame." They said: "And did we not forbid thee from mankind?"[7] Said he: "Here are my daughters if ye are going to act thus." By thy life, in the intoxication of their lust they were out of their senses, So the Shout[8] took them as they arose at sunrise, And We turned their city upside down,[9] and rained upon them stones of hardened clay. In that, indeed, there are signs to those who mark the signs, And the city [that was overturned] was on a way that still remains. Truly, in that there is a sign for those who believe.

❧·Also the people of the Grove [in the land of Midian] were wrongdoers, So We took vengeance on them. Verily they are both in a Codex that makes clear.[10] And the people of al-Hijr counted the envoys false. We brought to them Our signs, but they were turning away from them, And were hewing out for themselves houses from the mountains, quite secure, But the Shout took them as they were arising in the morning, And what they had been gaining availed them not.[11]

❧·We have not created the heavens and the earth and what is between them both save in truth. Also the Hour is surely coming, so, O Mohammed, pardon with a gracious pardon those who have been inimical. Thy Lord, He, indeed, is the One Who creates, the One Who knows. We have given thee seven from the *Mathani*[12] and the mighty Koran. So let not thine eyes look longingly at what We have given divers of them to enjoy, and grieve not over them, but lower thy wing to those who believe, And say: "As for me, I am the clear warner."

❧·Like that which We sent down upon those who make decisions,[13] Who have made the lesson [*qur'an*] into separate parts, So by thy Lord We shall assuredly question them all About what they have been doing. So, O Mohammed, declare what thou art bidden, and turn from the polytheists. Verily We shall attend to the scoffers for thee, Those who set up another deity along with Allah. Anon they will know. We know, indeed, that thou dost feel a straitening of thy breast at what they are saying, But give glory, with praise of thy Lord, and be one of those who do obeisance, And worship thy Lord till the certainty come to thee.

Surat al-Kahf: The Cave

The three main legends—that of the Seven Sleepers, that of Moses and al-Khidr, and that of Alexander the Great—and the two parables, which form the nucleus of this Sura, are of Middle Meccan material, but odd bits, some of earlier and some of later date, have been interpolated, perhaps by the compilers, and Medinan material has been used both for the introduction and the conclusion. All three of the legends were derived from Christian sources, though that of Moses goes back to a Jewish original, at least in part.

IN THE NAME OF ALLAH,
THE MERCIFUL, THE COMPASSIONATE

Praise be to Allah, Who has sent down upon His servant the Book, and has put in it no crookedness, But has made it direct, that He may warn of grievous vengeance from His presence, and give good tidings to the believers who do righteous works, that for them there is an excellent reward, Wherein they will abide for ever, And warn those who say: "Allah has taken for Himself a son." They have no knowledge thereanent nor had their fathers. It has grown big as a word that comes out from their mouths, but they say naught but a lie. Maybe thou art going to wear thyself out in vexation following their footsteps if they do not believe this discourse. We, indeed, have appointed whatever is on the earth to be an adornment thereof that We might test them, which of them is best in works, But We are assuredly going to make what is on it a barren expanse of earth.[1] Or hast thou considered, O Mohammed, how the Companions of the Cave and of ar-Raqim[2] were a wonder from among Our signs? When the youths fled for refuge to the cave, they said: "O our Lord, grant us a mercy from Thyself, and prepare for us a right direction for our affair." So We smote upon their ears in the cave for quite a number of years. Then We raised them up that We might know which of the two parties[3] was the better at reckoning the time they had tarried there. We shall relate to thee their story in truth. They were youths who believed in their Lord, and whom We increased in guidance. And We girded up their hearts when they stood up and said: "Our Lord is Lord of the heavens and the earth, never will we call upon any deity other than Him, for in that case we should have said something outrageous. These people of ours have taken for themselves deities other than Him. Would that they could bring some clear authority for them, for who does greater wrong than one who devises some lie about Allah? Now, since ye have separated yourselves from them and that which they worship in place of Allah, flee for refuge to the cave. Your Lord will extend to you of His mercy, and will prepare for you some settlement of your affair." Thou mightest see the sun when it arose incline to the right-hand side of their cave, and when it set turn off to the left-hand side of them, while they were in an open part thereof. That is one of Allah's signs. The one whom Allah guides is really guided; and whom He sends astray, for him thou wilt never find a patron who will direct aright. And thou wouldst have thought them awake while they were asleep, and We were making them turn over now to the right, now to the left, while their dog at the threshold was stretching out its paws. Hadst thou caught sight of them thou wouldst have turned from them in flight, and been filled with terror of them. Thus did We raise them up that they might question among themselves. Said one of them who spoke: "How long have ye tarried?" They said: "We have tarried a day, or part of a day." They said: "Your Lord knows best how long ye have tarried. Send now one of you with this money of yours into the city. Let him observe where therein the food is purest, and let him bring you provision therefrom; also let him speak courteously and not discover you to anyone, For they, indeed, if they get hold of you will stone you, or will force you to return to their religion, in which case ye will never prosper at all." Thus, then, did We make folk acquainted with them, that they might know that Allah's promise is true, and that the Hour is something about which there is no doubt: When the people [of Ephesus] were disputing among themselves about their affair, they said: "Build over them a building. Their Lord knows best about them." Said those who prevailed in their matter: "We shall surely set up over them a place of worship."⁴ Some will say: "Three, their dog the fourth of them." Others will say: "Five, their dog the sixth of them," making a shot at the unknown. Others will say: "Seven, their dog the eighth." Say: "My Lord knows best what their number was." None but a few know about them, so do not thou, O Mohammed, dispute about them save where the issue is obvious, and do not ask anyone from among them [i.e., the Christians] for an opinion about them. And never say about anything, "I am going to do that tomorrow" Without adding: "Should it be that Allah wills." And make mention of thy Lord when thou hast forgotten, and say: "Maybe my Lord will guide me to something nearer right direction than this." Now they tarried in their cave three hundred years and added thereto nine.⁵ Say: "Allah knows best how long they tarried." His are the unknown things of the heaven and the earth. How well He sees and hears! They have no patron other than Him, and He associates no one in His wisdom. So recite what is revealed to thee from the Book of thy Lord. There is no one who may make alterations in His words, nor wilt thou ever find a refuge other than Him. So content thy soul in patience along with those who call upon their Lord in the morning and in the evening, seeking His face, and let not thine eyes be turned away from them seeking the splendour of this present world, and obey not him whose heart We have made careless of remembering Us, who follows his desire, and whose affair has become iniquitous. And say: "The truth is from your Lord, so whosoever wills let him believe, and whosoever wills let him disbelieve." Truly, We have prepared for the wrongdoers a Fire, whose canopies will surround them, and should they ask for moisture they will be moistened with water like molten metal which will scald their faces. How terrible a drink, and how evil a place in which to recline! As for those who have believed and done righteous works, We shall not suffer the reward of one who has worked well to be lost. Such have gardens of Eden beneath which rivers flow, in which they will be adorned with golden bracelets, be clothed with green robes of satin and brocaded silk, reclining there on couches. What a wondrous reward, and how excellent a place in which to recline!

❧ Now set forth for them a parable about two men, for one of whom We appointed two gardens of grapevines, both of which We girt about with palm trees and between them set plots for cultivation. Each of the two gardens yielded its edible fruits and did not come short thereof in anything, and between the two of them We caused a stream to flow; Thus he had fruit, so he said to his friend, as he was conferring with him: "I have more wealth than thou hast, and a mightier family." So he entered his garden, doing wrong to himself. He said: "I do not think that this will ever perish, Nor do I think that the Hour will ever come, and even should I be sent back to my Lord I shall surely find something better than it in exchange." His friend said to him while he was conferring with him: "Dost thou disbelieve in Him Who created thee from dust, then from a drop, then fashioned thee as a man? Indeed, He is Allah, my Lord, and I shall not associate anyone with my Lord. Why didst thou not, when entering thy garden, say: 'What Allah has willed: There is no strength save with Allah'? Even though thou seest that I am thy inferior with regard to wealth and children, It may be that my Lord will give me something better than thy garden, and send upon thy garden a thunderbolt from the sky so that by the morning it is a slippery expanse of earth, Or by morning its water has become so deeply sunk thou wilt never be able to reach it." So his fruit was encompassed by destruction, and he was that morning wringing his hands over what he had spent on it, for the vines were wasted on their trellises, and he was saying: "O would that I had not associated anyone with my Lord!" And there was no party to help him in place of Allah, and he was not one who could help himself. There the protecting is Allah's affair, the True One Who is best when it comes to reward, and best when it comes to the final outcome.

❧ Set forth also for them a parable of this present life. It is as water which We send down from the skies so that there is a mingling with the vegetation of the earth, but in the morning it is stubble which the breezes scatter, for Allah has power over everything. Wealth and children belong to the adornment of this world's life, but in thy Lord's sight the things that abide, righteous works, are better in matter of reward and better in matter of hope. On the Day when We shall set the mountains moving, thou wilt see the earth an extended plain, where We have assembled them and have not omitted one of them. When they have been drawn up before thy Lord in ranks, We shall say: "Truly ye have come to Us as We created you the first time. Nay, but ye claimed that We should never set for you an appointed time." Then the Book will be placed before Him, and thou wilt see the sinners alarmed about what is in it, and they will say: "O woe to us! What a Book this is that omits nothing either small or great but has made count of it!" And they will find what they have done there present, and thy Lord will not wrong anyone.

❧Also make mention of when We said to the angels: "Do obeisance to Adam." They did obeisance, save Iblis who was of the jinn and revolted against the command of his Lord. Is it that ye will take him and his progeny as patrons instead of Me? Why, they are inimical to you. How poor an exchange for the wrongdoers! I did not have them witness the creation of the heavens and the earth, nor the creation of themselves, nor was I taking as helpers those who lead astray. On a Day He will say: "Summon those whom ye claimed were My partners." So they will summon them but they will not answer them, for We will have set a gulf between them. Then the sinners will see the Fire and will imagine that they are about to be flung into it, and will find no place to which to turn from it.

❧Truly We have set forth for the people in this Koran every kind of parable, but man, more than anything else, is a caviller. And naught prevented the people from believing when the guidance came to them, and from asking forgiveness from their Lord, save that they were going to follow the custom of former peoples, or that punishment would come to them openly. We do not send envoys save as bringers of good tidings and as warners, but those who disbelieve cavil with vain arguments that thereby they may attempt to refute the truth; and they take My signs, and that by which they are warned, as a jest. So who does greater wrong than one who is reminded of the signs of his Lord, but turns away from them, forgetting what his hands have sent forward? We have set veils over their hearts lest they should understand it, and in their ears a heaviness, so if thou summonest them to the guidance, even then they will never be guided. Yet thy Lord is the Forgiving One, One Who has mercy. Were He to take them to task for what they have earned, He would hurry on for them the punishment. But they have an appointed time, and they will never find a refuge apart from Him. Those towns We destroyed when they did wrong, and We set an appointed time for their destruction.

❧ Also make mention of when Moses said to his servant: "I shall not stop till I reach the confluence of the two seas,[6] or if I do not reach that, I shall go on for a long time. Then when the two of them reached the confluence, between them they forgot their fish, so it took its way to the sea by a path.[7] Then when the two of them had passed on he said to his servant: "Bring us our morning meal, for we have become weary from this journey of ours." Said he: "Didst thou notice when we went to the rock for rest? It was then I forgot the fish—and none but Satan made me forget to mention it—and it took its way wondrously to the sea." He said: "That is the very thing of which we were in quest," so they went back, retracing their steps, And they found one of Our servants[8] to whom We had granted a mercy from Ourselves, and whom We had taught knowledge such as We have. Moses said to him: "Shall I follow thee on condition that thou teachest me somewhat of the right guidance that thou hast been taught?" Said he: "Thou wouldst never be able to be patient with me. Indeed, how shouldst thou be patient about that concerning which thou hast no information?" Said Moses: "If Allah wills thou wilt find me patient, and I shall not disobey thee in any matter." Said he: "Well, if thou followest me thou art not to question me about anything until I make mention of it to thee." So the two of them went along till when they embarked on a ship, al-Khidr staved it in. Said Moses: "Hast thou staved it in in order to drown its company? Truly thou hast done a grievous thing." Said he: "Did I not say that thou wouldst never be able to be patient with me?" Said Moses: "Do not chide me because I forgot, and do not lay too difficult a thing upon me in my affair." So the two of them went along till, when they met a youth, al-Khidr slew him. Said Moses: "Hast thou put to death a guiltless soul? Truly, thou hast done an unheard-of thing." Said he: "Did I not say to thee that thou wouldst never be able to be patient with me?" Moses said: "If I question thee about anything after this let me be thy companion no more, for truly thou hast now from me an excuse." So the two of them went along till, when they came to the people of a town, they asked its people for food, but they disdainfully refused to take them as guests. So they found therein a wall just ready to fall down but al-Khidr set it upright. Moses said: "Hadst thou so wished thou mightest have taken payment for it." Said he: "This is the separation between me and thee. I shall now inform thee of the interpretation of that about which thou couldst not be patient. As for the ship, it belonged to poor men who laboured in the sea, and I desired to damage it because behind them was a king who was seizing every ship by force. And as for the youth, his two parents were believers, and we feared that he might cause them trouble by his transgression and unbelief, So we wanted their Lord to give them in exchange a son better than him in purity and closer in affection. And as for the wall, it belonged to two youths in the city who were orphans, and beneath it was a treasure of theirs. Now their father was a righteous man, so their Lord wanted them to reach their years of strength and bring forth their treasure as a mercy from their Lord. Thus I did not do it at my own bidding. That is the interpretation of that about which thou wast not able to be patient."

❧ Also they will ask thee about Dhu'l-Qarnain.⁹ Say: "I shall recite to you some mention of him." Truly, We made him powerful in the earth and gave him a way to everything, So he followed a way, Until he reached the setting-place of the sun. He found it setting in a muddy spring, beside which he found a people dwelling. We said: "O Dhu'l-Qarnain, two ways are open to thee: either that thou punish these people, or that thou take among them a way of kindness." Said he: "As for anyone who does wrong, we shall anon punish him and he will be sent back to his Lord, who will also punish him with an unheard-of punishment, But as for him who believes and acts righteously, his is the reward of that which is better, and we shall say to him that of our command which is easy." Then he followed a way, Till when he reached the place where the sun rises he found it rising on a people for whom We had set no curtain over against it. Thus it was, and truly, We had full information about what was with him. Then he followed a way, Till when he reached the place between the two mountain ramparts he found over against them a people who could hardly understand speech.[10] They said: "O Dhu'l-Qarnain, truly Gog and Magog are working corruption in the land, so shall we pay thee tribute on condition that thou settest up a rampart between us and them?" Said he: "That in which my Lord hath made me powerful is better, so assist me with such strength as ye have, and I shall set firm a wall between you and them. Bring me lumps of iron" — until, when he had made a level place between the two mountain sides, he said: "Blow your bellows," till, when he had made it red hot he said: "Bring me molten brass that I may pour on it." So they [the hosts of Gog and Magog] were not able to scale it, nor were they able to dig through it. He said: "This is a mercy from my Lord, but when the promise of my Lord comes He will make it powdered dust, and the promise of my Lord is true."

And We shall leave them on that Day surging like waves against one another; then there will be a blast on the Trump, and We shall assemble them all together. On that Day We shall present Gehenna in all its extent to the sinners, Whose eyes have been veiled against My reminder, and who have become incapable of hearing. Is it that those who disbelieve consider that they can take My servants as patrons instead of Me? Truly, We have made Gehenna ready as a reception for the unbelievers. Say: "Shall we inform you about those who will be losing their works the most? Whose effort in this present life has gone astray, while they consider that their works are going well? These are they who disbelieve in the signs of their Lord, and in the meeting with Him, so their works have been in vain, for We shall assign them no weight at the weighing on the Resurrection Day. That is their recompense, Gehenna, because they have disbelieved and taken My signs and My messengers as matter for jest." Verily those who believe and do righteous works, the gardens of Firdaus[11] are a reception for them, Wherein they shall abide for ever, for they will desire no change therefrom. Say: "Were the ocean ink for writing down the words of my Lord, the ocean would fail ere the words of my Lord fail, even though We were to bring as much as it again in addition."[12] Say: "I am, indeed, only a man like you. It has been revealed to me that your god is One God, so let whosoever hopes to meet his Lord work a righteous work and associate no one in the worship of his Lord."

106

Surat Ya Sin: Y.S.

The Sura derives its name from the mysterious letters with which it opens. For some reason not entirely clear it has become the Sura popularly recited at funerals, during periods of mourning, and at the visitation of graves. There are eschatological pieces in it, but the nucleus is the parable in the third section, which is Middle Meccan, as are the passages illustrating the signs. The other pieces that were inserted, however, are later, and the introduction is certainly Medinan.

Sura
36

IN THE NAME OF ALLAH,
THE MERCIFUL, THE COMPASSIONATE

Y.S. By the wise lesson [*qur'an*], Thou, O Mohammed, art indeed one of the envoys, Upon a straight path, Bringing a revelation [*tanzil*] of the Sublime, the Compassionate, That thou mayest warn a people whose fathers were not warned, so they were heedless.

Verily the sentence has come true on most of them, so they will not believe. We, indeed, have set shackles on their necks, which reach to the chins, so that they perforce hold up their heads. And We have set a rampart before them and a rampart behind them, and We have covered them over so that they do not see. Thus it is alike to them whether thou warn them or warn them not, they will not believe. Only such as follow the reminder wilt thou warn, such as fear the Merciful in the Unseen; so to such give good tidings of forgiveness and of a generous reward. It is We Who bring to life the dead, and write down what they have sent ahead and the traces they have left behind. Everything have We reckoned up in a Codex[1] that makes clear.

Set forth for them, O Mohammed, a parable: The people

of a certain town[2] were there when the envoys came to it, When We sent to them two; but they counted them both false, so We strengthened the mission by a third. Then the messengers said: "We are indeed Allah's envoys to you." The people said: "Ye are naught but humans like ourselves; and the Merciful has not sent down a thing. It is only that ye are lying." The messengers said: "Our Lord knows that we are indeed His envoys to you, But we have no obligation beyond the clear proclamation of the message." The people said: "We augur[3] ill of you. If ye do not desist we shall most assuredly stone you, and assuredly there will touch you from us a painful punishment." The messengers said: "Your ill augury is with yourselves. Since ye have been warned, will ye still be unbelieving? Nay, but ye are prodigal people." Then there came from the farthest end of the city a man running.[4] Said he: "O my people, follow ye the envoys, Follow those who do not ask of you any wage, and who are rightly guided. Why should I not worship Him Who created me? It is to Him ye are to be brought back. Am I to take other gods instead of Him? Should the Merciful wish to harm me their intercession would not avail me a thing, nor would they deliver me. I should then indeed be in manifest error. Lo! I have believed in your Lord, so hearken ye to me." It was said to him: "Enter the Garden."[5] Said he: "Would that my people could know How my Lord has forgiven me my sins and made me one of the honoured ones!" Now We did not send down upon his people after him any army from the skies, nor have We been sending such down, There was naught but a single shout, and lo! They were extinct. O what sorrow for humans![6] There comes not to them any messenger but they are making mock of him. Have they not seen how many generations before them We have destroyed? They, indeed, will not return to them, Yet assuredly all will be brought together before Us.

❧Moreover the dead earth is a sign to them. We gave it life and brought forth from it grain, so that of it they eat, And We set therein gardens of date palms and grapevines, and therein caused springs to gush forth, That they might eat of its fruits and of that for which their hands have laboured. Will they not then be thankful? Glory be to Him Who created all the pairs from which the earth has its productivity, and is the Creator of themselves, and of things they know not.[7] The night also is a sign for them. We strip from it the day, and behold! they are in darkness. Also the sun which runs to a place of rest it has. That is the decreeing of the Sublime, the Knowing One. And for the moon We have decreed stations, so that it comes back like an ancient bent palm branch. It behooves not the sun to overtake the moon, nor the night to outstrip the day, but, each in an orbit, they swim along.

❧Also a sign for them is the fact that We carried their progenitors[8] in the fully-laden ark, And We have granted for them the like whereon they embark; And if We will We drown them, so no cry for help will avail them, nor will they be rescued, Unless as an act of mercy from Us, and as an enjoyment for a while. Yet, when it is said to them: "Fear ye what is before you and what is behind you, maybe ye will obtain mercy," they pay no heed. Not a sign of the signs of their Lord comes to them but they turn away from it. And when it is said to them: "Give a contribution out of that with which Allah has provided you," those who disbelieve say to those who believe: "Shall we feed one whom Allah could feed if He so willed? Ye are only in clear error." And they are saying: "When will this threat come to pass, if ye are those who speak the truth?" What do they expect save a single shout?[9] It will seize them while they are still disputing. So they will be able to make no testamentary deposition, nor will they return to their families, But there will be a blast on the Trump, and lo! from the sepulchres to their Lord will they be speed-ing. They will say: "Ah! alas for us! Who has raised us from our place of rest? This is what the Merciful promised, and the envoys spoke the truth." There is naught but a single blast, and behold! all of them are brought into Our presence. Today no soul will be wronged in anything, and ye will not be recompensed save for what ye have been doing. Verily, the inmates of the Garden are today joyously busy, They and their spouses are in shade, reclining on couches. They have therein fruit, and they have whatsoever they call for. "Peace!" —a word of greeting from a compassionate Lord. But to the others He will say: "Separate yourselves out today, O ye sin-ners. Did I not make a covenant with you, O ye sons of Adam, that ye should not serve Satan?"—he, indeed, is a manifest enemy to you—And did I not say: "Worship ye Me. This is a straight path?" But now, indeed, he has led astray a great host of you. Did ye then have no sense? This is Gehenna with which ye were threatened. Roast in it today because of the way ye were disbelieving. Today We shall set a seal upon their mouths, and their hands will speak to Us, and their feet will bear witness to what they have been acquiring. And did We please We should put out their eyes, so that they would be trying to get ahead on the path, but how would they see? And did We please We should metamorphose them where they stand, so that they would not be able to move on, nor go back. And no matter to whom We give long life, him shall We reverse in nature.[10] Is it that they do not have intelligence?

✺We have not taught him [i.e., Mohammed] poetry, nor would that beseem him. It is naught but a reminder and a lesson [qur'an] that makes clear, That he may warn whoso-ever is alive, and that the sentence against the unbelievers may be justified.

❧Do they not see that We have created cattle for them out of what Our hands have made, so that they have dominion over them? And We have made them subject to them, so that from them they may have their riding beasts, and from them they may eat, And have of them advantages and beverages. Will they not be thankful? Yet they have taken for themselves deities apart from Allah, that mayhap they may be aided by them. They are not able to aid them, though they are for them a host that will be brought forward. So do not let their speech grieve thee. We know, indeed, what they keep secret and what they reveal.

❧Does not man see that We have created him from a drop? Yet, behold, he is a manifest disputer, And has set forth for Us a parable, and forgotten his creation, saying: "Who will bring the bones to life when they are decayed?" Say: "He will bring them to life Who produced them the first time, since He knows about every created thing, He who gave you fire from the green tree, so that, behold, ye kindle flame from it. Is not He who created the heavens and the earth powerful enough to create their like? Yea, indeed, He is the Creator, the Knower. His only command when He desires anything is to say to it: 'Be!' and it is. So glory be to Him in whose hand is the dominion over everything, seeing that to Him ye will be brought back."

Surat Nuh: Noah

As the title indicates, the message of this Sura is the story of Noah, the main portion of which is Middle Meccan. Bell has suggested that the greater part of the first section, which really has nothing to do with the Noah story, is part of a Meccan meditation of Mohammed, which is here put into the mouth of Noah as appropriate to the occasion.

Sura

71

❧ We, indeed, sent Noah to his people, saying: "Warn thy people before a painful punishment come upon them." He said: "O my people, I am to you a plain warner. Worship Allah and act piously towards Him, and obey me, Then He will forgive you your sins and defer you till a fixed time. Truly, Allah's time, when it comes, is not to be deferred, did ye only know." He said: "O my Lord, I have summoned my people night and day, But my summoning has only increased them in their eagerness to be fleeing. Indeed, whenever I summon them that Thou mayest forgive them, they put their fingers in their ears, and wrap their garments around them, and they persist in their evil ways and act disdainfully. Then I, indeed, summoned them plainly, Then I addressed them in public, and secretly I addressed them in private, And I said: 'Ask pardon of your Lord, for He has become forgiving. He will send down the skies upon you in copious rain, And will expand you in wealth and children, and will appoint for you gardens, and appoint for you streams. What is the matter with you that ye put no hope in Allah's benevolence, Seeing that it was He Who created you stage by stage? Have ye not seen how Allah created the seven heavens one above the other? And in them set the moon as a light and set the sun as a lamp? Allah also made you spring plantlike out of the earth, Then He will make you return into it, and will bring you out again. Also Allah has set the earth for you like a carpet spread, That thereon ye may walk in open paths."

❧ Said Noah: "O my Lord, they have disobeyed me, and they have followed one whose wealth and children have increased him only in loss, And they have worked out a mighty stratagem, And say: 'Leave not your deities! Leave not Wadd, nor Suwa, nor Yaghuth and Ya'uq and Nasr!'[1] And they have, indeed, led many astray, though they increase the wrongdoers in naught but error." Because of their sins they were drowned, and were made to enter a fire,[2] for they did not find for themselves any helpers apart from Allah. Said Noah: "O my Lord, leave not on the earth any house of the unbelievers, For shouldst Thou leave them they will lead Thy servants astray and beget only wicked unbelievers. O my Lord, forgive me and my parents, and every believer who enters my house, and the male and female believers, but increase not the wrongdoers save in destruction."

Surat al-Isra: The Night Journey

Here we have a Sura made up of a great number of little pieces of revelation material, most of it Meccan, but some of it clearly Medinan additions. It contains a number of very interesting passages. There is an imitation of the Decalogue, adapted to the new religion. There are some curious reminiscences of Jewish history in the second and the next-to-last sections, a reference to the Psalms at Reference 8, an echo of the discussion about the Spirit, and an important verse of instruction to Moslems on the matter of prayer. The opening verse, from which the Sura gets its name, is, as has often been observed, quite unconnected with what follows, but is important as the basis for the well-known legend of the Prophet's ascension.

IN THE NAME OF ALLAH,
THE MERCIFUL, THE COMPASSIONATE

Glory be to Him Who took His servant by night from the sacred shrine to the further shrine[1] Whose environs We have blessed, that We might show him some of Our signs. He it is Who is the One Who hears, the One Who sees.

Sura

17

113

❧Now We gave Moses the Book which We appointed to be a guidance for the Children of Israel, saying: "Take for yourselves no guardian beside Me, O ye progeny of those whom We carried in the ark along with Noah. He, indeed, was a grateful servant." And We decreed for the Children of Israel in the Book: "Ye will assuredly cause corruption in the land, and ye will assuredly mount to a great height.[2] So when the menace of the first of the two periods of corruption comes We shall send against you servants of Ours, possessors of mighty prowess, and they will search the inner apartments of the houses, so that it becomes a menace accomplished. Then We shall give you the turn again over them and extend you in wealth and children, and make you a more numerous host, And We shall say: 'If ye do well it is to your own souls ye do well, and if ye do evil it is to your own souls.' Then when the menace of the other period of corruption comes, it will come that they may make your faces ashamed and may enter the sanctuary as they entered it the first time, and that they may destroy utterly whatever they lay hands on. Maybe your Lord will have mercy on you, and will say: 'If ye turn back We shall turn back, but We have set Gehenna as a prison for the unbelievers.'" Verily, this Koran guides to that which is more upright, and it gives good tidings to the believers, who perform righteous acts, that for them there is, indeed, a great reward; And that for those who do not believe in the Hereafter We have prepared a painful punishment. But man prays for evil as he prays for good, for man is hasty.

❧Now We have appointed the night and the day as two signs; then We blot out the sign of the night and set up the sign of the day to make things visible, so that ye may seek bounty from your Lord, and that ye may know the number of the years and the reckoning of time, and everything have We made clearly distinct. Each man's bird of fate[3] have We fastened on his neck, and on the Day of Resurrection We shall produce for him a Book which he will meet wide open, And the Judge will say: "Read thy Book! Thou thyself wilt suffice today to assess the reckoning against thee." Whosoever submits to guidance submits only his own soul to the guidance, and he who goes astray leads astray only it. No burdened soul will bear the burden of another. It has not been Our wont to punish till We send a messenger, And whenever We desire to destroy a town We give command to its affluent folk and they act wickedly therein, so the sentence against it is justified, and We destroy it utterly. How many generations of those after Noah have We destroyed? And thy Lord is sufficiently informed and observant of the sins of His servants. Whosoever is desirous of this life which hastens away, We hasten to him therein what We will, to whom We will; then We appoint for him Gehenna where he will roast, disgraced, rejected. But whosoever desires the Hereafter and strives for it as it should be striven for, and is a believer, these will find that their striving has been gratefully received. To all, both to these and to those, do We extend of the bounty of thy Lord, for the bounty of thy Lord has not been hindered. Look how We have given some preference over others, but the Hereafter has greater degrees and greater preferment.

❧Set not up some other deity along with Allah, for by doing so thou wilt sit disgraced, abandoned. Thy Lord hath decreed that ye humans shall worship none save Him, and that ye act kindly with parents, whether only one of them reach old age with thee or both of them. Say not thou to them: "Uff!"[4]—neither reproach them, but speak to them with respectful speech, And lower thou to them the wing of humility in mercy, and say: "O my Lord, show mercy to them both since they brought me up when I was but little." Your Lord well knows what is in your souls if ye are upright, and He, indeed, is forgiving to those who resort to Him. And give thou to the kinsman his due, and to the unfortunate, and to the son of the road, and be not a squanderer. Verily, squanderers are brothers of the satans, and Satan was ungrateful to his Lord. But shouldst thou turn from them out of a desire for a mercy from thy Lord of which thou hast hope, nevertheless speak to them with gentle speech. Keep not thy hand bound fast to thy neck, yet do not open it out too liberally,[5] so that thou sittest there as one who is blamed and beggared. Verily, thy Lord provides openhandedly for whom He wills, or gives limited measure. He, indeed, is well-informed about and observant of His servants. Put not your children to death out of fear of want. We shall make provision for them and also for you. Truly, the putting them to death is a great sin. And draw not near to fornication. It is, indeed, a wicked thing and an evil way. Do not kill, save where it is justified, any soul[6] that Allah has made inviolate. We have given authority to the next-of-kin of anyone who is wrongfully killed, but let him not be excessive in the killing, for he himself has been aided. And draw not nigh to the property of orphans, except as is right and proper, till he reaches his maturity; and fulfill the covenant you have made, for a covenant is something about which one will be questioned.[7] Give full measure when ye measure, and weigh with a just balance. That is better and the fairer interpretation. Follow not that about which thou hast no knowledge. Verily, hearing, seeing, heart, all those are things about which one will be questioned. And walk not insolently in the land. Thou wilt never pierce a hole through the earth, nor wilt thou ever reach the mountains in height. All that is something whose evil is an odious thing with thy Lord. That which is set forth above belongs to the wisdom which thy Lord hath revealed to thee, so set not up some other deity along with Allah, lest thou be cast into Gehenna, blamed, rejected. Has then your Lord for preference granted you sons and taken from the angels for Himself females? Ye are, indeed, uttering a mighty saying. We have made use of various things in this Koran that they might be reminded, but it increases them in naught but flight from the truth. Say: "Were there deities along with Him, as ye say, they would in that case have certainly sought a way unto the Possessor of the Throne. Glory be to Him! and exalted be He a great height from what they are saying. The seven heavens and the earth and all that is in them give glory to Him. Indeed, there exists nothing that does not give glory with praise of Him, but ye do not understand how they give glory. He, indeed, is forbearing, forgiving."

❧·And when thou recitest the lesson [qur'an], O Mohammed, We set between thee and those who do not believe in the Hereafter a veil spread as a curtain. And We have set upon their hearts a covering lest they should understand it, and in their ears a heaviness; and when thou makest mention of thy Lord alone in the lesson they turn tail in flight. We well know how they will listen, when they listen to thee, and when they are in private, when the wrongdoers say: "Ye follow but a man who has been ensorcelled." Look how they set forth parables for thee; but they are astray, and are unable to find a way. And they say: "When we have become bones and grains of dust are we going to be raised up a new creation?" Say: "Be ye stones, or iron, Or any created thing that in your breasts ye think big." They will say: "Who is going to restore us?" Say: "He Who created you the first time." But they will wag their heads at thee and say: "When is this to be?" Say: "Maybe it is near, The Day He will summon you, and ye will respond with praise of Him, and ye will think that ye have tarried in the grave but a little while." And say thou to My servants that they should speak what is right and proper. Truly, Satan stirs strife among them, for Satan is, indeed, a manifest enemy to man. Your Lord well knows about you. If He will He may show you mercy, or if He will He may punish you. We have not sent thee, O Mohammed, to be a guardian over them. Thy Lord well knows who is in the heavens and on the earth, and We have given some of the prophets superiority over others, and We gave to David the Psalter.[8]

❧·Say: "Summon those whom ye claim to be deities apart from Him. They have no power to relieve your distress or to make any change." Those upon whom they call are themselves seeking a way of access to their Lord, to see which of them will be nearer than the others. They themselves are hoping for His mercy and are afraid of His punishment. Truly, the punishment of thy Lord is something against which to guard. There is no town but We are going to destroy it before the Day of Resurrection, or punish it with grievous punishment. That has been written in the Book. Naught has prevented Us from sending signs save that the former peoples counted them false. We gave Thamud the she-camel as a visible thing, but they did wrong to her. We do not send signs save to arouse fear. And when We said to thee: "Verily thy Lord is round about the people," We did not appoint a vision which We caused thee to see save as a testing for the people,[9] and the tree accursed in the Koran. We frighten them but it increases them in naught save great presumption.

❧·And when We said to the angels: "Do obeisance to Adam," then they did obeisance, save Iblis, who said: "Shall I do obeisance to one whom Thou hast created of clay?" He said: "Seest Thou this creature whom Thou hast honoured above me? If thou wilt give me respite till Resurrection Day I shall certainly devour his progeny save a few." Said Allah: "Go! and should any of them follow thee, then Gehenna is your recompense, an ample recompense. So entice such of them as thou art able by thy voice, and attack them with thy cavalry and thy infantry, and go partners with them in wealth and in children, and make them promises." Yet Satan promises them naught but vain hopes. "Really thou hast no authority over My servants, and thy Lord is a sufficient guardian."

❊It is your Lord Who speeds along the ships for you in the sea that ye may seek of His bounty. He is, indeed, compassionate with you. And when troubles touch you at sea, whosoever it may be ye summon to your aid save Him, is astray; but when He has brought you safely to the shore, ye turn away. Man is ungrateful. Are ye then so sure that He will not make the side of the shore swallow you up, or send against you a sandstorm? Then ye will find for yourselves no guardian. Or are ye sure that He will not return you to the sea a second time, and send against you a hurricane of wind, so that He drowns you because of your ingratitude? Then ye will not find for yourselves any helper against Us therein. And, indeed, We have honoured the children of Adam, and have borne them by land and by sea, and have provided for them of the good things of Our creation, and We have given them obvious superiority over many of the things We have created. One Day We shall summon all men with their exemplar.[10] Then such as are given their book in their right hand, those will read their book and they will not be wronged a *fatil*,[11] But he who in this life has been blind will also be blind in the Hereafter, and even further astray from the path.

❊Truly, they had almost beguiled thee from that which We revealed to thee, that thou mightest invent something other than it against Us, in which case they would certainly have taken thee as a friend;[12] And had We caused thee to stand firm thou wouldst almost have leaned a little towards them, In which case We should have made thee taste a double portion of the woes of life, and a double portion of those of death.

Then thou wouldst not find for thyself any helper against Us. Indeed, they had almost driven thee from the land, that they might expel thee from it, in which case they themselves would not have remained after thee but for a little while. This has been the custom in the case of those of Our messengers whom We sent before thee, and thou wilt not find any change in Our custom.[13]

❊·Observe prayer from the declining of the sun till the darkening of the night, and the dawn recitation. Verily the dawn recitation is witnessed, And some of the night, so keep thou vigil therein as something in addition for thyself. It may be that thy Lord will raise thee to a highly praised position. And say: "O my Lord, make me enter with a right entrance and come forth with a right exit, and appoint for me from Thyself a helpful authority." And say: "The truth has come, and the false has vanished." Verily, the false has become a vanishing thing. So We are sending down of the Koran that which is a healing and a mercy to the believers, but it increases not the wrongdoers save in loss. When We bestow favour on man he turns away and goes to one side, but when evil troubles him he is in despair. Say: "Each acts after his own manner, and your Lord well knows about who is best guided in the path."

❊·They will question thee about the Spirit.[14] Say: "The Spirit is part of the affair of my Lord, and ye have not been given save a little knowledge of these matters."

❊·Did We so will We could certainly take away that which We have revealed to thee. Then thou wouldst find for thyself no guardian against Us in that, Save a mercy from thy Lord. Truly His bounty to thee has been great. Say: "Even though men and jinn were to combine to produce the like of this

Koran they would not produce its like though the one group were helping the other." We have, indeed, set out for men in this Koran every kind of parable, but the most part of the people refused aught but disbelief. And they say: "We shall never believe for thee till thou makest a spring gush forth for us from the earth, Or till thou hast a garden of palms and grapevines, and thou makest streams to gush forth so as to run through the midst of them, Or makest the skies to fall down in pieces upon us as thou pretendest,[15] or bringest Allah and the angels as surety, Or thou hast a house with gilt embellishment, or thou mountest up into the sky, though we shall never believe in thy mounting up till thou sendest down to us a Book that we may read." Say: "Glory be to my Lord! Am I anything more than a man who has come as a messenger?" Naught hinders the people from believing when guidance has come to them save that they say: "Has Allah sent a man as a messenger?" Say: "Had it been angels who were walking about tranquilly on the earth, We should have sent down to them from heaven an angel as a messenger." Say: "Allah suffices as a witness between me and you. He, indeed, is well informed about and observant of His servants." Whomsoever Allah guides, he is, indeed, guided; and whomsoever He leads astray, for them thou wilt never find patrons apart from Him, and We shall assemble them on the Resurrection Day on their faces, blind, dumb, and deaf. Gehenna will be their refuge-place, where as often as it dies down We shall make Sa'ir[16] burn more fiercely for them. That is their recompense because they disbelieved in Our signs and said: "Is it that when we have become bones and grains of dust we are going to be raised up a new creation?" Have they not perceived that Allah who created the heavens and the earth is able to create their like? Also He has appointed for them a term about which there is no doubt, yet the wrongdoers have refused aught but disbelief. Say: "Were ye in possession of the treasuries of my Lord's mercy ye would certainly in that case keep a tight hold, afraid of expending, for man is niggardly."

❧ Now We gave Moses nine evidential signs, so ask the Children of Israel. When he came to them as Allah's messenger, and Pharaoh said to him: "I, indeed, consider thee, O Moses, as ensorcelled," He said: "Surely thou knowest that none other than the Lord of the heavens and the earth sent down these signs as visible evidences? I, indeed, consider thee, O Pharaoh, as lost." So he wanted to drive them out from the land, but We drowned him and those with him altogether, And after that We said to the Children of Israel: "Dwell ye in the land." But when the promise of the Hereafter comes We shall bring you along a mixed crowd.

❧ With the truth have We sent the message down, and with the truth it came down, and We have not sent thee, O Mohammed, save as a bringer of good tidings and a warner. And as a lesson [qur'an] We have separated it out that thou mayest recite it to the people bit by bit, and We sent it down as a revelation [tanzil]. Say: "Believe in it or believe not, the fact is that those who were previously given knowledge of Scripture, when it is recited to them, fall down on their chins doing obeisance, And they say: 'Glory be to our Lord! The promise of our Lord has come to pass.' And they fall down upon their chins weeping, and it increases their humility." Say: "Invoke Allah, or invoke the Merciful. Whichever of them it is ye invoke, He has the beautiful names." And do not, O Mohammed, utter loudly thy praying, yet do not utter it in too low a voice, but seek a way between these, And say: "Praise be to Allah, Who has not taken for Himself a son, and Who has no partner in the kingdom, and Who has no one to protect Him from abasement," and magnify Him with a magnificat.[17]

Late Meccan
Suras

Surat as-Sajda: The Prostration

Here a collection of Late Meccan material has been worked over to make up a Sura, and provided with an introduction which is Medinan. There seem also to be some Medinan insertions, e.g., the first three verses of the last section. It is interesting that the Moslem Masoretes were well aware that this Sura was a mixture of Meccan and Medinan material.

IN THE NAME OF ALLAH,
THE MERCIFUL, THE COMPASSIONATE

A.L.M. The revelation [*tanzil*] of the Book, there is no doubt about it, is from the Lord of mankind. Or do they say: "He has invented it?" Nay, but it is the truth from thy Lord, that thou mayest warn a people to whom no warner has come before thee, that maybe they will submit to guidance.

Allah is He Who created the heavens and the earth and what is between them both in six days, then took His seat upon the Throne. Ye have no patron apart from Him and no intercessors. Will ye not then be reminded? He arranges the matter[1] from the heaven to the earth, then it will mount up to Him on a Day the measure of which is a thousand years of those ye reckon. That is He Who knows the unseen and the seen, the Sublime, the Compassionate. Who made everything that He created very good, and commenced the creation of man with clay. Then He appointed that his posterity should issue from an extract from contemptible water.[2] Then He fashioned him and breathed into him of His spirit. Also He made for you hearing and seeing and hearts. How little thankful ye are!

But they say: "Is it that when we have lain hidden in the

earth we are going to be in a new creation?" Nay, but they are those who disbelieve in the meeting with their Lord. Say: "The angel of death will cause you to die, he who has been put in charge of you. Then to your Lord will ye be returned." Couldst thou but see, O Mohammed, when the sinners hang their heads in the presence of their Lord, and say: "O our Lord, we have seen, and we have heard, so send us back and we shall act righteously. We are indeed convinced." Had We willed We could have given every soul its guidance, but that saying from Me is true: "I shall assuredly fill Gehenna with jinn and men together," So taste ye the punishment. Because ye were forgetful of the meeting, on this Day of yours We are forgetful of you, so taste ye eternal punishment because of what ye have been doing. Only those believe in Our signs who when mention is made of them fall down doing obeisance, and give glory with praise of their Lord, and they do not show arrogance. As their sides are withdrawn from their couches they invoke their Lord in fear and in desire, and from the provision We have made for them they give in charity. No soul knows what coolness for the eyes has been reserved for them as a reward for what they have been doing. Shall then he who has been a believer be as he who has acted wickedly?[3] They shall not be alike. As for those who have believed and done righteous works, for them are gardens of resort as an abode, because of what they have been doing. But as for those who have acted wickedly, their resort will be the Fire. As often as they attempt to get out of it they will be sent back into it. To them it will be said: "Taste ye the punishment of the Fire which ye were counting as false." And, indeed, We shall make them taste the nearer punishment before the greater punishment that perchance they may return. And who does greater wrong than the one to whom are mentioned the signs of his Lord, then he turns from them? We, indeed, are going to take vengeance on the sinners.

Now We gave Moses the Book—and be not thou in doubt about the meeting with Him—and We appointed it as guidance for the Children of Israel, And We appointed from among them leaders,[4] who should guide by Our command when they had themselves endured patiently and were convinced of Our signs. Truly thy Lord is He who will make distinction among them on the Day of Resurrection with regard to that on which they have been differing. Is it no guidance to them to remember how many generations before them We have destroyed, in whose dwelling-places they walk? Truly, in that there are signs. Will they then not hearken? Have they not seen how We drive the water to the parched earth so that thereby We bring forth vegetation from which their cattle eat, as also they themselves? Will they then not observe? Yet they say: "When will this opening-up take place,[5] if ye are those who speak the truth?" Say: "On the day of the Opening-up their faith will not avail those who have disbelieved, nor will they be respited." So turn thou from them, O Mohammed, and wait in expectancy. They, indeed, are waiting expectantly.

Surat an-Nahl: The Bee

This is another Sura made up of Meccan pieces worked over and put together in Medina, and given a Medinan introduction. The earliest passages are those dealing with the signs, from one of which the Sura gets its name. The amr *and the Spirit occur again here, and there are some interesting passages reflecting the growing controversy with Jews and Christians. It is in this Sura that we have (in the last section but one) the famous declaration that Mohammed's religion is really a continuation of the religion of Abraham.*

❧ Allah's affair [*amr*] has come, so seek ye not to hasten it. Glory be to Him! Exalted be He above what they associate with Him! By the Spirit He sends down the angels concerning His affair [*amr*][1] upon whom He wills among His servants, that they may warn. The fact is, there is no deity save Me, so show piety towards Me.

❧ He created the heavens and the earth in truth. Exalted be He above what they associate with Him! He created man from a drop, yet behold! he is a manifest caviller. The cattle also He has created for you. In them are warmth and varied benefits, and of them ye may eat. In them there is also beauty for you when ye fetch them home and when ye take them out to pasture. Also they carry your heavy loads to a land ye would not be able to reach save by overtaxing yourselves. Your Lord is, indeed, kindly, compassionate. And He created horses, and mules, and asses, that ye may ride on them and that they may be an adornment. Also He creates things of which ye know not. It is for Allah to give direction on the way. Some turn aside from it, but had He willed He would have guided you all. He it is who has sent down water from the skies for you. Of it is your drink, and from it are the bushes on which ye pasture your flocks; By it He makes the grain to grow for you, and the olives, and the date-palms, and the grapevines, and all kinds of fruits. In that, indeed, is a sign for a people who will ponder. Also He has subjected to you[2] the night and the day, and the sun and the moon and the stars, made subject by His command. In that, indeed, are signs for a people who are intelligent. And all the varied kinds of things He has multiplied in the land for you. In that, indeed, there is a sign for a people who will recollect. He it is who has made the sea subject so that from it ye may eat fresh flesh, and that ye may extract from it ornaments that ye can wear. And thou seest the ships ploughing along therein, and all this is so that ye may seek of His bounty, and maybe ye will be thankful. Also He cast mountains upon the earth lest it should move with you, and rivers and paths, that perchance ye might get guidance, And landmarks, though by the skies also they get guidance. Is then One Who creates as one who does not create? Will ye not recollect? Should ye attempt to number up Allah's favours ye would not be able to count them. Allah is indeed forgiving, compassionate, And Allah knows what ye keep secret and what ye make public. But those they invoke apart from Allah do not create a thing, for they themselves are created. Dead, not alive, they are not aware when they will be raised.

❈ Your God is One God,[3] but those who do not believe in the Hereafter, their hearts are given to denial and they are arrogant. There is no doubt but that Allah knows what they keep secret and what they make public. He, indeed, loves not the arrogant. And when they are asked: "What is that which your Lord has sent down?" they say: "Tales of the ancients." This is so that they may bear their burdens completely on the Resurrection Day, and part of the burdens of those whom, without knowledge, they led astray.[4] Is not that which they will bear an evil thing? Those who preceded them made their stratagems, but Allah came at their building from the foundations, so that the roof over them fell in upon them, and the punishment came upon them from whence they were unaware. Then on the Day of Resurrection He will put them to shame, and will say: "Where are My associates over whom ye were causing divisions?" Those to whom the knowledge of true religion has been given will say: "Verily, the shame and the evil are today on the unbelievers." Those whom the angels take in death while they are wronging their own souls, and who make an offer of submission, saying: "We were not doing any evil," will hear in reply: "Nay, indeed, Allah has knowledge of what ye have been doing, So enter ye the gates of Gehenna, therein to abide for ever." So how bad is the abiding-place of the overweeningly proud!

To those who have shown piety it will be said: "What is this that your Lord has sent down?" They will say: "A good thing." For those who do well there is a fine reward in this world, nevertheless the dwelling of the Hereafter is better, and how excellent is the dwelling of those who show piety; Gardens of Eden which they will enter, beneath which rivers flow, in which they may have whatsoever they wish. Thus does Allah recompense those who show piety. To those whom the angels take in death while they are doing good to their own souls they will say: "Peace be upon you! Enter ye the Garden because of what ye have been doing." Do they expect anything other than that the angels will come to them, or that the command of thy Lord will come? Thus did those who preceded them act, and Allah wronged them not, but they were wronging their own souls. So the evil of what they had done finally reached them, and there encompassed them that of which they had been making jest. Those who have associated other deities with Allah say: "Had Allah willed we should not have worshipped anything apart from Him, neither we nor our fathers, and not a thing should we have declared unlawful apart from Him." Thus did those who preceded them act, but are the messengers responsible for anything more than a clear proclamation? In every community We have raised up a messenger to say: "Worship ye Allah and avoid idolatry." So among them were some whom Allah guided and among them were some for whom error was the right thing. So journey in the land and see how the final outcome was for those who counted the message false. If thou art anxious, O Mohammed, about their guidance, know that Allah does not guide those whom He sends astray, and for them there are no helpers.

※.Now they have sworn by Allah, the strongest oath they possess, that Allah will not raise up anyone who dies. Nay, but it is a promise He must bring true; yet most of the people do not know. His message comes that He may make clear to them that about which they differ, and that those who have disbelieved may know that they were speaking falsely. Our word to a thing when We have willed it is only that We say to it: "Be!", and it is.

※.For those who have emigrated[5] for Allah's sake after they had been treated unjustly, We shall assuredly provide an excellent place in this world, though the reward of the Hereafter is greater, did they but know, For those who patiently endure and put their trust in their Lord.

※.Before thee, O Mohammed, We have sent none but men to whom We gave revelation—so ask the people of the Reminder[6] if ye do not know—With evidential signs and Scriptures, and We have sent down to thee the reminder, that thou mayest make clear to the people what has been sent down to them, that perchance they may ponder. Are then those who have plotted evil things so sure that Allah will not make the earth sink with them, or that punishment will not come to them whence they are unaware? Or that He will not take them in their comings and goings? for they are not able to resist Him, Or that He will not take them by some terrifying thing? Yet your Lord is kindly, compassionate. Have they not looked at those things which Allah has created, whose shadows turn about from right to left, doing obeisance to Allah, while they are of no account? Whatever is in the heavens, and whatever animals are on earth, and the angels, do obeisance to Allah, and they are not arrogant. They fear their Lord Who is above them, and do what they are bidden.

✤ Allah has said: "Take not for yourselves two deities"[7]—He is only One God—"Me, therefore, reverence Me." His is whatsoever is in the heavens and the earth, and His is the religion unceasingly. Will ye then show piety to other than Allah? Whatever favours ye have are from Allah: then, when trouble touches you, to Him ye are lowing like cattle. Then when He removes the trouble from you, behold! one party of you associates other deities with their Lord, That they may show their ingratitude for what We have given them. Enjoy yourselves then, for anon ye will know. And they appoint for that which they know not a share out of that with which We have provided them. By Allah, ye will most assuredly be questioned about what ye were inventing. And they appoint daughters for Allah—Glory be to Him!—yet they have what they long for.[8] So when one of them is given the announcement of a daughter his face is clouded with black looks and he is inwardly grieving; He hides himself from the people because of the evil of what has been announced to him. Shall he keep it with disgrace, or shall he bury it in the dust? Is not that which they judge an evil thing? For those who believe not in the Hereafter there is an evil similitude, but for Allah is the highest similitude, and He is the Sublime, the Wise. Were Allah to take men in their wrongdoing He would not leave on earth a beast, but He postpones them to a term appointed, and when their term has come they will not retard it an hour, nor will they advance it. They appoint for Allah what they themselves loathe,[9] and their tongues set forth what is false, namely, that for them is the better lot. Yet there is no doubt but that for them is the Fire, and thereto will they be hastened. By Allah, We have sent messengers before thee to communities, but Satan made their works fair-seeming to them, so he is today their patron, and for them is painful punishment. And We have not sent down the Book to thee save that thou mightest make clear to them that about which they differ, and to be a guidance and a mercy to a people who believe.

✳Allah has sent down water from the skies and thereby quickened the earth after its deadness. In that, indeed, there is a sign to a people who will hearken. And, truly, for you in the cattle there is a lesson. We provide drink for you from what is in the bellies thereof, from between the filth and the blood, pure milk, a pleasing beverage for those who drink, And from the fruits of the date-palms and the grapevines from which ye take for yourselves intoxicating drink and excellent provision. In that, indeed, there is a sign for those who have intelligence. Also thy Lord has spoken by revelation to the bee, saying: "Take for thyself houses in the mountains and in the trees and in the hives men construct, Then eat from all the fruits and move humbly along the paths of thy Lord." From their bellies comes forth a drink of varied colour in which is healing for men. In that, indeed, there is a sign for those who ponder.

✳Allah has created you; then He will cause you to die, though among you are some who will be kept back till the most decrepit stage of life where one will not know a thing after having had knowledge. Allah, indeed, is knowing, powerful. And Allah has favoured some of you above others in the matter of provision; yet those who have been favoured do not impart of their provision to those whom their right hands possess [their slaves] so that they share equally therein. Is it then that they dispute Allah's boon? Allah has appointed for you wives from among yourselves, and from your wives has appointed you sons and helpers, and has provided for you from the good things of the earth. Is it then that they will believe in the false and be ungrateful for Allah's boons? And they worship apart from Allah that which possesses not a thing in the heavens or the earth as provision for them, nor are they able to gain possession of such.

❉ So do not set forth similitudes for Allah, for Allah knows and ye do not know. Allah has set forth a parable, a slave, possessed by a master, who has no power over anything, and one to whom We have given excellent provision from Ourselves, so that therefrom he disburses charity secretly and openly. Are they on an equality? Praise be to Allah! Nay, but most of them do not know. And Allah has set forth a parable of two men, one of whom is dumb, who has no power over anything and is a burden to his master, for no matter where he sends him he brings no good. Is he on an equality with one who enjoins what is equitable and is on a straight path? Allah's is the unseen of the heavens and the earth, and the matter of the Hour is as near as the twinkling of an eye, or even nearer. Allah, indeed, is powerful over everything. Allah has brought you forth from the bellies of your mothers ye not knowing anything, and has arranged hearing and seeing and hearts for you, that perchance ye might be thankful. Have they not looked at the birds under service in the sky's vault? No one holds them in hand save Allah. In that, indeed are signs for a people who will believe. Also Allah has appointed for you in your houses a habitation, and appointed for you houses from the skins of your flocks that ye may find them light of weight on the day you strike tents and on the day you set them up, and from their wool and their fur and their hair, furnishings and enjoyment for a while. And Allah has appointed for you, from that which He has created, things for shade, and from the mountains He has appointed for you places of shelter, and He has appointed for you garments which will protect you from the heat, and garments which will protect you from your violence towards one another. Thus does He perfect His favour to you that perchance ye may be submissive. So if they turn their backs, thou, O Mohammed, art responsible only for a clear proclamation of the message. They recognize Allah's favour, then they deny it, and the most part of them are unbelievers.

✻ On the Day when We raise up from each people a witness, then no permission to speak will be given to those who disbelieve, and they will not be invited to make themselves acceptable. And when those who have done wrong see the punishment it will not be lightened for them, nor will they be respited. When those who have associated other deities with Allah see their associate-gods, they will say: "O our Lord, these are our associate-gods whom we invoked instead of Thee." But the associate-gods will cast the words back at them, saying: "Indeed, ye are speaking falsely." On that Day they will offer submission to Allah; and there will stray from them that which they were inventing. Those who have disbelieved and turned others from the path of Allah, for them We shall increase punishment on top of punishment because of the corruption they have been causing, And on the Day We shall raise up in each people a witness against them from among themselves. We have brought thee, O Mohammed, as a witness against these Meccans, and We have sent down to thee the Book as an explanation for everything, and a guidance and a mercy, and good tidings to those who submit themselves.

✻ Allah, indeed, enjoins equity, and the doing of good, and giving to kinsfolk, and He forbids dishonourable conduct, and what is reproved, and iniquity. He admonishes you that maybe ye will be reminded. So fulfil Allah's covenant when ye have made a covenant, and break not an oath after ye have pledged it, for ye have appointed Allah as surety over you. Truly, Allah knows what ye do. Be not like her who untwisted her spinning into threads after it had been strongly spun,[10] taking your oaths as but a pretence among yourselves, that one community may be more numerous than another. Allah is only thereby making trial of you, and on the Day of Resurrection He will most assuredly make clear to you that about which ye differ. Had Allah so willed He would have made you a single community, but He leads astray whom He wills and guides whom He wills, and ye will most assuredly be questioned about what ye have been doing. So do not take oaths as pretence among yourselves lest a foot slip after it has been firmly planted, and ye taste evil because ye have turned others from the path of Allah, and for you there is a mighty punishment. And do not purchase by Allah's covenant some paltry value. Verily, that which is with Allah is better for you, did ye but know. That which is with you will pass away, but what is with Allah abides, and We shall most assuredly recompense those who have patiently waited for their reward, rewarding them with the best of what they have been doing. Whosoever acts righteously, whether male or female, and is a believer, him We shall most assuredly quicken to a good life, and recompense him with the best of what he has been doing as his reward.

❧ Now when thou recitest the lesson [*qur'an*], O Mohammed, take refuge with Allah from Satan the stoned.[11] The fact is, he has no authority over those who believe and who put their trust in their Lord. His authority is only over those who take him as their patron, and those who associate other deities with Him.

❧ And when We substitute a verse in place of a verse[12]—and Allah well knows what He sends down—they say: "Thou art only an inventor of revelations." Nay, but the most part of them do not know. Say: "The Spirit of Holiness brought it down from thy Lord with truth, in order that it might establish firmly those who believe, and be guidance and good tidings to those who submit themselves." We know that they are saying: "It is only a man who teaches him." The speech of him at whom they hint[13] is foreign, but this is clear Arabic speech. Verily those who do not believe in Allah's signs, Allah will not guide them, and for them is a painful punishment. The only ones who invent falsehood are those who do not believe in Allah's signs. Those are they who speak falsely.

❋ Whosoever disbelieves in Allah after having been a believer —save one who is compelled to recant though his heart remains tranquil in the faith—but whosoever eases his breast by unbelief, on him is anger from Allah, and for him is a mighty punishment. That is because they have loved the life of this present world more than the Hereafter, and because Allah does not guide the unbelieving people. Those are they upon whose hearts and hearing and sight Allah has set a seal, and those are the careless ones. There is no doubt but that in the Hereafter they are the ones who lose. Then, verily, to those who emigrated after the trials they suffered, then strove hard and endured patiently, truly thy Lord after that is forgiving, compassionate.

❋ On the Day when every soul will come making its plea for itself, each soul will be fully paid for the deeds it has done, and they will not be wronged.

❋ Now Allah has set forth a parable: a town[14] which was safe, tranquil, whose provision came to it abundantly from every place, but it was ungrateful for Allah's bounties, so Allah made it taste of the vesture of hunger and fear because of what its townsfolk had been doing. Then there came to them a messenger from among themselves, but they considered him false, so the punishment took them while they were doing wrong.

✿So eat what is lawful and good of that with which Allah has provided you, and be thankful for Allah's bounty, if ye are those who worship Him. He has made forbidden to you only what has died of itself, blood, swine's flesh, and that which has been offered to any other than Allah,[15] but should anyone be compelled, not lusting for it nor wilfully transgressing, then truly Allah is forgiving, compassionate. And say not, in accordance with what your tongues would falsely assert: "This is lawful and this is forbidden," framing up falsehood against Allah. Truly, those who frame up falsehood against Allah will not prosper. A little enjoyment will be theirs, then for them is a painful punishment. To those who were Jews We made forbidden that which We formerly related to thee,[16] and We did not wrong them though they were wronging themselves. Then, truly, to those who in ignorance have wrought evil, then after that have repented and reformed, truly thy Lord, after that, is certainly forgiving, compassionate.

✿Verily Abraham was a community in himself,[17] obedient to Allah, a Hanif, and was not one of those who associate other deities with Allah, but was Thankful for His bounties. He chose him and guided him to a straight path. And We gave him in this world an excellent portion, and in the Hereafter he will, indeed, be among the righteous. Then We spoke to thee by revelation, O Mohammed, saying: "Follow thou the religion[18] of Abraham, a Hanif, and one who was not of those who associate."

✿The Sabbath was instituted only for those who differed about it.[19] Verily, thy Lord will deliver judgment between them on Resurrection Day in regard to that about which they differ. Summon thou to the way of thy Lord with wisdom and goodly admonition, and dispute with them in a most goodly manner. Verily, thy Lord well knows about him who errs from His way, and He well knows about those who submit to guidance. If ye Moslems exact vengeance,[20] then exact it to the measure it has been exacted from you; but truly if ye patiently endure, that is better for those who patiently endure. So, do thou, O Mohammed, patiently endure, though thy patiently enduring is only through the favour of Allah, and grieve not over them, and be not narrowly distressed at the stratagems they plot. Allah is indeed with those who show piety and with those who are doers of good.

Surat ar-Rum: The Byzantines

The name of the Sura comes from the opening verses, which seem to refer to some conflict in North Arabia in which the Byzantines were involved, probably a conflict with the Sassanians or their allies, and which Mohammed took as a sign of the ultimate victory of true believers. This introduction is Medinan, and there are some Medinan insertions, but the bulk of the material is Late Meccan. It will be noticed how many points of contact there are with Sura 16, and how the Hanif connection again comes in. The sign-passages are perhaps the earliest material, though some of the unconnected pieces which have been attached at the end may also be early.

IN THE NAME OF ALLAH,
THE MERCIFUL, THE COMPASSIONATE

A.L.M. The Byzantines have been defeated[1] In the nearer part of the land, but they, after their defeat, will be victorious In a few years. The affair is Allah's both before and after, and on that day the believers will rejoice In the help of Allah. He helps whom He will, and He is the Sublime, the Compassionate.

❀·It is Allah's promise, and Allah does not fail of His promise, though the most part of the people do not know. They know what is apparent of the life of this present world, but of the Hereafter they are negligent. Have they never pondered with themselves that Allah did not create the heavens and the earth and what is between them both save in truth and with a fixed period? Yet many of the people are disbelieving in the meeting with their Lord. Have they never journeyed in the land so that they might see how the final issue was for those before them who were mightier in strength than they are, who ploughed up the earth and cultivated it far more than they have cultivated it, to whom messengers came with evidential signs? So Allah was not one to wrong them but they were wronging themselves. Then the final issue for those who were evil was evil, because they counted Allah's signs false and were making them a jest. Allah originates a creature, then He makes it return to its original dust, then to Him will ye be brought back at the Last Day. And on the Day when the Hour arrives the sinners will be in despair, For there will be no intercessor for them from among the associate-gods, and they will be disbelieving in their associate-gods. On the Day when the Hour arrives, on that Day they will be separated out. As for those who believed and did works of righteousness, they will be in a meadow making joyful; But as for those who disbelieved, and counted false Our signs and the meeting in the Hereafter, such will be handed over to punishment.

❀·So say: "Glory be to Allah!" when ye come to evening hour and when ye rise at morn, And say: "To Him be praise in the heavens and the earth!" both at twilight and when ye come to noon.[2] He brings forth the living from the dead, and brings forth the dead from the living, and He quickens the earth after its deadness, and thus will ye be drawn forth. Among His signs is the fact that He created you from dust, and then, lo! ye are men spreading yourselves abroad. Also among His signs is the fact that He created for you from yourselves wives that ye may dwell with them, and He instituted between you love and mercy. In that, indeed, there are signs for a people who will ponder. And among His signs are the creation of the heavens and the earth, and the differences among you in speech and in colour. In that, indeed, there are signs for those who know. And among His signs are your sleeping by night and by day, and your going in quest of His bounty. In that, indeed, there are signs for those who will hearken. And among His signs is the fact that He causes you to see the lightning with both fear and desire, and sends down from the skies water whereby He quickens the earth after its deadness. In that, indeed, there are signs for a people who have intelligence. And among His signs is the fact that the skies and the earth stand firm at His command. Then when He summons you from the earth with a summons, behold! ye will come forth. His are those who are in the heavens and the earth, all obedient to Him. He it is Who originates a creature, then makes it return to its original dust, and that is very easy for Him. His is the highest similitude in the heavens and the earth, and He is the Sublime, the Compassionate. He has set forth for you a similitude from yourselves. Do ye have from among those whom your right hands possess [i.e., your slaves] any associates in that with which We have provided you so that ye are on an equality therein? Do ye fear them as ye fear yourselves? Thus do We set out the signs for a people who have intelligence. Nay, but those who do wrong follow their own desires without knowledge. So Who will guide him whom Allah has sent astray, seeing that for them there are no helpers? So set thou thy face, O Mohammed, towards religion as a Hanif, Allah's creation according to which He has created man, and there is no changing Allah's creation.[3] That is the right religion, though the most part of men do not know. So be ye such as turn in penitence to Him, and show ye piety and observe prayer, and be not of those who associate other deities with Allah, Of those who have divided up their religion and become sects, each party rejoicing in what they have of their own. But when some trouble touches the people they invoke their Lord, turning in penitence to Him. Then when He gives them to taste a mercy from Himself, lo! a group of them associate others with their Lord. That they may be ungrateful for that which We have given them. So take ye your enjoyment for anon ye will know. Or have We sent down to them some authority, and it speaks in favour of what they have been associating with Him? When We give the people to taste of some mercy of Ours they rejoice therein, but if some evil come upon them because of what their hands have sent forward, lo! they are stricken with despair. Have they not seen that Allah provides openhandedly for whom He wills, or gives limited measure?[4] In that, indeed, there are signs for a people who believe.

❧ Give the kinsman that to which he has a right, and to the unfortunate and to the son of the way. That is better for those who desire Allah's face, and those are they who prosper. What ye give out at usury, that it may gain increase amidst the people's wealth, gains no increase with Allah, but what ye give as alms, desiring the face of Allah—those are they who make double gain.

❧ Allah is the One Who created you, then made provision for you, then will put you to death, then will quicken you. Is there any among your associate-gods who can do anything such as that? Glory be to Him, and high exalted be He from that which they associate with Him! Corruption has appeared by land and by sea because of what the hands of people have gained, that He may make them taste somewhat of what they have done, that perchance they may return. Say: "Journey ye in the land and see how the final issue was for those of former days, the most part of whom were associators."

❧ Set thy face then, O Mohammed, to the right religion, before a Day arrives which naught can prevent Allah from bringing on. On that Day they will be divided into two groups: Whoso has disbelieved, on him will be his disbelief; and whoso have acted righteously are making things smooth for their own souls, That from His bounty He may recompense those who have believed and have done deeds of righteousness. The fact is, He loves not the unbelievers.

❧ Also among His signs is the fact that He sends the winds as bringers of good tidings, and that He may give you to taste of His mercy, and that the ships may run along at His command, and that ye may go questing for His bounty, and maybe ye will be thankful.

❧ Before thee, O Mohammed, We have sent messengers to their people; so they brought them the evidential signs, and We took vengeance on those who sinned, and it was a duty for Us to aid the believers.

❧ Allah is the One who sends the winds[5] so that they bring up a cloud which He spreads out in the skies just how He wills, and breaks it up so that thou seest the rain coming forth from the midst thereof. Then when He pours it down upon whom He wills of His servants, lo! they are full of joy, Even though they were before that—before it was sent down to them—in despair. So look at the traces of Allah's mercy, how He quickens the earth after its deadness. Truly that One is the quickener of the dead, and He is powerful over everything. But if We send a wind so that they see the vegetation gone yellow, nevertheless even after that they would continue un-believing.

❊·Yet indeed thou, O Mohammed, wilt not make the dead to hear, nor wilt thou make the deaf hear the summons when they turn away, turning their backs. Nor art thou going to guide the blind out of their error. Nor wilt thou make any hear save such as believe in Our signs, for they are submitting themselves.

❊·Allah is the One Who has created you in weakness, then after weakness has appointed strength, then after strength has appointed weakness and grey-headedness. He creates what He wills, and He is the Knowing, the Powerful.[6]

❊·On the Day when the Hour arrives the sinners will swear they have not tarried in the grave more than an hour. Thus were they being involved in falsehood.[7] But those who have been given the knowledge and the faith will say: "Ye have tarried, according to what is written in Allah's Book, till the Day of the raising up, and this is the Day of the raising up, but ye were unknowing. On that Day their making excuses for themselves will not benefit those who have done wrong, and they will not be invited to make themselves acceptable.

❊·Truly, We have set forth for the people in this Koran every kind of similitude, yet if thou bringest to them a verse those who disbelieve will certainly say: "Ye are only dealing in vanities." Thus does Allah set a seal upon the hearts of those who know not. So do thou, O Mohammed, bear up patiently. Verily the promise of Allah is true, so let not those who have no sure conviction make light of thee.

Surat Luqman: Luqman

*Luqman, or Lokman, is the Arabic Aesop. He is mentioned
only in this Sura, which speaks of his sage advice to his son.
The collection of stories which circulates as the* Fables of Luqman *contains material derived from the Greek Aesop, but the
name would seem to have been given to the collection from its
occurrence in this Sura. The Sura itself is a mixture of Meccan
and Medinan material. The Luqman passage is Late Meccan,
as is the signs-passage (eighth section); but the introduction
is Medinan and there are Medinan insertions.*

IN THE NAME OF ALLAH,
THE MERCIFUL, THE COMPASSIONATE

❀ A.L.M. Those are the signs of the wise Book, A guidance
and a mercy to those who do good, Who observe prayer and
pay the legal alms, and have sure conviction about the Hereafter. Such are under guidance from their Lord, and those are
they who will prosper.

❀ Among the people there is one who will purchase an amusing tale that he may lead people astray from Allah's way without knowledge,[1] and take the way of Allah as a matter of jest.
Those are they for whom is a shameful punishment. And
when Our signs are recited to him he turns proudly away as
though he heard them not, as though in his ears were a heaviness. So give him tidings of a painful punishment. Verily for
those who believe and do works of righteousness, for them
there are gardens of delight, In which they will eternally
abide. This is Allah's true promise, and He is the Sublime,
the Wise.

❀ He created the heavens without any pillars that ye can see,
and He cast mountains upon the earth lest it should move with

you, and scattered therein all kinds of beasts, and sent down from the skies water, so that We have caused to grow up therein every noble species of plant. This is Allah's creation, so show ye Me what those whom ye worship apart from Him have created. Nay, but the wrongdoers are in manifest error. Now We gave Luqman wisdom, saying: "Be thankful to Allah, for whosoever gives thanks gives thanks only to his own soul's good; and should anyone be grateful, why, Allah is rich, praiseworthy." And remember when Luqman[2] said to his son; as he was admonishing him: "O my son, associate naught with Allah. Truly, association of other deities with Allah is a mighty wrong."

We have laid an injunction on man with regard to his two parents. His mother carried him in weakness on weakness, and his weaning was after two years. So be thankful to Me and to thy parents. To Me is the journey back.[3] But if they [i.e., thy parents] are importunate with thee that thou associate with Me that concerning which thou hast no knowledge, then obey them not. Nevertheless live in friendliness with them in this world as is right and proper, but follow thou the path of him who turns in penitence to Me. Then to Me is your return, and I shall assuredly inform you about what ye have been doing.

"O my son," said Luqman, "the fact is that even though it be but the weight of a grain of mustard seed, and should it be on a rock, or in the heavens, or in the earth, Allah will bring it to light. Allah, indeed, is gentle, well-informed. O my son, observe prayer, bid what is right and proper and forbid what is disapproved, and be patiently enduring under whatever befalls thee. Truly, that belongs to what determines affairs. And do not curl thy cheek at people in disdain, and walk not insolently in the land, for, indeed, Allah loves not any arrogant boaster. So steer a middle course in thy walking, and keep thy voice low, for truly the most displeasing of voices is the voice of asses."

❊ Have ye not seen that Allah has subjected to your service whatever is in the heavens and whatever is on the earth, and has caused His grace to abound towards you outwardly and inwardly? Yet among the people are those who dispute concerning Allah without any knowledge or guidance or enlightening Book, And when it is said to them: "Follow ye what Allah has sent down," they say: "Nay, but we shall follow that at which we found our fathers." What! even though Satan is summoning them to the punishment of as-Sa'ir?[4] But whosoever submits his face to Allah, while doing that which is good, he has laid hold on the firmest handle, although with Allah is the ultimate issue of affairs. And should anyone disbelieve, let not his disbelief grieve thee, O Mohammed. To Us is their returning and We shall inform them of that which they have done. Allah, indeed, has knowledge about the secrets of the hearts. We shall give them to enjoy a little, then We shall force them to a harsh punishment.

❊ Shouldst thou ask them who created the heavens and the earth they would assuredly say: "Allah." Say: "Praise be to Allah!" Nay, but the most part of them do not know. Allah's is whatsoever is in the heavens and the earth. Allah, indeed, He is the Rich, the Praiseworthy. Were whatever trees are on the earth pens, and the sea an ocean of ink,[5] which seven seas thereafter swell, the words of Allah would not fail. Allah, indeed, is sublime, wise.

❊ Your creation and your resurrection are as but that of a single person. Allah, indeed, is He Who hears, He Who sees. Hast thou not seen that Allah makes the night penetrate into the day and the day penetrate into the night, and has subjected to your service the sun and the moon, each running along to a fixed term, and that Allah is informed about what ye do? That is because Allah is the True One, and because what they invoke apart from Him is vain, and because Allah, He is the High One, the Great One. Hast thou not seen that the ships run in the sea by Allah's favour, that He may show you of His signs? Truly, in that there are signs for every truly patient, thankful one. When waves overshadow them like tent coverings they invoke Allah, making religion solely His, but when He brings them safely to shore, some of them are halting between two opinions, yet no one disputes about Our signs save every perfidious, ungrateful one.

❋ O ye people! show piety towards your Lord, and fear a Day when no parent will make atonement for his child, nor a child atone in any way for his parent. Verily, the promise of Allah is true, so let not the life of this present world deceive you, and let not the Deceiver[6] deceive you about Allah. With Allah, indeed, is knowledge of the Hour, for He sends down the gentle showers and He knows what is in the wombs, though no soul knows what it will gain on the morrow, nor does any soul know in what land it will die.[7] Allah, indeed, is knowing, informed.

Surat Yusuf: Joseph

This is the only Sura of any length in the Koran which deals with a single subject. The material of the Joseph story is for the most part Late Meccan, but it has been given an introduction and a conclusion which, at least in their present form, are Medinan. Bell thinks that the Benjamin story is a later addition and that several other passages were subjected to necessary altera-tions when the Benjamin story was added. The curious frag-mentation of the story may be due to the fact that it was repro-duced just as Mohammed could remember it, or it may be that

Sura

12

in the process of revision bits were left out. What is of particular interest is that the Prophet's informants were, as Schapiro has shown in detail, well acquainted with Midrashic legends about Joseph.

IN THE NAME OF ALLAH,
THE MERCIFUL, THE COMPASSIONATE

❧A.L.R. These are the signs of the Book that makes clear. We have sent it down as an Arabic lesson [*qur'an*]. Maybe ye will understand. We are relating to thee, O Mohammed, one of the best of stories in revealing to thee this lesson, though before it thou wert one of the heedless.

❧When Joseph said to his father: "O my Father, I indeed have seen eleven stars and the sun and the moon. I saw them doing obeisance to me,"[1] Said he: "O my son, relate not thy vision to thy brethren, lest they plot against thee a stratagem. Verily, Satan is a manifest enemy to man. Thus is thy Lord choosing thee, and He will teach thee the interpretation of hard sayings, and will perfect His favour upon thee, and upon the House of Jacob, as He perfected it earlier on thy two forefathers, Abraham and Isaac. Verily, thy Lord is knowing, wise." Now indeed in Joseph and his brethren were signs for those who question. When they said: "Joseph and his brother are dearer to our father than we are, though we are a band. Verily, our father is in manifest error. Kill ye Joseph, or drive him out of the country, then the face of your father will be free for you, and ye may be thereafter honest people," A speaker from among them said: "Kill ye not Joseph, but cast him into the bottom of a cistern.[2] One of the passing caravans will pick him up if ye do that." They said: "O our father, what is the matter with thee? Thou dost not trust us with Joseph although we are his sincere advisers. Send him with us tomorrow. He will enjoy himself and play, and we shall be watching over him." Said he: "It assuredly grieves me that ye should go off with him, and I fear that the wolf may eat him while ye are careless of him." They said: "Should the wolf eat him while we are a band, in that case we should indeed be losers." So when they went off with him, and agreed together to put him in the bottom of the cistern, then We spoke by revelation to him, saying: "Thou wilt most assuredly inform them of this matter of theirs at a time when they are not aware." Then in the evening they came to their father weeping. They said: "O our father, we went off to race one another and we left Joseph with our baggage, but the wolf ate him. Yet thou wouldst not be believing us even were we telling the truth." And they brought lying blood upon his shirt. Their father said: "Nay, indeed! your souls have enticed you into an affair; but patience is a seemly thing, and Allah is the One to be asked for help against what ye tell." Now a caravan came along, and they sent ahead their water-drawer, who let down his water-bucket. Said he: "O best of news! Here is a youth," and they concealed him as a piece of merchandise.[3] But Allah was well aware of what they were doing. So they sold him for a trifling price, some dirhams counted out, for they were but rough appraisers with regard to him. The Egyptian who bought him said to his wife: "Lodge him honourably, for it may be that he will be useful to us, or we may take him as a son." Thus did We make a place for Joseph in the land, and that was so that We might teach him the interpretation of hard sayings. Allah has the mastery over His affair, though the most part of the people do not know. Now when he reached his mature strength We gave him wisdom and knowledge. Thus do We reward those who do well. But she in whose house he was, lusted for his person. She locked the doors and said: "Come along!" Said he: "Allah forbid! Truly, my Lord[4] has lodged me in excellent fashion. Moreover, wrongdoers will not prosper." But she wanted him, and he had wanted her had it not been that he saw a demonstration of his Lord.[5] It was thus in order that We might turn from him evil and turpitude. He, indeed, was one of Our single-hearted servants. The two of them raced for the door, and she tore his shirt from behind. At the door they met her husband. Said she: "What is the recompense for one who has desired evil of thy household, unless it be that he be put in prison, or suffer a painful punishment?" Joseph said: "She lusted for my person." A witness[6] from her household bore witness, saying: "If his shirt has been torn in front then she has told the truth and he is among the liars, But if his shirt has been torn from behind then she is lying and he is of those who tell the truth." So when he saw that his shirt had been torn from behind, he said: "This, indeed, is of your female scheming. Verily the scheming of you women is great. O Joseph, shun this. And do thou, O woman, seek pardon for thy sin, for thou hast indeed been among those who commit faults." Women in the city said: "The prince's wife lusts after her servant's person. He has made her sick with love. In our opinion she is in manifest error." Now when she heard of their plotting she sent them a message and prepared for them a banquet. When they came she gave to each one of them a knife. Then she said: "Come forth to them, O Joseph." When they saw him they were amazed at him and cut their hands. They said: "Allah forbid! This is no man. This is naught but a noble angel." She said: "That is the one with regard to whom ye were blaming me. I, indeed, did lust for his person but he abstained. Yet if he does not do what I bid him he will most assuredly be imprisoned and be one of the paltry ones." He said: "O my Lord, to me the prison is preferable to that to which they are inviting me. Yet if Thou dost not avert from me their scheming I shall act the youth with them, and shall be one of the ignorant." So his Lord answered him, and averted from him their scheming. He, indeed, is the Hearer, the

Knower. Then it seemed good to them, after they had seen the signs, to imprison him for a while. Now there entered the prison with him two youths. Said one of them: "As for me, I see myself pressing out wine." Said the other: "As for me, I see myself carrying on my head bread of which the birds are eating. Tell us its interpretation. We, indeed, consider thee one of those who do good." Said he: "No food with which ye are provided will come to you ere I have told you its interpretation before it comes to you. That is part of what my Lord has taught me. I, indeed, have forsaken the religion [*milla*] of a people who do not believe in Allah and who are disbelieving in the Hereafter, And I have followed the religion [*milla*] of my fathers, Abraham and Isaac and Jacob. It was not for us to associate anything with Allah. That is Allah's bounty to us and to the people, but the most part of the people do not render thanks. O my two prison companions, are various Lords better, or Allah, the One, the All-overcoming? What ye worship apart from Him are naught but names which ye and your fathers have named. Allah has sent down no authority for them. Wisdom is with Allah alone. He has given command that ye worship none but Himself. That is the right religion, but the most part of the people do not know. O my two prison companions; as for one of you, he will pour out wine for his lord; as for the other, he will be crucified and birds will eat from his head. Decreed is the matter about which ye made enquiry." Then he said to the one of them he thought was going to escape: "Mention me before thy lord." But Satan made him forget to mention him to his lord,[7] so he continued in prison for some years. Said the king: "I see in my dream seven fat cows which seven lean ones devour, and seven green ears of grain and others dried up. O courtiers, instruct me with regard to my vision, if ye are such as can expound visions." They said: "Confusions of dreams! We are not such as know about the interpretation of dreams."[8] Said the one of them who had escaped, remembering after a time: "I will get you information as to its interpretation, so send me." Going to the prison he said: "O Joseph, O thou trusty one, instruct us about seven fat cows which seven lean ones devour, and seven green ears of grain and others dried up. Perchance I may return to the people that maybe they will know." Said he: "Seven years will ye sow according to custom, but what ye harvest leave in its ear, save a little from which ye may eat. Then there will come after that seven hard years which will devour what ye have laid up for them, save a little of what ye preserve in store. Then, after that, there will come a year in which the people will have abundant rain, and in which they will express the juice of grapes." Said the king: "Bring him to me." But when the messenger came to him, he said: "Return to thy lord, and ask him what was the matter with the women who cut their hands. My lord, indeed, knows about their scheming." The king said: "What is this affair of yours when ye lusted after Joseph's person?" They answered: "Allah forbid! We know no evil against him." The wife of the prince said: "Now has the truth come to light. It was I who lusted after his person, and he, indeed, is one of those who speak the truth." "That," said Joseph, "is that he may know that I did not betray him in his absence, and that Allah guideth not the plotting of those who are betrayers. Yet I do not declare myself innocent. Verily, the soul has a natural inclination towards evil, save in so far as my Lord shows mercy. Truly, my Lord is forgiving, compassionate." Said the king: "Bring him to me! I appropriate him for myself." So when he spoke with him he said: "Behold, thou art today before us in a position established, secure." He said: "Appoint me over the storehouses of the land. I, indeed, am a knowing keeper." Thus did We make a place for Joseph in the land that he might settle down therein wheresoever he might desire. We make Our mercy alight on whom We will, and We allow not the reward of those who do good to be lost. Nevertheless the reward of the Hereafter is better for those who believe and have been pious. Now when the days of famine arrived, Joseph's brethren came and entered to him, and he recognized them but they were ignorant of who he was. When he supplied them with their needed supplies, he said: "Bring me a brother of yours from your father. Do ye not see that I give full measure, and that I am the best of hosts? But if ye do not bring him to me there will be no measure for you with me, nor will ye draw near me." They said: "We shall beseech his father for him. We are those who will do it." He said to his servants: "Put their merchandise back in their packs. Maybe they will recognize it when they get back to their families, and maybe they will return." Now when they returned to their father they said: "O our father, measure is refused us, but send our brother along with us and we shall get measure, and we shall be sure guardians of him." Said he: "Shall I entrust you with him save as I entrusted you formerly with his brother? But Allah is the best guardian, and He is the most merciful of those who shew mercy." Then when they opened up their belongings they found that their merchandise had been returned to them. They said: "O our father, what more could we desire? This merchandise of ours has been returned to us, so we can supply our families, and preserve our brother, and get an extra camel-load of measure. That will be an easy measure." Said he: "Never will I send him with you until ye give me an assurance from Allah that ye will bring him back to me, unless ye are prevented." Then when they had given him their assurance, he said: "Allah is trustee over what ye say." He said: "O my sons, enter not in by a single gate, but enter by different gates. Yet I avail you naught against Allah. The judgment is with Allah alone. On Him have I set my trust, and on Him let those who trust set their trust." So when they entered according as their father had bidden them, it availed them naught against Allah, though it satisfied a need in Jacob's soul; and he, indeed, was a possessor of knowledge because of what We had taught him, but the most part of the people do not know. When they entered to Joseph he took his brother to be with him, saying: "I, truly, am thy brother, so be not distressed at what they have been doing." Then when he prepared for them what they wanted prepared, he put the king's drinking-cup in his brother's saddlebag. Then a herald made cry: "O caravan! ye are surely thieves." Said they, as they approached them: "What do ye find missing?" They said: "We miss the king's goblet.[9] To him who brings it will be given a camel's load, and I am surety for that." They said: "By Allah, ye well know that we did not come to do evil in the land, and we are no thieves." They said: "And what will be the recompense for it if ye be lying?" They answered: "Let the recompense for it be that he in whose saddlebag it is found be himself the recompense for it. Thus would we recompense wrongdoers." He made a beginning with their packs before coming to his brother's pack. Then he drew it forth from his brother's pack. Thus did We work a scheme for Joseph. Because of the king's religion he could not have taken his brother, had not Allah so willed. We raise the ranks for whom We will, and above every possessor of knowledge there is One who knows. They said: "If he has stolen, nevertheless a brother of his stole before,"[10] but Joseph kept it secret to himself and did not let it appear to them. He said: "Ye are in an evil spot, and Allah knows best about what ye tell." They said: "O prince, he has a father, a very old man, so take one of us in his stead. We, indeed, see that thou art one of those who do good." Said he: "Allah forbid that we should take anyone save him with whom we found our property, for otherwise we should be oppressors." So when they despaired of him they drew aside to take counsel in private. Said the eldest of them:[11] "Know ye not that your father has taken an assurance against you from Allah, and how previously ye acted iniquitously with regard to Joseph? I shall never leave the land till my father gives me permission, or till Allah gives judgment for me, for He is the best of those who give judgment. Go back to your father and say: 'O our father, thy son hath stolen, and we testify only to that which we know, nor could we have guarded against the unseen. So question the town in which we were, and the caravan in which we have come, for we, indeed, are those who speak the truth.'" This they did, but their father said: "Nay! but your souls have framed up a matter for you. Patient endurance, however, is a beautiful thing. Maybe Allah will bring them all to me together. He it is Who is the Knowing, the Wise." Then he turned from them and said: "O what grief is mine for Joseph!" And his eyes went white from sorrow,[12] and he was inwardly grieving. They said: "By Allah, thou wilt keep on making mention of Joseph till thou art become decrepit, or art become one of those about to perish." Said he: "I take my complaint of my sorrow and my grief to Allah alone, but I know from Allah what ye know not. O my sons, go and seek for news of Joseph and his brother, and despair not of Allah's mercy. None, indeed, despair of Allah's mercy save the unbelieving people." Then when they came in to Joseph they said: "O prince, distress has touched us and our households, and we have brought but scanty merchandise, but give us full measure, bestowing it as charity upon us, for Allah, indeed, recompenses those who give in charity." He said: "Know ye what ye did with Joseph and his brother when ye were ignorant of what ye were doing?" They said: "Art thou, can it be that thou art Joseph?" Said he: "I am Joseph, and this is my brother. Allah has been gracious to us. The fact is, if one shows piety and patiently endures: Allah lets not the reward of those who do good perish." They said: "By Allah, Allah has, indeed, given thee the preference over us, and we have been those who were committing faults." Said he: "Let there be no blame upon you this day. Allah will forgive you, for He is the most merciful of those who shew mercy. Go ye with this shirt of mine[13] and cast it on my father's face, and he will see again. And bring to me your households, all of them." When the caravan set out from Egypt their father said: "I should declare that I perceive the smell of Joseph, were it not that ye would think me doting." They said: "By Allah, there thou art at thine ancient error." But when the bearer of good tidings came he cast it on his face, so he saw again. Said he: "Did I not say to you: 'I know from Allah what ye know not'? " They said: "O our father, ask pardon for us for our sins. We have been those who were committing faults." Said he: "Anon I shall ask pardon for you from my Lord. He it is Who is the Forgiving, the Merciful." When they entered to Joseph he took his two parents[14] to be with him, and he said to the others: "Enter ye Egypt in safety, if Allah wills." Then he brought his two parents up to the throne. They all fell down before him doing obeisance. He said: "O my father, this is the interpretation of my dream heretofore. My Lord has made it come true. He has treated me well indeed, since he brought me out of prison, and has brought you from the desert, after Satan had stirred up strife between me and my brothers. My Lord, indeed, is kindly disposed in what He wills. He it is Who is the Knowing, the Wise. O my Lord, Thou hast given me dominion and taught me the interpretation of hard sayings. O Creator of the heavens and the earth, Thou art my guardian in this world and the next. Cause me to die as one who submits, and join me with the Just."

This is one of the announcements of the Unseen. We reveal it to thee, O Mohammed, for thou wast not with them when they agreed on their matter and were scheming. But the most part of the people, even though thou art urgent, are not believers. Yet thou askest no reward for it. It is naught but a reminder to mankind. How many a sign in the heavens and the earth they pass by, yet they are turning away from them. Most of them believe not in Allah without associating others with Him. Are they then secure from there coming upon them a calamity of Allah's punishment, or from the Hour coming on them suddenly, when they are not aware? Say: "This is my way. I summon to Allah by way of clear proof, I and whosoever follows me. So glory be to Allah, I am not one of the associators." We have not sent before thee any save men of the townspeople to whom We gave revelation. Have they not travelled in the land and seen what the final issue was for those who preceded them? The abode of the Hereafter is better, indeed, for those who show piety. Will ye not then understand? Until the messengers were in despair and thought they were being counted as false, Our help came to them. Thus We rescue whomsoever We will, and Our violence is not to be turned back from the sinful people. Now, indeed, there has been in their story[15] a lesson for such as are possessed of insight. It was not a tale newly invented, but a confirmation of that which is there present, and an explanation of everything, a guidance and a mercy to a people who believe.

Surat Maryam: Mary

Though this Sura was revised in Medina its material is mostly from the Late Meccan period. The latter half of it, consisting of odd pieces which have been put together and attached to the Prophet-stories, is apparently older than the Prophet-stories themselves, at least in their present form. The Abraham story in Section 5 has a special interest in that here his father is represented as a worshipper of Satan. This may point to the Christian origin of this story, especially as the John and Jesus stories with which the Sura begins were drawn from Christian informants familiar with the Apocryphal Gospels.

IN THE NAME OF ALLAH,
THE MERCIFUL, THE COMPASSIONATE

❊K.H.Y.ʿ.S. A remembrance of the mercy of thy Lord to His servant Zachariah, When he called upon his Lord a secret calling. He said: "O my Lord, my bones have indeed grown weak within me, and my head has kindled a hoary white, yet never have I been unfortunate in prayer to Thee, O my Lord. But now I have fears as to kindred after me, since my wife has become barren, so do Thou grant me from Thyself a successor, Who will inherit from me, and inherit from the family of Jacob, and make him, O my Lord, one who is well-pleasing to Thee." Said the angel:[1] "O Zachariah, indeed I give thee good tidings of a youth (*ghulam*) whose name is John, We did not appoint for him such a name before."[2] Said he: "O my Lord, how shall I have a son, seeing that my wife has become barren, and I have already reached an advanced age?" He said: "Thus it shall be. Thy Lord has said: 'It is easy for Me. Why, I created thee before when thou wast not anything.'" He said: "O my Lord, appoint for me a sign." Said the angel: "Thy sign shall be that thou shalt not speak to the people for three days on end." Then he went out to his people from the sanctuary and spoke to them by signs, saying: "Give glory to Allah morning and evening." Said Allah: "O John, take the Book with strength,"[3] and We gave him wisdom as a child, And grace from Ourselves, and purity, and he was pious, And dutiful towards both his parents, and never was he proud, disobedient. So peace be upon him the day he was born, the day he dies, and the day he will be raised alive!

❋ And make mention in the Book,[4] O Mohammed, of Mary, when she went apart from her people to an eastern place, And set up for herself over against them a curtain. Then We sent to her Our Spirit, who for her took the shape of a comely human.[5] She said: "I, indeed, take refuge with the Merciful from thee, if thou art pious." Said he: "I am only a messenger of thy Lord, sent to thee that I may give thee a pure son." She said: "How shall I have a child when no man has touched me, and I have never been unchaste?" Said he: "It shall be so. Thy Lord has said: 'It is easy for Me, and truly We shall make him a sign to the people, and a mercy from Us. The matter has been decided.'" So she became pregnant with him and went apart with him to a remote place. Then the birth pangs drove her to a palm-tree trunk. She said: "O would that I had died ere this, and become forgotten, quite forgotten." Then one from beneath her called to her,[6] saying: "Do not grieve. Thy Lord has set beneath thee a rivulet. So shake towards thyself the palm-tree trunk, it will let fall on thee fresh ripe dates, So eat and drink and be of good cheer, and shouldst thou perchance see anyone of human kind, then say: "Truly, I have vowed to the Merciful a fast, so I shall not speak today to any man." Then she brought him to her people, carrying him. They said: "O Mary, thou hast come with a strange thing. O sister of Aaron,[7] thy father was no man of wickedness, nor was thy mother unchaste." So she pointed to him.

They said: "How shall we speak with one who is in the cradle, a babe?" The babe said: "Truly, I am a servant of Allah. He has given me the Book and has made me a prophet, And made me blessed wherever I may be, and laid on me the obligation of prayer and legal alms, so long as I remain alive, And that I be dutiful to my mother. And He has not made me a proud, a wretched fellow, So peace be upon me the day I was born, the day I die, and the day I am raised alive!"

❧That is Jesus, son of Mary, a statement of the truth concerning a matter about which they are in doubt. It was not for Allah to take any son. Glory be to Him! When He determines a matter He has only to say to it: "Be!" and it is, And, verily, Allah is my Lord and your Lord, so worship Him. This is the straight path.

❧Now the sects came to differ among themselves, but woe to those who disbelieve, woe from the witness-place of a mighty Day! How quick they will be to hear, how quick to see, on the Day when they come to Us! But today the wrong-doers are in manifest error. So warn them of the Day of Sighing, when the matter is accomplished while they are in heedlessness. Yet they will not believe. It is We Who will inherit the earth and whosoever are upon it, and to Us will they be brought back.

❧And make mention in the Book, O Mohammed, of Abraham. He, indeed, was a trustworthy man, a prophet, When he said to his father: "O my father, why dost thou worship that which neither hears nor sees, and profits thee not a thing? O my father, truly there has come to me a certain knowledge that has not come to thee, so follow me. I shall guide thee on an even path. O my father, worship not Satan. Verily Satan has come to be in rebellion against the Merciful. O my father, I fear, indeed, that there may touch thee a punishment from the Merciful, and that thou mayest become a vassal to Satan." He said: "Art thou averse to my gods, O Abraham? If thou dost not leave off I shall most assuredly stone thee. So begone from me for a season." Abraham said: "Peace be upon thee! I shall seek forgiveness for thee from my Lord. Truly, He has been gracious to me, But I shall separate myself from you people and that upon which ye call instead of Allah, and I shall call upon my Lord. Maybe I shall not be unhappy in calling upon my Lord." Then when he separated himself from them and from what they were worshipping instead of Allah, We gave him Isaac and Jacob, and each of them We made a prophet, And gave to them of Our mercy, and appointed for them a high tongue of truth.[8]

❧ And make mention, in the Book, of Moses. He, indeed, was single-hearted, and was a messenger, a prophet, And We summoned him from the right side of at-Tur,[9] and brought him near for private talk, And of Our mercy We gave him his brother Aaron as a prophet. And make mention in the Book of Ishmael. He was one who was true to his promise, and was a messenger, a prophet, And used to enjoin on his household prayer and legal alms, and with his Lord was one well-approved. And make mention, in the Book, of Idris.[10] He, indeed, was a trustworthy person, a prophet, And We raised him up to a high place. These are they among the prophets of Adam's posterity to whom Allah has shown favour, and of those whom We carried with Noah, and of the posterity of Abraham and Israel,[11] and of those whom We guided and whom We chose. When the signs of the Merciful are recited to them they fall prostrate, doing obeisance and weeping, But others came in succession after them who were unmindful of prayer and followed their lusts, so anon they will meet destruction. Save such as repent and believe and act righteously, for those will enter the Garden of Paradise, and in naught will they be wronged: Gardens of Eden which the Merciful has promised to His servants in the Unseen. His promise has ever been fulfilled. They will not hear therein any foolish talk, but only "Peace," and therein they will have their provision morning and evening. That is the Garden which We have given to be inherited by Our servants, and by everyone who has been pious.

❈·Said Gabriel: "We do not come down save by commandment of thy Lord. His is whatever is before us, whatever is behind us, and whatever in between them, and thy Lord is not forgetful; Lord of the heavens and the earth and what is between them both, so worship thou Him, and continue patiently in His service. Dost thou know any other with the same name as His?"

❈·Now man says: "Is it that when I have died I shall anon be brought forth alive?" Does not man remember that We, indeed, earlier created him when he was nothing? So, by thy Lord, We shall assuredly assemble them and the satans also. Then We shall also have them present kneeling around Gehenna. Then We shall separate out from each party those of them who were most insolent in rebellion against the Merciful. Then, truly, We shall know best about those who are worthiest for roasting therein. There is no one among you but will go down to it: that, with thy Lord, is something settled, determined. Then We shall rescue those who have shown piety, but We shall leave the wrongdoers kneeling therein. Yet when Our signs are recited to them as evidential signs, those who disbelieve say to those who believe: "Which of the two parties has the best position and the finest ruling council?"[12] But how many a generation have We destroyed before them, people who surpassed them in possessions and reputation? Say: "Whoso is in error let the Merciful give him an extension so that when they see what they are promised, whether it be the punishment or the Hour, then they will know who is in the worse position and has the weakest army." Yet Allah will increase guidance for those who have submitted to guidance, and those things that remain, the righteous works, are better in thy Lord's sight in respect to reward and are a better issue.

❧·Hast thou seen him,[13] O Mohammed, who disbelieved Our signs, and said: "I shall assuredly be given wealth and children?" Has he mounted up to the Unseen? or has he taken some covenant from the Merciful? Nay, indeed, We shall write down what he says and lengthen out for him the punishment. We shall inherit from him that about which he speaks, and he will come to Us all by himself. Yet they take for themselves instead of Allah deities that these may be a strength to them. Nay, indeed, on the Day these false gods will disavow their worship and will be in opposition to them. Hast thou not seen, O Mohammed, that We have sent the satans on the unbelievers to incite them to evil? So be not thou in haste over them. We do but number to them a number of days, Till the Day when We assemble unto the Merciful those who show piety as a delegation, And drive the sinners to Gehenna as a herd.[14] They will have no power of intercession, save such of them as have taken a covenant with the Merciful. Yet they say: "The Merciful has taken for Himself a son." They have certainly brought a monstrous thing, At which the heavens are well-nigh rent asunder, and the earth is split open, and the mountains fall in fragments, That they ascribe to the Merciful a son. It were unseemly for the Merciful to take for Himself a son. There is no one either in the heavens or the earth but comes as a servant to the Merciful. Truly, He has counted them up and numbered them a number, And each of them will come to Him by himself on the Day of Resurrection. Verily, to those who have believed and done righteous works, to them the Merciful will vouchsafe love.

❧ We have made it easy for thy tongue, O Mohammed, that by it thou mayest give good tidings to those who show piety, and by it warn a contentious people. How many a generation before them have We destroyed! Canst thou perceive a single one of them, or hear even a whisper of them?

Medinan
Suras

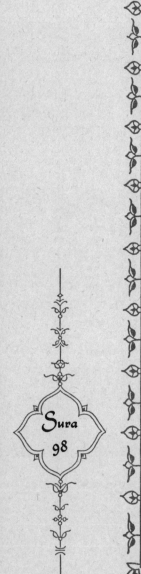

Surat al-Bayyina: The Demonstration

The Demonstration is the coming of a messenger from Allah with a Book of Scripture. It was the coming of Jesus with his new revelation which separated Christians from Jews, and so it is Mohammed's preaching of his revelation which separated his community both from those of the People of the Book and from the pagan Arab polytheists. The passage thus clearly comes from the early Medinan period when the Prophet was busy developing his theory that the Hanif religion was a return to the religion of Abraham.

IN THE NAME OF ALLAH, THE MERCIFUL, THE COMPASSIONATE

Those among the People of the Book and the associators [polytheists] were not to be set apart till the Demonstration should come to them, Namely, a messenger from Allah reciting purified pages In which are true Scriptures.[1] Those who were given the Book did not separate from one another till after the Demonstration had come to them. They were enjoined naught save that they should worship Allah, making religion exclusively His, as Hanifs, and to observe prayer and pay the legal alms, for that is the true religion. Verily those among the People of the Book and the associators who have disbelieved will be in the fire of Gehenna, therein to abide eternally. Such are the worst of creation, Whereas those who believe and perform righteous acts, they are the best of creation. Their recompense is with their Lord, Gardens of Eden beneath which rivers flow, therein to abide eternally for ever. Allah will be well-pleased with them and they well-pleased with Him. That is for whosoever fears his Lord.

Sura 98

Surat at-Taghabun:
The Mutual Deception

At-Taghabun is one of the many names of the Last Day, which is said to be so called because those who thought that they would have much will be surprised at how little they have, while those who thought they would have but little will be surprised at how much they have. So it is like a case of mutual deception. The material belongs to the early period of the Prophet's ministry in Medina, and in part is concerned with his difficulties in establishing his community there.

Sura 64

IN THE NAME OF ALLAH,
THE MERCIFUL, THE COMPASSIONATE

Whatsoever is in the heavens, and whatsoever is on earth, gives glory to Allah. His is the kingdom and His is the praise, and He is powerful over everything. He is the One Who created you, but some of you are unbelievers, and some of you are believers. Yet Allah is observant of what ye are doing. He created the heavens and the earth in truth, and not only formed you but made excellent your forms, and to Him is the journey back. He knows whatever is in the heavens and the earth, and He knows what ye keep secret and what ye reveal publicly. Indeed, Allah knows about the secrets of the breasts.

Has there not come to you the account of those who in former times disbelieved, and so tasted the grievousness of their affair? for theirs was a painful punishment. That was because their messengers had come to them with evident signs, but they said: "Is is that men will guide us?" So they disbelieved and turned their backs. But Allah could do without them, for Allah is rich, praiseworthy. Those who have disbelieved claim that they will never be raised up. Say: "Yea, indeed, by my Lord, ye will assuredly be raised up; then ye will just as surely be informed about what ye have done. That is an easy thing for Allah." So believe in Allah and in His messenger and in the light that We have sent down. Allah is informed about what ye do. On the Day when He assembles you to the Day of Gathering, that is the Day of mutual deception. Then he who believes in Allah and acts righteously, for him He will expiate his evil deeds, and make him enter gardens beneath which rivers flow, therein to abide eternally for ever. That is the great felicity. But those who have disbelieved and counted Our signs false, those are the people of the Fire, therein to abide eternally, and how evil a destination!

❧No misfortune ever happens save by Allah's permission. He who believes in Allah, his heart will He guide, and Allah knows everything. So obey Allah and obey the messenger. If then ye turn your backs Our messenger is responsible only for the clear proclamation of the message—"Allah, there is no deity save Him, so in Allah let the believers put their trust."

❧O ye who believe, in your wives and your children there is an enemy to you, so beware of them. However, if ye pass it over and pardon and forgive, Allah too is forgiving, compassionate. Your wealth and your children are only a trial, and Allah has with Him a wondrous reward. So show piety towards Allah as ye are able, to hearken and obey and make charitable contributions as something good for your souls, for whoso is saved from the miserliness of his soul, such are they who prosper. If ye lend Allah a goodly loan He will increase it double for you and will forgive you, for Allah is grateful, kindly, He Who knows both the unseen and the seen, the Sublime, the Wise.

Surat al-Fath: The Victory

It was early recognized that passages in this Sura were concerned with the victory and treaty of Hudaibiyya in the year 6 A.H. It is much concerned with problems of expeditions, the division of spoils, troubles with the Bedouin, discontents within his own community, and so it must come from a relatively advanced period of his Medinan years and looks forward to the conquest of Mecca. The references to the Torah and the Gospel in the concluding verse reveal a growing acquaintance with Scripture.

IN THE NAME OF ALLAH, THE MERCIFUL, THE COMPASSIONATE

Verily We opened to them a manifest opening[1] [at Hudaibiyya] That Allah might forgive both thy former and thy latter sins, and might perfect His grace to thee, and guide thee in a straight path, And that Allah might aid thee with mighty succour. He is the One Who sent down the spirit of tranquillity[2] into the hearts of the believers that they might have an increase of faith along with their faith, for Allah's are the armies of the heavens and the earth, for Allah is knowing, wise; That He may make the believers, male and female, enter gardens between which rivers flow, wherein they are to abide eternally, and that He may expiate for them their evil deeds, and that, with Allah, is the great felicity; And that He may punish the hypocrites, male and female, and the associators [polytheists], male and female, who think evil with regard to Allah. For them is a circuit of evil, for Allah is angered with them and has cursed them, and has prepared Gehenna for them —how evil a destination! Allah's are the armies of the heavens and the earth, for Allah is sublime, wise.

We have sent thee, O Mohammed, as a witness, a bringer

Sura 48

of good tidings and a warner, That ye folk may believe in Allah and in His messenger, that ye may assist him, show him due respect, and give glory to Him[3] morning and evening. In truth, those who are swearing fealty to thee are actually but swearing fealty to Allah. Allah's hand is above their hands, so he who breaks oath breaks it only against himself; and to him who fulfils that concerning which he has made covenant with Allah, to him He will give a great reward.

Those of the Bedouin who have been left behind will say to thee: "Our properties and our families kept us occupied, so ask thou forgiveness for us." They say with their tongues what is not in their hearts. Say: "So who will avail aught for you against Allah if He either wishes you harm or wishes your advantage? Nay, but Allah was informed about what ye were doing. Nay, but ye thought that the messengers and the believers would never return from the battle to their families. That was made to seem fine in your hearts, so ye thought evilly and became a reprobate people. Such as believe not in Allah and in His messenger, We have got Sa'ir[4] ready for such unbelievers. Allah's is the kingdom of the heavens and the earth. He grants forgiveness to whom He will, and He punishes whom He will, though Allah is forgiving, compassionate.

Those who have been left behind will say when ye go forth for the spoils, that ye may take them, "Let us follow you," desirous of changing Allah's word. Say: "Never will ye follow us. Thus has Allah said before."[5] They will say: "Nay, but ye are jealous of us." Nay, but they were not understanding save a little. Say to those of the Bedouin who were left behind: "Ye are going to be called out against a people possessed of unwavering courage. Ye will fight them or they will submit. So if ye obey, Allah will give you an excellent reward, but if ye turn your backs as ye turned your backs on a previous occasion, Allah will punish you with a painful punishment." No blame rests on the blind, and no blame rests on the lame, and no blame rests on the sick for not responding to the call. Whoso obeys Allah and His messenger, him He will make enter gardens beneath which rivers flow, but whoso turns his back, him He will punish with a painful punishment. Allah was well-pleased with the believers when they were swearing fealty to thee beneath the tree,[6] for He knew what was in their hearts and He sent down the spirit of tranquillity upon them, and rewarded them with a speedy victory [*fath*], And much spoils they might take, for Allah is sublime, wise. Allah promised you much spoils that ye might take, so He hurried this along for you and restrained the hands of the people from you,[7] so that it might be a sign to the believers, and might guide you in a straight path. But other spoils ye were not able to take, those hath Allah compassed, for Allah is powerful over everything. Had those who disbelieved fought you they would have turned their flanks; then they would find no guardian, no helper. This is Allah's custom which was put into effect in earlier times, and thou wilt never find any changing in Allah's custom.

He is the One Who restrained their hands from you and your hands from them in the interior of Mecca after He had given you the victory over them,[8] and Allah was observing what ye were doing. They were the ones who disbelieved and kept you away from the sacred shrine, so that the offering was prevented from reaching its place of sacrifice. And had it not been for men and women believers of whom ye did not know and whom ye might have trampled down, and a crime come upon you because of them unknowingly, that Allah may cause to enter His mercy whom He will, Allah would have settled all this. Had they been separated out We should have punished those among them who disbelieved with a painful punishment.[9] When those who disbelieved set fierce zeal in their hearts, the fierce zeal of paganism, then did Allah send down His spirit of tranquillity upon His messenger and upon the believers, causing them to cleave to the word of piety, seeing that they were the best entitled to it and the most worthy of it. Allah is knowing about everything, Allah has brought true for His messenger the vision in which He had said: "Ye will assuredly enter the sacred shrine safely, if Allah wills, some of you with your heads shaven, others with hair short-cropped, without your being afraid." He knew what ye did not know, and He appointed even before that an early victory [*fath*]. He is the One who has sent His messenger with guidance and the religion of truth, that He may make it victorious over all religions. Allah sufficeth as a witness. Mohammed is Allah's messenger, and those with him are strong against the unbelievers, compassionate among themselves. Thou seest them bowing, prostrating in obeisance, desiring some bounty from Allah and His acceptance. Their faces are marked by the traces of prostration. That is their similitude in the Torah, and their similitude in the Gospels[10] is that they are like a seed planted which puts forth its shoot, then strengthens it so that it grows stout and stands upright on its stalk, amazing the husbandman, that He may by them make the unbelievers wroth. Allah has promised those among them who believe and do works of righteousness forgiveness and a great reward.

Surat at-Tahrim:
The Declaring Prohibited

*The small pieces, easily distinguishable by the rhyming endings,
which make up this Sura are all Medinan, but there is no clue
as to why they were put together thus. The opening verses are
concerned with the famous scandal in the Prophet's harem over
Mary the Copt, and his embarrassment thereat. Almost equally
famous, however, are the similitudes of the unrighteous women
and the righteous women at its close.*

IN THE NAME OF ALLAH,
THE MERCIFUL, THE COMPASSIONATE

O Prophet, wherefore dost thou make prohibited that which
Allah has made allowable for thee? Why art thou seeking to
please thy wives? But Allah is forgiving, compassionate. Allah
has sanctioned for you Moslems the annulment of your oaths,
and Allah is your patron, and He is the Knowing, the Wise.
When the Prophet spoke in secret to one of his wives about
a recent happening,[1] then when she gave information about
it to another of his wives, and Allah made this apparent to
him, he made known a part of it but held back a part. Then
when he informed her about it she said: "Who told you this?"
He said: "The Knowing, the Well-informed told me." If ye
two wives repent towards Allah, then your hearts have inclined towards what is right; but if ye support one another
against him, then Allah is his patron, also Gabriel and the
righteous believers, and beyond that the angels are a support.
Should he divorce you[2] maybe his Lord will give him in exchange wives who are better than you, submissive, believers,
obedient, penitent—women who worship, women who fast,
both those who have known men and virgins.

Sura
66

❧ O ye who believe, protect yourselves and your families from a Fire whose fuel is men and stones,[3] over which are angels rough and strong who do not disobey Allah in that which He has commanded them, but perform what they are bidden. O ye who have disbelieved, make no excuses for yourselves to-day, ye are only being recompensed for what ye have been doing.

❧ O ye who believe, repent with a sincere repentance towards Allah, perchance your Lord will expiate your evil deeds and make you enter gardens beneath which rivers flow, on the Day when Allah will not humiliate the Prophet and those with him who have believed. Their light will hasten on before them and at their right hands. They will say: "O our Lord, make perfect for us our light, and grant us forgiveness. Thou, indeed, art powerful over everything." O Prophet, contend against the unbelievers and the hypocrites,[4] and be rough with them. Gehenna is their place of resort, and how evil a destination.

❧ Allah has set forth as a similitude of those who disbelieve, the wife of Noah[5] and the wife of Lot. These both were under marital bonds with two of Our righteous servants, but they betrayed them both, and their husbands availed them naught against Allah, so it was said: "Enter ye two women the Fire along with those who enter." Also Allah has set forth as a similitude of those who believe, the wife of Pharaoh,[6] when she said: "O my Lord, build for me near Thee a dwelling in the Garden, and deliver me from Pharaoh and what he is doing, and save me from the wrongdoing people," And Mary, the daughter of Amram, who guarded her private parts, so We breathed therein of Our Spirit, and she gave credence to the words of her Lord and to His Books and was one of the obedient.[7]

Surat al-Baqara: The Cow

Sura 2 is the longest Sura in the Koran, and there is some reason to believe that its earlier passages were being put together by the Prophet to be the beginning of his Book. For this reason it introduces the story of Adam quite early, so as to begin at the beginning. Its main interest to us is in its passages of controversy with the Jews and Christians, and for its many legislative passages which are of great importance for the understanding of the Islamic religious system. It may have some Meccan material included in it, but for the most part it comes from the earlier years of the Prophet's labours in Medina.

IN THE NAME OF ALLAH,
THE MERCIFUL, THE COMPASSIONATE

A.L.M. That is the Book. There is no doubt about it. It is a guidance to those who shew piety, Who believe in the Unseen, and observe prayer, and give generously in charity of that with which We have provided them, And who believe in what has been sent down to thee, O Mohammed, and in what was sent down before thee, and concerning the Hereafter have sure conviction. Such have guidance from their Lord, and those are they who prosper. As for those who disbelieve it is all the same to them whether thou hast warned them or didst not warn them, they will not believe. Allah has put a seal on their hearts, and on their hearing, and over their seeing is a veil, so for them is a mighty punishment. Among the people are some who say: "We believe in Allah and in the Last Day," but they are not believers. They would deceive Allah and those who believe, but they are deceiving no one but themselves, though they perceive it not. In their hearts is

Sura

2

a sickness, so Allah will increase the sickness, and for them is a painful punishment because of what they have been treating as false. When it is said to them: "Cause no corruption in the land," they say: "Why, we are only setting things right." Is it not that they are the ones who are causing corruption? but they perceive it not. When it is said to them: "Believe as others of the people have believed," they say: "Shall we believe as the foolish ones have believed?" Is it not that they are the foolish ones? But they know it not. When they meet those who have believed they say: "We believe;" but when they are alone with their satans[1] they say: "We are really with you, we were only making jest." Allah will make jest of them and will extend their blind wandering in their wicked transgression. Those are they who have purchased error at the price of guidance, so their trafficking has been no profit, and they have not been guided.

❀·When thy Lord said to the angels: "I am going to set a vicegerent on the earth," they said:[2] "Wilt Thou set one thereon who will cause corruption therein and shed blood? whereas we give glory with Thy praise and we sanctify Thee."[3] He said: "I, indeed, know what ye do not know." Now He taught Adam the names of His creatures, all of them. Then He presented them to the angels and said: "Inform Me of the names of these if ye are those who speak the truth." They answered: "Glory be to Thee! We have no knowledge save what Thou hast taught us. It is Thou who art the Knowing, the Wise." Said He: "O Adam, inform them of their names." Then when he had informed them of their names, He said: "Did I not say to you that I know the unseen things of the heavens and the earth, and I well know both what ye show openly and what ye have been concealing?" And when We said to the angels:

"Do obeisance to Adam," then they did obeisance, save Iblis, who disdainfully refused, thinking himself too big, and was among the unbelievers. And We said: "O Adam, dwell thou and thy spouse in the Garden, and eat ye both to your fill thereof wheresoever ye will, but draw ye not near to this tree, lest ye be among the wrongdoers." But Satan caused them both to slip from obedience, so that he brought about their banishment from that blissful state in which they had been. We said: "Get ye down, the one of you an enemy to the other,[4] and there will be for you on the earth an abiding-place and enjoyment for a while." Now Adam learned from his Lord some words,[5] for He relented towards him. The fact is, He is the One Who relents, the Compassionate. We said: "Get ye down from it, the lot of you, but should there ever come to you guidance from Me, then on such as follow My guidance, on them shall be no fear, nor will they grieve. But those who disbelieve, and count false Our signs, those are the people of the Fire, wherein they will abide eternally.

❊·Neither those among the People of the Book who disbelieve nor the associators [or polytheists] like it that any good is sent down upon you Moslems from your Lord, but Allah singles out for His mercy whom He will, and Allah is the possessor of great bounty. We do not abrogate a verse or make thee forget it, O Mohammed, but We replace it with one better than it, or one like it.[6] Knowest thou not that Allah is powerful over everything? Knowest thou not that Allah's is the kingdom of the heavens and the earth, and that apart from Allah ye have no guardian and no helper? Or do ye desire to question your messenger as Moses was formerly questioned? Whosoever takes unbelief in exchange for belief has certainly gone astray from the even way. Many among the People of the Book would like to turn you back to unbelief after your belief, out of selfish envy which they have even after the truth has been made clear to them, but pardon ye it and pass it over till Allah comes with His affair. Allah, indeed, is powerful over everything. So observe prayers and pay the legal alms, for whatsoever good ye send ahead for yourselves ye will find with Allah. Allah, indeed, is observant of what ye do. And they say: "No one will ever enter the Garden of Paradise save him who is a Jew or a Christian." Those are their desires. Say: "Bring ye your proof if ye are speaking the truth." Nay, indeed, whosoever has submitted his face to Allah, and is a doer of good, has his reward with his Lord. On such there is no fear, nor will they be grieved. The Jews say: "The Christians are on no basis," and the Christians say: "The Jews are on no basis," and yet they both read the Book. Likewise those who have no knowledge [i.e., the pagans] say the like of what they say. But Allah will give judgment between them on Resurrection Day concerning that about which they have been differing among themselves. Yet who acts more wrongfully than those who prevent Allah's name from being made mention of in His shrines, and are eager to ruin them? Such ought not to enter them save in fear. For them there is in this world humiliation and for them in the Hereafter is a mighty punishment. Allah's are both the East and the West, so whithersoever ye turn there is the face of Allah. Allah is, indeed, wide-reaching, knowing. The Christians say: "Allah has taken for Himself a son." Glory be to Him! Nay, but His is whatsoever is in the heavens and the earth, where all are obedient to Him. He is the originator of the heavens and the earth, so when He determines some matter He only says to it: "Be!" and it is. Those who have no knowledge[7] say: "Unless Allah speaks to us, or a sign comes to us." Thus those who preceded them said the like of what they say. Their hearts are alike. We have already made the signs clear to a people who have sure conviction. We have, indeed, sent thee with the truth, O Mohammed, as a bringer of good tidings and as a warner, and thou wilt not be questioned about the people of al-Jahim.[8] Neither the Jews nor the Christians will ever be pleased with thee till thou followest their religion.[9] Say: "Allah's guidance is the guidance," for shouldst thou follow their desires after that knowledge which has come to thee, thou wilt have from Allah neither guardian nor helper. Those to whom We have given the Book, and who read it as it ought to be read, such believe in it, and such as disbelieve in it they are the losers.

They say: "Be Jews or Christians and ye will be rightly guided." Say: "Nay, but the religion of Abraham, a Hanif,[10] and he was not one of the associators [or polytheists]." Say ye: "We believe in Allah and in what has been sent down to us, and what was sent down to Abraham, and to Ishmael and Isaac and Jacob and the Patriarchs, and in what was given to Moses and Jesus, and in what was given to the prophets from their Lord. We make no distinction between any of them, and to Him we submit ourselves." So, if they believe in the like of what ye believe then they are indeed guided, and if they turn away it is only they who are in schism. Allah will be thy sufficiency against them. He is the One Who hears, the One Who knows. Allah's *sibgha*,[11] and who has a better *sibgha* than Allah? Him are we worshipping. Say: "Will ye dispute with us about Allah, when He is both our Lord and your Lord? We have our works and ye have your works, and we devote ourselves singleheartedly to Him. Or do ye say: 'Verily Abraham, and Ishmael, and Isaac, and Jacob, and the Patriarchs were Jews or Christians.' " Say: "Are ye the more learned or Allah? Who is a greater wrongdoer than he who conceals a testimony he has from Allah? Allah is not heedless of what ye are doing." That is a community which has passed away. It has what it earned, and ye will have what ye have earned, and ye will not be questioned about what they were doing.

The foolish among the people will say: "What has turned them from the kiblah they were wont to make use of?"[12] Say: "To Allah belong both the East and the West. He guides whom He wills to a straight path." Thus We have appointed you Moslems as an intermediate community, that ye may be witnesses against the people, and that the messenger may be a witness against you. We appointed the kiblah ye used to make use of only that We might know who would follow the Messenger from him who would turn on his heel. If it be a great matter it is not so to those whom Allah has guided. Allah is not One to let your faith come to naught. With the people Allah is indeed gentle, compassionate. We, indeed, see thee turning thy face towards the skies, so We shall assuredly make thee, O Mohammed, turn around to a kiblah that will please thee. Turn, therefore, thy face towards the sacred shrine; and wherever ye Moslems may be, turn your faces towards it. Verily those to whom the Book has been given know that it is the truth from their Lord, and Allah is not heedless of what they are doing. Even shouldst thou bring to those to whom the Book has been given every sign they would not follow thy kiblah. Thou art not now a follower of their kiblah, even as some of them are not followers of the kiblah of others, and shouldst thou follow their desires after the knowledge that has come to thee, thou wouldst in that case be among the wrongdoers. Those to whom We have given the Book recognize it as they recognize their own sons, yet a party among them conceals the truth, and they know that they are doing so. The truth is from thy Lord, so on no account be thou among those who doubt. To each has been given a direction to which he turns in prayer, so strive for pre-eminence in the good things. Wheresoever ye may be, Allah will bring you all together. Allah, indeed, is powerful over everything. So from wherever thou hast gone forth, turn thy face to the sacred shrine; for it, indeed, is the truth from thy Lord, and Allah is not heedless of what ye are doing. So from wherever thou hast gone forth, turn thy face towards the sacred shrine; and wheresoever ye Moslems may be, turn your faces towards it, that the people may have no argument against you, save those among them who do wrong. Do not fear them, fear Me; and do this that I may perfect My favour upon you, and maybe ye will be guided. Accordingly We have sent among you a messenger from among yourselves to recite to you Our signs, and purify you, and teach you the Book and the Wisdom, and teach you what ye did not know. So remember Me, I shall remember you, and give thanks to Me, and be not ungrateful to Me.

❧·Verily, those who conceal the evidential signs and the guidance that We have sent down, after We have made it clear to the people in the Book, they are the ones Allah will curse, and those who curse will also curse them, Save those who repent and reform and make this clear, for they are those towards whom I shall relent, for I am He Who relents, the Compassionate. They, indeed, who disbelieve and die as infidels, they are those on whom is the curse of Allah, of the angels, and of the people altogether, Under which they will be for ever, their punishment never lightened for them, and having no expectancy of deliverance. Your God is One God, there is no deity save Him, the Merciful, the Compassionate.

Assuredly in the creation of the heavens and the earth, in the alternation of night and day, in the ships that run in the sea with what may be useful to people, in the rain that Allah sends down from the sky, whereby He quickens the earth after its deadness and spreads abroad in it every kind of animal, in the changing about of the winds, and in the clouds set to serve between sky and earth, in all these are signs for a people who have intelligence. Yet among the people are some who in place of Allah take substitutes which they love as one loves Allah. Nevertheless those who believe have an even stronger love for Allah. Could those who do wrong but see that Day when they will see the punishment, see that the power is wholly with Allah, and that Allah is severe in punishment! It will be a Day when those who have been followed[13] will declare themselves innocent of those who have followed, and they will see the punishment, while all means of relief are cut off from them. And those who have followed will say: "Could we but have another chance we would keep ourselves free from them, as they declare themselves free from us." In this way doth Allah show them their works. For them are in store sighings, but they will not get out from the Fire.

O ye people! eat of what is lawful and good in the earth, but do not follow in the footsteps of Satan, for he is a manifest enemy to you. He enjoins on you only evil and wickedness, and that ye say about Allah what ye do not know. When it is said to them: "Follow what Allah has sent down," they say: "Nay, but we shall follow what we found our fathers at." What! even though their fathers understood naught and had no guidance? The similitude of those who disbelieve is that of one who addresses a creature which hears nothing but a summons and a call. Deaf, dumb, blind are they, so they do not understand. O ye who believe! eat of the good things which We have given you as provision, and be thankful to

Allah, if ye really worship Him. He has made forbidden to you only that which is dead,[14] and blood, swine's flesh, and that which has been offered to any other than Allah;[15] though should anyone be compelled, not lusting for it nor wilfully transgressing, then there is no guilt on him if he eat of such food, for Allah, indeed, is forgiving, compassionate.

❧ Verily, those who conceal what Allah has sent down of the Book and thereby purchase a little gain, such take naught but fire as food into their bellies. Then on the Resurrection Day Allah will not speak to them, and will not clear them, but for them will be a painful punishment. Those are the ones who purchase error at the expense of guidance, and punishment at the expense of forgiveness. How patiently enduring will they be at the Fire! That is because Allah sent down the Book with the truth, so those who differ among themselves about the Book are indeed far gone in schism.

❧ Being upright does not consist in turning your faces to the East or to the West, but being upright is to believe in Allah, and the Last Day, and the angels, and the Books, and the Prophets, and in bestowing one's wealth, in spite of love for it, upon relatives, upon the orphans, the unfortunate, the son of the way, the beggars, and for ransoming those enslaved, to observe prayer, and pay the legal alms. Those are upright who fulfil their covenants when they have entered into such, who patiently endure under adversities and hardships and when under attack. These are they who are sincere, and those are the ones who are pious.

❧ O ye who believe! fasting is prescribed for you as it was prescribed for those who preceded you. Maybe ye will show piety. It is for a calculated number of days, but should anyone of you be sick, or on a journey, then a number of other days. For those who are able yet do not perform it a redemption is provided: the feeding of an unfortunate, though it is better for one to do good voluntarily, and that ye should fast is better for you did ye know it. It is for the month of Ramadan,[16] in which the Koran was sent down as a guidance for men, and as evidential signs of the guidance, and the *Furqan*.[17] So whoever of you observes the month let him fast during it, but should anyone be sick, or on a journey, then a number of other days. Allah desires it to be easy for you, with no desire that it be difficult, and that ye may complete the number of days, and that ye may magnify Allah for the way He has guided you, and perchance ye will be thankful. Now if My servants ask thee, O Mohammed, about Me, why, I am near at hand. I answer the call of him who calls when he calls upon Me. So let them respond to Me, and let them believe on Me; perchance they will be rightly guided. Going in to your wives on the night of the fast is lawful for you. They are a clothing for you, and ye are a clothing for them. Allah knows that ye have been defrauding yourselves, so He has relented towards you and has pardoned you. So now lie with them and seek what Allah has prescribed for you, and eat and drink till at the dawning a white thread is distinguishable by you from a black thread. Then fulfil the fast till night, and do not be lying with them when ye should be occupying your place in the houses of worship. These are the limits set by Allah, so draw not near to them. Thus does Allah make clear His signs to men; maybe they will show piety.

❧·Now fulfil ye the *hajj* and the *umra* to Allah,[18] but if ye are hindered then send along such sacrificial gift as may be easy for you, and shave not your heads till the sacrificial gift has reached its place. Should anyone of you be sick, or have an injury to his head, then he must pay compensation by fasting, or by distributing charitable alms, or performing some sacrificial rite. But when ye are safe, should anyone use for himself the period from the *umra* to the *hajj* then let him offer such sacrificial gift as may be easy; and should anyone not find a gift to be possible, then a fast for three days during the pilgrimage and seven when ye have returned home; that will be ten full days. This is for anyone whose family is not present at the Sacred Shrine, so show piety towards Allah, and know that Allah punishes severely. The pilgrimage [*hajj*] is during specified months, so if anyone undertakes the duty of pilgrimage therein let there be no sex indulgence, no transgression, and no disputing during the pilgrimage. Whatever good ye do, Allah knows it. Take provision for the journey, but the best provision is piety, so show piety towards Me, O ye who possess intelligence. It is no crime on your part that ye seek bounty from your Lord, so when ye pour forth from Arafat[19] remember Allah at the sacred monument, and remember him as He gave you guidance, even though ye formerly were of those astray. Then pour forth from where the people have poured forth, and seek Allah's forgiveness. Allah, indeed, is forgiving, compassionate.

O ye who believe! contribute from that which We have given you as provision, before there comes a Day on which there will be no bargaining, no amity, no intercession. The unbelievers, they are the wrongdoers. Allah, there is no deity save Him, the Living, the Self-subsistent. Slumber takes Him not, nor sleep.[20] His is whatever is in the heavens and whatever is on earth. Who is it that will intercede with Him save by His leave? He knows what is before them and what is behind them, whereas they comprehend naught of His knowledge save what He wills. Wide stretches His Throne over the heavens and the earth, yet to guard them both wearies Him not, for He is the High, the Mighty.

The similitude of those who contribute of their wealth in the way of Allah is that they are like a seed which produces seven ears, in every ear of which are a hundred seeds, seeing that Allah gives double to whom He will, and Allah is wide-reaching, knowing. Those who contribute of their wealth in the way of Allah, and do not follow up what they have contributed with reminders or annoyance, they have their reward with their Lord; no fear will be upon them, nor will they grieve. Polite language and forgiveness are better than charitable alms followed by annoyance. Allah is rich, forbearing. O ye who believe! do not spoil your charitable almsgiving by reminders and annoyance, like one who contributes of his wealth to be seen of men, and has no belief in Allah and the Last Day. His similitude is that he is like a hard rock on which is earth and which, when rain falls on it, is left bare. Such have no power over anything of what they have gained, and Allah does not guide the unbelieving people. But the similitude of those who contribute of their wealth out of a desire that Allah be well-pleased, and that they themselves be strengthened, is that they are like a garden on a hill on which rain falls and it yields double produce, and even if no rain falls on it there is dew. And Allah is observant of what ye are doing. Would any one of you like it if he had a garden of date-palms and grapevines beneath which streams flow, in which he has all kinds of fruits, yet old age comes on him and the progeny he had are weaklings, when a fiery whirlwind comes upon it so that it is burned up? Thus does Allah make clear to you the signs that maybe ye will ponder. O ye who believe, contribute of the good things ye have gained and out of that which We have produced from the earth for you, and do not choose the filthy parts thereof to contribute, such as ye yourselves would not accept unless ye were conniving therein. Be it known to you that Allah is rich, praiseworthy. Satan promises you poverty while bidding you commit crimes, whereas Allah promises you forgiveness from Himself and bounty, and Allah is wide-reaching, knowing. He gives wisdom to whom He will, and whosoever has been given wisdom has indeed been given much good; yet none are admonished save those possessed of intelligence. Whatsoever contribution ye make, or whatsoever vow ye vow, Allah assuredly knows about it, and for the wrongdoers there are no helpers. If ye give charitable alms publicly it is good, but if ye do it privately, and give it to the poor, that is better for you, and it will atone for some of your evil deeds, for Allah is well-informed about what ye do. Guiding them is no responsibility of thine, O Mohammed; Allah will guide whom He will, and whatever good ye Moslems contribute is for your own souls, seeing that ye contribute with no desire for anything save the face of Allah, and whatever good ye contribute will be fully repaid you, and ye will not be wronged. It is for the poor who have been restricted in the way of Allah, being unable to move around in the land. The ignorant man considers them rich because of their modest demeanour. By their marks thou mayest know them. They do not beg importunately from folk. Whatever good ye contribute, Allah, indeed, knows about it. Those who contribute of their wealth by night and by day, privately or publicly, such have their reward with their Lord; no fear will be upon them, nor will they grieve. Those who devour usury will not arise on the Day save as he will arise whom Satan has affected by his touch. That is because they said: "Usury is only like bargaining," though Allah has made bargaining licit but usury illicit. So whoever has a warning from his Lord come to him and stops, he may have what is past, and his affair is with Allah; but he who returns to it, such are the companions of the Fire, in which they will eternally abide. Allah is wiping out usury but is making charitable alms bear interest, and Allah does not love any guilty infidel. Verily, those who believe and perform works of righteousness, who observe prayer and pay the legal alms, such have their reward with their Lord; no fear will be upon them, nor will they grieve. O ye who believe! shew piety towards Allah, and leave what still remains of the usury,[21] if ye are believers, But if ye do not do this then expect war from Allah and His messenger, though if ye repent yours is the capital of your wealth, and ye are neither wronging nor being wronged. Also should the debtor be a man in difficulties, then allow him a respite till things are easier, but that ye should give it as charitable alms would be better for you, did ye but know. And fear ye a Day wherein ye will be made to return to Allah. Then every soul will be fully paid whatever it has earned, and they will not be wronged. O ye who believe! when ye contract a debt payable at a fixed term, write it down. Let a scribe write it down fairly between you, and let no scribe refuse to write, as Allah has taught him. Let him do the writing and let the one who owes the debt dictate, and let him fear Allah, his Lord, and not diminish aught thereof. Should he who owes the debt be feeble in mind or body, or be unable himself to dictate, then let his guardian dictate with fairness, and call to witness two witnesses from among your men, or if there be not two men available then a man and two women from among those looking on whom ye think suitable, that if one of them should err the other may remind her. Let not the witnesses refuse when they are called upon. Disdain not to put it in writing, whether it be little or much, with its agreed-upon term. That is more equitable for you with Allah, more accurate for the witnessing, and more likely to save you from doubts about it. This is the proper procedure unless it be a matter of present merchandise which you are circulating among yourselves. In that case it is no fault on your part if ye do not write it down, but be sure to have witnesses when ye are buying and selling with each other. Let not either scribe or witness do any injury to the parties involved, for if ye do, that is a crime on your part. Show ye piety towards Allah and Allah will instruct you, for Allah knows about everything. Should ye be on a journey and find no scribe, then let there be a pledge taken; but should any one of you trust another, let him who is trusted pay back what has been entrusted to him, and let him fear Allah, his Lord. Do not conceal the evidence. Whosoever conceals it, his heart is guilty, and Allah knows what ye are doing. Allah's is whatever is in the heavens and whatever is in the earth. Whether ye disclose what is in your souls or conceal it, Allah will reckon with you for it. He forgives whom He will, and He punishes whom He will, and Allah is powerful over everything. The Messenger believes in what has been sent down to him from his Lord, as do the believers. Each believes in Allah, and in His angels, and His Books, and His messengers. We make no distinction between one and another among His messengers. And they say: "We hear and we obey. Grant us Thy forgiveness, O our Lord, for to Thee is the return." Allah does not impose upon a soul more than it is capable of bearing. To its credit is what it has earned, and against it is what it has stored up. O our Lord, do not take us to task if we should forget or make a mistake. O our Lord, do not burden us with what is beyond our capacity, but pardon us, and forgive us, and have mercy upon us. Thou art our Patron, so assist us against the unbelieving people."

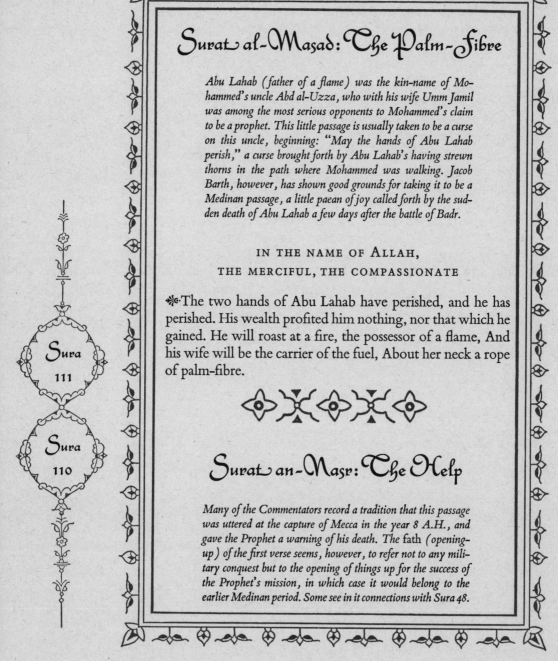

Surat al-Masad: The Palm-fibre

Abu Lahab (father of a flame) was the kin-name of Mohammed's uncle Abd al-Uzza, who with his wife Umm Jamil was among the most serious opponents to Mohammed's claim to be a prophet. This little passage is usually taken to be a curse on this uncle, beginning: "May the hands of Abu Lahab perish," a curse brought forth by Abu Lahab's having strewn thorns in the path where Mohammed was walking. Jacob Barth, however, has shown good grounds for taking it to be a Medinan passage, a little paean of joy called forth by the sudden death of Abu Lahab a few days after the battle of Badr.

IN THE NAME OF ALLAH,
THE MERCIFUL, THE COMPASSIONATE

The two hands of Abu Lahab have perished, and he has perished. His wealth profited him nothing, nor that which he gained. He will roast at a fire, the possessor of a flame, And his wife will be the carrier of the fuel, About her neck a rope of palm-fibre.

Surat an-Nasr: The Help

Many of the Commentators record a tradition that this passage was uttered at the capture of Mecca in the year 8 A.H., and gave the Prophet a warning of his death. The fath (opening-up) of the first verse seems, however, to refer not to any military conquest but to the opening of things up for the success of the Prophet's mission, in which case it would belong to the earlier Medinan period. Some see in it connections with Sura 48.

Sura
111

Sura
110

IN THE NAME OF ALLAH,
THE MERCIFUL, THE COMPASSIONATE

When Allah's help and the opening-up have come, And thou seest the people entering Allah's religion in troops, Then give glory, with praise of thy Lord, and seek His forgiveness. He, indeed, has always been One who relents.

Surat at-Takathur: Multiplying

We have here a fragment from a Medinan sermon, possibly from a relatively early period in the Prophet's sojourn in Medina. Like Sura 107 it is concerned with the lukewarmness of many of his followers who are more interested in other things than in religion. To what the "multiplying" refers is uncertain. The favourite explanation is that it refers to increasing in riches, though others consider that the reference is to clan rivalries in Medina, each clan desiring to outdo the others in numbers and strength.

IN THE NAME OF ALLAH,
THE MERCIFUL, THE COMPASSIONATE

The business of multiplying occupies you, Until ye have visited the graves. Nay, indeed, ye will know. Again, nay, indeed, ye will know, Nay, indeed, ye will know with certain knowledge. Ye would see al-Jahim[1] even now with the mind's eye, But after death ye will assuredly see it with the eye of certainty. Then on that Day ye will assuredly be questioned[2] about your pleasant life.

Sura 102

Sura
107

Surat al-Ma'un: The Assistance

This fragment from a Medinan passage belongs to the period when the Prophet was having trouble with his community in Medina, many members of which, while interested in the political implications of this new movement, were less than lukewarm with regard to its religious aspects.

IN THE NAME OF ALLAH,
THE MERCIFUL, THE COMPASSIONATE

❋Hast thou seen him who considers the religion false? That fellow is the one who repulses the orphan, And does not stir up folk to feed the unfortunate. So woe to those who pray But are careless about their praying, Who are all for making a show, But withhold assistance from the needy.

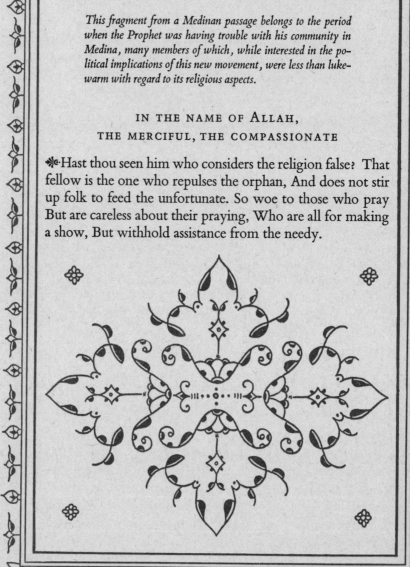

Surat an-Nisa: The Women

The material of this Sura comes, as a whole, from a somewhat later stage in the Medinan period than that in Sura 2. It is important for its legislative material, so passages have been selected which illustrate the laws of inheritance and the marriage laws, and from the latter part of the Sura a passage illustrating the still-developing controversy with the Jews and Christians.

IN THE NAME OF ALLAH,
THE MERCIFUL, THE COMPASSIONATE

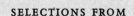O ye people! show piety towards your Lord who created you from a single person and from that person created his spouse, from which pair He spread abroad many men and women. So, show piety towards Allah about Whom ye question one another, and show reverence for blood relationships. Allah, indeed, is keeping watch over you. Give the orphans their property and do not exchange the worthless for the good. And devour not their property after adding it to your property, for that is a great crime. And if ye are afraid that ye may not deal justly with the orphans, then marry such women as may seem good to you, two or three or four, but if ye are afraid that ye may not be equitable, then one, or such slave-girls as your right hand may possess. That is more likely to keep you from swerving. Give the women their dowries freely, but should it please them to give you somewhat therefrom, then enjoy it with profit and advantage. But do not give to the weak-minded your property which Allah has appointed as a support for you, but provide for them therefrom, and clothe them, and speak to them with befitting speech. And make trial of the orphans so that when they reach the age of

Sura
4

marriage, if ye perceive they are going rightly ye then may hand over their property to them, but see that ye do not devour it in extravagance and in haste ere they grow up. Should a guardian of orphans be rich, let him keep himself from it altogether, but should he be poor let him make use of it as is befitting. Then when ye hand over their property to them take witnesses against them, though Allah is a sufficient accountant. Men have a right to a share of what their two parents and kinsfolk leave, and women have a right to a share of what parents and kinsfolk leave, a legally assigned share of whatever it is, whether little or much. So when there are present at the division those who have ties of kinship, the orphans, the unfortunate, make provision for them therefrom and speak to them with befitting speech. And let those be afraid who, were they to leave behind them weak progeny, would be fearful on their behalf. Let them show piety towards Allah and let them make an opportune proposal. Verily, those who devour wrongfully the property of orphans only take fire as food into their bellies, and anon they will roast at Sa'ir.[1]

❊ Allah lays commandment on you in the matter of your children. The male is to have the same portion as two females. Should they be women [i.e., if there is no male heir], if there are more than two they are to have two-thirds of what he has left, but if she be an only daughter she is to have half. His parents are to have each of them a sixth of what he has left if he has a child, but if he has no child then his two parents are his heirs and his mother is to have a third. If, however, he has brothers, his mother is to have a sixth—all the above after any bequests he may have made or any debts have been paid. Since ye do not know whether your fathers or your sons are more entitled to benefit from you, this is an ordinance from Allah. Allah, indeed, is knowing, wise. Ye are to have half of what your wives leave if they have no child, but if they have a child ye are to have a fourth of what they have left, after any bequests they may have made or any debts have been paid; and they are to have a fourth of what ye leave if ye have no child, but if ye have a child then they are to have an eighth of what ye have left after any bequests ye may have made or any debts have been paid. Should the inheriting be from a man or a woman with no direct heir, then if there be a brother or a sister, each of them is to have a sixth, and should there be more than that then they are to be partners in a third, after any bequests he may have made or any debts have been paid, without doing injury to anyone; a commandment from Allah, and Allah is knowing, forbearing. These are the bounds set by Allah, so such as obey Allah and His messenger He will make enter gardens beneath which rivers flow, in which they will abide forever. That is the great felicity. But whoso disobeys Allah and His messenger and breaks His bounds He will make enter the Fire, therein to abide forever, and for him there is a shameful punishment.

❧ Now those among your women who commit whoredom, against them bring as witnesses four from among you; and if they testify to the whoredom, shut those women up in the houses till death take them or Allah appoints a way for them. And those couples among you who commit it, punish them both; but if they repent and amend, turn away from them. Allah, indeed, is He Who relents, is compassionate. Nevertheless, relenting on Allah's part is only towards those who do evil in ignorance and then soon repent. Towards such Allah will relent, for Allah is knowing, wise. The relenting is not for those who do evil deeds till, when death comes nigh one of them, he says: "Now, indeed, I repent;" nor is it for those who die while they are infidels, since for those We have made ready a painful punishment.

❧ O ye who believe! it is not lawful for you to inherit from women against their will, so do not act harshly with them that ye may get away with part of what ye have given them as dowry, unless it be that they commit open whoredom; but live with them as is right and proper, for if ye are averse to them maybe ye are averse to something in which Allah has set great good. And should ye desire to make an exchange of one wife in place of another, and have given one of them a hundredweight[2] of goods as dowry, take naught from it. Would ye take it by calumny and manifest guilt? Moreover, how could ye take it when ye have had marital relations with one another and they have accepted from you a solid compact? Do not take in wedlock women whom your fathers have taken in wedlock—save what is already past[3]—for that is foulness and abomination and an evil way. Forbidden to you are your mothers, your daughters, your sisters, your paternal aunts and maternal aunts, brothers' daughters and sisters' daughters, foster mothers who have suckled you, foster sisters, mothers of your wives, wards who are under your care from women unto whom ye have gone in [i.e., step-daughters]—though if ye have not gone in to them there is no blame on you for taking their daughters—the lawful spouses of your sons who are from your loins. Also it is forbidden that ye take two sisters together—save what is already past. Allah, indeed, is forgiving, compassionate. Also such women as are under marriage protection, save what your right hands possess.[4] This is Allah's prescription for you. Whatever is beyond that, it is permissible for you to seek in accordance with your wealth, but under marriage protection, not for fornication. To those of them ye have enjoyed thereby give their hire as stipulated, though there is no blame on you should ye be pleased to give beyond what was stipulated. Allah, indeed, is knowing, wise. Such among you as cannot wait to take believing women in wedlock under marriage protection, let them take from those whom your right hands possess among your serving-maids. Allah well knows your faith. Ye are part of one another, so take them in wedlock with the permission of their families and give them their hire as is right and proper, under marriage protection, not for fornication, and not taking mistresses for yourselves. Then when the slave-girls are under marriage protection, should they commit whoredom, inflict on them half the punishment inflicted on a free woman under marriage protection. All that is for him among you who fears committing sin, but that ye should patiently endure were better for you. Nevertheless, Allah is forgiving, compassionate. Allah desires to make things clear to you and to guide you to the customs of those who preceded you, and to relent to you, for Allah is knowing, wise. Allah desires to relent towards you, but those who follow their lusts desire that ye should turn mightily aside from His bounds. Allah desires to make things light for you, for man was created a weak creature.

❧We have, indeed, sent down to thee, O Mohammed, the Book with the truth, that thou mayest judge between the people according to what Allah has shown thee, so be not an advocate for treacherous men, But seek Allah's forgiveness, for Allah, indeed, is forgiving, compassionate. And stand not up on behalf of those who are traitors to themselves. Allah, indeed, loves not one who is a traitor, a guilty person. They may conceal themselves from the people, but they do not conceal themselves from Allah, for He is with them when they spend the night at speech that is not seemly, and Allah comprehends what they are doing. There ye are! Ye have stood up for these in this worldly life, but who is going to stand up for them against Allah on Resurrection Day? or who then will be an advocate for them? Whosoever does evil, or wrongs himself, then asks Allah's forgiveness, will find Allah forgiving, compassionate; But whoso makes a guilty gain, gains it only to his own hurt, for Allah is knowing, wise. Whoso makes a sinful or a guilty gain, then casts it on an innocent person, has indeed laid on himself calumny and manifest guilt. Had it not been for Allah's bounty and mercy to thee, O Mohammed, a party of them would have succeeded in leading thee astray, but they lead astray none but themselves, and they will not harm thee in any way. Allah has sent down to thee the Book and the Wisdom, and has taught thee what thou knewest not, so Allah's bounty to thee has been great.

❦The People of the Book will ask thee, O Mohammed, to bring down a Book for them from the skies. Yet they asked Moses something greater than that, for they said: "Show us God openly."[5] So the thunderbolt took them in their wrongdoing. Then they took for themselves the calf even after the evidential signs had come to them, but We pardoned that and gave Moses clear authority. And We raised up the mountain over them at their covenanting, and We said to them: "Enter ye the gate, doing obeisance;" and We said to them: "Transgress not on the Sabbath," and We took from them a firm covenant. So because of their violating their covenant, and their disbelieving in Allah's signs, and their unjustified killing of the prophets,[6] and their saying: "Our hearts are uncircumcised"—nay, but Allah has set a seal upon them because of their unbelief, so that they believe not, save a few—And because of their unbelief and their speaking against Mary a dreadful calumny, And their saying: "Truly we killed the Messiah, Jesus the son of Mary, the messenger of Allah," whereas they did not kill him and they did not crucify him, but a likeness was made for them. Truly, those who differ about it are in doubt about him. They have no real knowledge about him but only follow opinion, for certainly they did not kill him. Nay, but Allah raised him to Himself, and Allah is sublime, wise. There are none of the People of the Book but will believe in him before his death,[7] and on the Day of Resurrection he will be a witness against them. Now because of wrongdoing on the part of those who became Jews We made illicit for them certain good things which had been licit to them, and this was because of their turning many aside from Allah's way. And because of their taking usury, though they had been forbidden that, and their wrongfully consuming the people's property, so We have got ready for the unbelievers among them a painful punishment. But for those among them firmly established in knowledge, and the believers who believe in what has been sent down to thee, and what was sent down before thee, and those who observe prayer and pay the legal alms, and those who believe in Allah and the Last Day, those We shall give a great reward.

Sura
5

Surat al-Ma'ida: The Table

Though passages of various date have been worked into this Sura, some passages must have been put together after the conquest of Mecca, for they assume that the Moslems are in control of the city. As a whole the Sura is generally regarded as the latest of the Medinan Suras. Two passages from the early part of the Sura have been chosen as illustrations of the controversy with the People of the Book, next some characteristic legislative passages, and then the concluding passage, the passage from which the Sura gets its name, giving Mohammed's final statement about the Christians.

IN THE NAME OF ALLAH,
THE MERCIFUL, THE COMPASSIONATE

O People of the Book! there has come to you Our messenger, making clear for you much of the Book that ye were concealing, and overlooking much, and there has come to you from Allah a light and a clear book, Whereby Allah will guide whosoever will follow His good-pleasure into ways of peace. Also it will bring them out of darkness to the light by His permission and guide them to a straight path. They indeed are in unbelief who say that Allah is the Messiah, the son of Mary.[1] Say: "Who then would control Allah at all, should He desire to destroy the Messiah, the son of Mary, and his mother, and those on the earth altogether? seeing that Allah's is the kingdom of the heavens and the earth and what is between them both. He creates whatsoever He wills, for Allah is powerful over everything." Now the Jews and the Christians say: "We are Allah's children and His beloved ones." Say: "Why then does He punish you for your sins? Nay but ye are humans, among the things He has created. He grants forgiveness to whom He will, and He punishes whom He will, for Allah's is the kingdom of the heavens and the earth and what is between them both, and to Him is the returning." O People of the Book! there has come to you Our messenger, making clear for you these matters after an interval[2] among the messengers, lest ye should say: "Neither bringer of good tidings nor warner has come to us," for now there has come to you a bringer of good tidings and a warner, and Allah is powerful over everything.

❧ And make mention of when Moses said to his people: "O my people! remember Allah's grace to you in that He instituted among you prophets, and made you kings, and has given you what He gave not to any others among mankind. O my people! enter ye the Holy Land which Allah has decreed is to be yours, and do not turn your tails so that ye become changed over from gainers to losers." They said: "O Moses, therein are a people who are giants,[3] and we shall never enter it till they go forth from it, but should they go forth from it then we may enter." Two men among those who truly feared, and to whom Allah had been gracious, said: "Enter the gate against them, for whensoever ye enter it ye will be the ones who overcome, so put your trust in Allah if ye are believers." They said: "O Moses, we shall never enter it at all so long as they are therein, so go up, thou and thy Lord, and do ye two fight, but as for us, we shall sit down here." Said he: "O my Lord, I rule over no one save myself and my brother, so pray distinguish between us and the impious people." Said He: "Verily, the Holy Land will be a forbidden thing to them for forty years, during which they will wander aimlessly in the land, so fret not over the impious people."

❧ Recite also to them truly, O Mohammed, the story of the two sons of Adam, when they both drew near with an offering which was accepted from one of them but was not accepted from the other. The one whose offering was not accepted said: "I shall most assuredly slay thee." Said the other: "Allah accepts only from those who show piety. Even shouldst thou stretch forth thy hand to kill me, yet I am not stretching forth my hand towards thee to slay thee. I fear Allah, Lord of mankind. I desire that thou shouldst be liable for the sin of slaying me as well as for thine own sin, so that thou becomest of the people of the Fire, for that is the recompense of those who do wrong."[4] Thus his soul inclined him to kill his brother. So he killed him and became one of the losers. Then Allah sent a raven to dig in the ground that it might show him how he might hide the shame of his brother.[5] He said: "Ah! woe is me! am I incapable of being like this raven and hiding the shame of my brother?" So he became one of those who repent. Because of that We ordained for the Children of Israel that: "Whosoever kills a person other than as penalty for killing another person, or for working corruption in the land, it is as though he had killed all men, and whosoever gives one life it is as though he had given life to all men."[6] So Our messengers came to them with evidential signs, but even then many of them after that are committing excesses in the land.

❖ ❖ ❖ ❖ ❖

[G] Truly, We sent down the Torah in which is guidance and a light. By it the Prophets who had submitted themselves to Allah gave judgment for those who became Jews, as did the Rabbis and the Divines by such portion as they were put in charge of the Book of Allah, and they were witnesses for it. So fear ye not the people, but fear Me, and sell not My signs at a little price. Whoso does not judge according to what Allah has sent down, they are the unbelievers. Now We ordained for them in the Torah: "A life for a life, an eye for an eye, a nose for a nose, an ear for an ear, a tooth for a tooth, and for wounds a retaliation,"[7] though should anyone charitably remit it, for him it is an expiation, but whoso does not judge according to what Allah has sent down, they are the wrongdoers. And We made Jesus, son of Mary, follow in their traces, confirming what of the Torah was there present, and We gave him the Gospel, in which is guidance and a light, confirming what of the Torah was there present, and a guidance and an admonition to those who show piety. So let the people of the Gospel judge by what Allah sent down therein, for whoso does not judge according to what Allah has sent down, they are the wicked transgressors. And We have sent down to thee, O Mohammed, the Book with truth, confirming what of Scripture was there present, and being a protector for it. So give judgment between them by what Allah has sent down, and do not follow their desires as against the truth that has come to thee. For each party of you We have instituted a rule of life[8] and a path; and had Allah so willed He would have made you one community, but He has made you different communities that He might test you by that which He has given you, so seek pre-eminence in things that are good. To Allah is where ye will all return, and He will inform you about that over which ye differ.

✽ɢ·O ye who believe! do not make illicit the good things that Allah has made licit for you,[9] yet do not transgress, for Allah loves not those who transgress. So eat of whatever licit good thing Allah has provided for you, and show piety towards Allah in Whom ye believe. Allah will not take you to task for foolishness in your oaths, but He will take you to task for pacts ye have made by oath should ye break them. The expiation for such is the feeding of ten unfortunates with the average amount ye feed to your own families, or the clothing them [i.e., the aforesaid unfortunates], or the freeing of a slave. However, should one not find the wherewithal to do that, the expiation is then fasting for three days. That is the expiation for oaths when ye have sworn, so watch your oaths. Thus does Allah make clear His signs for you, that perchance ye may be thankful. O ye who believe! wine and *maisir*,[10] and idol-stones and divining arrows are only filth of Satan's working, so avoid it that maybe ye may prosper. Satan desires only that he may cause enmity and hatred to occur among you through wine and *maisir* and turn you away from remembrance of Allah and from prayer, so will ye abstain? So obey Allah, and obey His messenger, and be on your guard. But should ye turn away then be it known to you that Our messenger is responsible only for clear proclamation of the message. There is no blame on those who believe and have done righteous works for anything they may have eaten, provided they show piety and believe and do righteous works, then show piety and believe, then show piety and do good, for Allah loves those who do good. O ye who believe! Allah will assuredly test you by some part of the game that your hands and your spears reach, that Allah may know who fears Him in the Unseen, so whoso transgresses after that, for him is a painful punishment. O ye who believe! do not kill game while ye are in a sacral state.[11] Should any one of you kill such intentionally, then from his own flocks he must pay as compensation the like of what he has killed, according as two just persons from among you decide, to be a sacrificial offering delivered at the Kaaba, or as an expiation in place of a compensation the feeding of unfortunates, or the equivalent thereof in fasting, that he may taste the heinousness of his affair. Allah has pardoned what is past, but should anyone do it again Allah will exact vengeance from him, for Allah is sublime, Lord of vengeance.

❧·Make mention, O Mohammed, when Allah said: "O Jesus, son of Mary, remember My bounty to thee and to thy mother. When I aided thee by the Holy Spirit thou didst speak to the people while in the cradle and as a grown man. And remember when I taught thee the Book and the Wisdom and the Torah and the Gospel,[12] and when thou didst create from clay as it were the figures of birds, by My permission, and thou didst breathe into them so that they became birds, by My permission. Also thou didst heal the born blind and the leper by My permission. And remember when thou didst bring forth the dead by My permission, and when I held back the Children of Israel from thee when thou didst bring to them the evidential signs, and those among them who disbelieved said: 'This is naught but manifest magic.'" And when I spoke by revelation to the disciples, saying: "Believe in Me and in My messenger," they said: "We believe; so bear witness that we have submitted ourselves." And make mention when the disciples said: "O Jesus, son of Mary, is not thy Lord able to send down to us a table from the skies?"[13] He said: "Show piety to Allah, if ye are believers." They said: "We desire to eat therefrom so that our hearts will be tranquil, and we shall know that thou hast spoken the truth to us, and we shall be among those who bear witness thereto." Jesus, son of Mary, said: "Allahumma! our Lord, send down to us a table from the skies to be a feast for us both the first and the last, and a sign from Thee. Make provision for us, for Thou art the best of providers." Allah said: "Indeed, I am going to send it down to you, and should any of you afterwards disbelieve, I shall punish him with such a punishment as I shall never punish anyone among mankind." And make mention when Allah said to Jesus, son of Mary: "Didst thou say to the people:

'Take me and my mother as two deities apart from Allah'?"[14] He said: "Glory be to Thee! it could not be for me to say what I know is not true. Had I said it Thou wouldst know it. Thou knowest what is in my soul whereas I know not what is in Thy soul. It is Thou Who art the Knower of things unseen. I did not say to them anything but what Thou didst bid me, namely: 'Worship ye Allah, my Lord and your Lord.' So I was a witness against them as long as I was among them, but when Thou didst cause me to pass away, it was Thou Who wert the watcher over them, for Thou art witness over everything. Shouldst Thou punish them, why they are Thy servants, and shouldst Thou grant them forgiveness, why it is Thou who art the Sublime, the Wise." Said Allah: "This is the Day on which their truth-telling will profit those who speak the truth. For them there will be gardens beneath which rivers flow, wherein they will abide eternally forever, Allah well-pleased with them and they well-pleased with Him, that is the great felicity. Allah's is the kingdom of the heavens and the earth, and His is whatsoever is in them, and He is powerful over everything.

Al-Mu'awwidhatan:
The Two Refuge Charms

These two short Suras (113 and 114) are in the nature of charms which, as it were, seal off the Book. Both are still commonly used on charms and amulets throughout Islam.

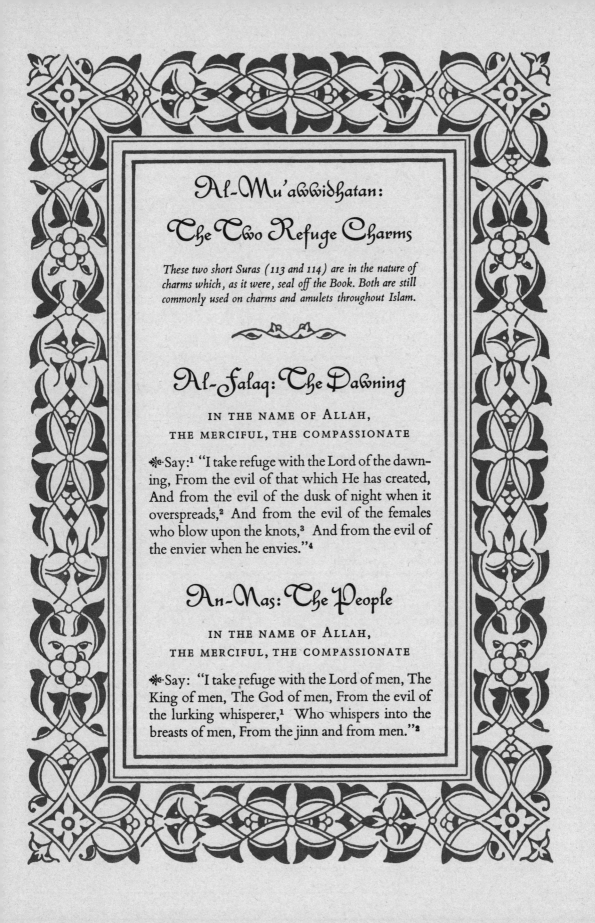

Al-Falaq: The Dawning

IN THE NAME OF ALLAH,
THE MERCIFUL, THE COMPASSIONATE

Say:[1] "I take refuge with the Lord of the dawning, From the evil of that which He has created, And from the evil of the dusk of night when it overspreads,[2] And from the evil of the females who blow upon the knots,[3] And from the evil of the envier when he envies."[4]

An-Nas: The People

IN THE NAME OF ALLAH,
THE MERCIFUL, THE COMPASSIONATE

Say: "I take refuge with the Lord of men, The King of men, The God of men, From the evil of the lurking whisperer,[1] Who whispers into the breasts of men, From the jinn and from men."[2]

Notes

Early Meccan Suras

Sura 96: page 25

1. *alaqa* is said to mean a minute nodule of clotted blood. The word is used in other passages which deal with the process of human reproduction, and seems intended to represent the earliest stage of formation of the embryo in the womb.
2. Some suggest that this refers to the art of writing. Others, with more likelihood, take it to mean that through the pen He was able to teach men by Scripture-revelation, gathered and written down, many things they would otherwise never have known.
3. The servant is usually considered to be Mohammed, but it is much more likely that the reference is to some humble member of the Prophet's following.
4. The *Zabaniyya* are said to be the infernal assistants of Malik (= Moloch), the Grand Chamberlain of Hell. This is the sole occurrence of the word in the Koran.

Sura 74: page 26

1. *kabbir*, lit. "make great," later came to mean "repeat the words *Allahu akbar*, 'Allah is very great,'" whence comes the technical term *takbir*, the pious act of ascribing greatness to Allah, i.e., "to magnify Him."
2. *naqur*, which is used only here for the trumpet on which the blast of Doom is sounded, and which is elsewhere generally called *sur*.
3. *Saqar* is one of the several names for Hell-fire, coming from a root meaning "to scorch." Tradition says that these 16 verses refer to Walid b. Mughira, a Meccan opponent of the Prophet.
4. There is a play on words here, for *bashar*, "epidermis," is the same word as was used for "a human" four lines back.
5. The "nineteen" are said to refer to the *Zabaniyya* of Sura 96, and the next three sentences seem to be a reply to those who have been discussing this matter of the guardians of Hell and the peculiar number of them.
6. Some refer the pronoun here to the reminder, others to *Saqar*.
7. I.e., death, which is a certainty for all.

Sura 106: page 28

1. I.e., the Kaaba, the central shrine at Mecca. In old Arabic, *bait*, "house," was used of sanctuaries just as was the Hebrew *beth*, as in Beth-el, a usage we still conserve in our "House of God."

Sura 108: page 29

1. This is commonly taken to be the name of a river in Paradise (*al-Kawthar*), which will be specially reserved for the use of Mohammed and his community in the next life. This, however, is a late conceit.
2. Lit. "tailless," used of an animal whose tail has been docked. Some think that this enemy had taunted Mohammed with the fact that he had no male children surviving, a state of affairs which was a great disgrace among the Arabs.

Sura 105: page 30

1. The word *ababil* occurs only here in the Koran and the translation is no more than a guess. Some Moslem commentators say that it is the name of the species of bird sent by Allah to drop clay pellets on Abraham's army and destroy it. The Egyptian sheikh Tantawi Jawhari, who died not many years ago, claimed that this is the first recorded case of aerial bombing in warfare.

Sura 92: page 31

1. *sa'y* is lit. "running," but is used for a man's life endeavour, and so means his life "course." What follows is a Koranic version of the famous doctrine of the Two Paths found in so

many religious texts from the ancient Near East.

Sura 90: page 32

1. Some authorities say that the particle *la* here and in the third verse is not the negative particle, but merely strengthens the oath, i.e., "I swear, indeed, by this land."

2. *najd* means an elevated path; *aqaba* in the next line means a steep mountain path. So here we have another statement of the doctrine of the Two Paths, the easy path of indulgence and the difficult path of duty and endeavour.

Sura 94: page 33

1. *wizr* means "burden," but in the Koran it is used technically of that burden which Mohammed insists no soul can bear for another, i.e., the burden of sin and guilt.

2. This verse may mean: "When thou hast finished with thy preaching be diligent in thy praying."

Sura 86: page 35

1. Some think that the reference is to the morning or the evening star, others that it means some shooting star or meteor. The word translated "shining" might also have been translated "burning," and another possible meaning from the same root is "piercing."

2. *ma'* is the word for "water," but it is often used for "semen," though some lexicographers think that that meaning is derived from its use in this passage.

3. The "return" in the preceding verse is said to refer to the annual recurrence of the celestial phenomena, and the "splitting" to the annual return of the vegetation shooting up through the soil.

Sura 91: page 36

1. *ma* means "what" or "that which," but here, as in many other passages, it is necessary to translate it "Him who," since the reference is obviously to Allah. The reason for the "that which" seems to be that it refers more particularly to the instrument whereby Allah performed the various acts of creation.

2. The story of Thamud is mentioned more than twenty times in the Koran, and is told in some detail in Suras 3 and 11. That the Thamud were a historical people is guaranteed by the fact that they are referred to in Assyrian inscriptions of the eighth century B.C. as well as by Greek and Latin writers. Their legend says that they were a mighty people of ancient Arabia who grew headstrong in their wickedness, so Allah sent to them one Salih as a prophet to preach monotheism to them and warn them of the sure fate of transgressors. When they demanded a miracle Salih struck a rock from which emerged a she-camel which gave birth to a camel calf. Salih made an equitable arrangement with them for her watering and pasturage, but one of them hamstrung the camel and killed the calf. As a result of their rejecting the messenger and his message, Allah sent on them destruction, from which only Salih and the few who believed in him escaped. Mohammed uses their legend as a warning example of what the Meccans are to expect if they in like manner reject him and his message.

3. Every messenger from Allah was "sent" to his community, and invariably complained that he was a person of no account, just some "wretched fellow" from among them.

Sura 80: page 37

1. Tradition, of course, gives the name of this rich man, but like that of the blind man, and most other names given in connection with passages in the Koran, they are all suspect of being late inventions.

2. The "it" here is the message.

3. See Sura 87, note.

4. *qaddarahu*, i.e., gave him what was decreed for him. The eased way in the next verse some take to mean an easy birth, others an easy way of life.

5. *sakhkha* occurs only here in the Koran. It means "a deafening noise," and doubtless refers to the Last Trump which announces the Day of Doom.

Sura 68: page 38

1. *Nun* is the twenty-fifth letter of the Arabic alphabet. Some twenty-nine Suras have such a letter or combination of letters at the commencement. Various explanations have been suggested for these mysterious letters, but no fully satisfactory solution has as yet been found.

2. *majnun*, "crazy," is literally "possessed by jinn," the jinn being invisible spirits, like Socrates' *daimon*, which could at times enter and "possess" humans. In pre-Islamic Arabia it was thought that poets, diviners, soothsayers, and such folk, had each his "familiar," which at times possessed him and enabled him to give utterance. Apparently Mohammed at first appeared to his Meccan contemporaries as just such a crazed, "possessed" man, and there is reason to believe that when he first felt his call to his mission after his great religious experience he was himself somewhat afraid that he was "jinn-possessed."

3. Tradition, again, knows the name of this person, but it is most likely a pure invention.

4. *khurtum* is the word for an elephant's trunk. Bell translates it "snout."

5. The commentators say that this means that when they vowed they would do this thing they did not add: "If Allah wills," and so they were punished for their presumption. However, a little farther on it is made clear that what they purposed was to go early and make so clean a gathering of the fruits there would be nothing for the poor to glean afterwards. This suggests that the parable had its source in something Mohammed had learned from the People of the Book.

6. *muslimun*, the plural of *Muslim*, i.e., one who has submitted or surrendered himself to Allah. The plural is used here as a common, not as a proper noun.

7. This and the following verses give colour to the theory of those who regard this passage as Medinan and addressed to the Jews.

8. *shuraka* means "associates," but here is a technical term for those beings, whether angels, demons, idols, false-gods, or what not, that men associated with Allah in their worship.

9. Eschatological tractates make much of this "uncovering of the leg" on the Last Day, the thought being that it is Allah who will uncover His Divine leg, and the evil-doers will be bidden to bow themselves in obeisance, but, though perfectly sound in body, they will find themselves as stiff as boards and unable to bow down as the righteous are doing. The Arabic phrase, however, originally meant no more than stripping for combat, and what Mohammed has in mind in this verse is apparently nothing more than the baring of the legs of those who are being hurried on to the place of judgment, on a Day when there can be no change in one's spiritual status, and those who were stiff-kneed about prayer and adoration in this life will find themselves still stiff-kneed in the presence of the Judge.

Sura 87: page 41

1. *suhuf* is literally "sheets," i.e., the sheets of parchment or papyrus on which Scripture Books were written, so it is one of the Koranic words for Scripture, often translated "scrolls." Many apocryphal works bearing the names of Abraham and Moses were in circulation among the Jews and Christians, so the reference may be to these. Or it may be that as Abraham and Moses were both prophets, Mohammed assumed that they must have had Scripture revelations, as he later learned for certain in the case of Moses, whose Torah he mentions frequently.

Sura 95: page 42

1. The land would be the Hejaz; or if *balad* means "town" then the refer-

ence would be to Mecca, and the word *amin* would refer to its inviolate character as a religious sanctuary. Some think, however, that coming after mention of Sinai the land is the Holy Land, of which the fig and the olive are so characteristic.

2. *taqwin* means "symmetry," and there seems to be some suggestion of a contrast between man's goodly physical form and his wretched moral stature.

3. Lit., "the judgliest of judges," if that were possible in English.

Sura 85: page 43

1. *buruj* (cf. Latin *burgus*) means "towers," but is said here to refer to the constellations in the heavens.

2. In 524 A.D. there was a great persecution of the Christians at Najran in South Arabia, of which we have accounts preserved by Simeon of Beth Arsham and in the curious *Book of the Himyarites* edited by Axel Moberg in 1924. The story as it came to Mohammed seems to have told that the bodies of the slain were burned in a trench *(ukhdud)*, and this serves to point a warning of the even worse fires of Gehenna.

3. This is sometimes rendered "Lord of the Glorious Throne," but the pointing of the text as we have it makes "glorious" an attribute of the Lord, not the Throne.

4. The reference is to the celestial archetype of Scripture.

Sura 73: page 44

1. *muzzammil* is from the verb *tazammala* "to wrap oneself in a cloak," and recalls the *muddaththir* of Sura 74.

2. *Qur'an* has here its original sense of "Scripture lesson," whereas in the concluding section it has the later meaning of the body of material Mohammed had been teaching them to use liturgically, as the Jews and Christians used Scripture liturgically.

3. *Jahim* means a fiercely burning fire, whence it comes to be one of the names for Hell-fire. See Sura 82, Note 4.

4. Apparently a reference to the fruits of the infernal tree *Zaqqum*, mentioned in Sura 37, on which the Damned are said to choke as they attempt to eat it.

Sura 99: page 46

1. It is a very ancient idea that as a preliminary to Judgment the earth will be flattened out so that there are no longer either hills or valleys. Thus all who are in their graves and all else hidden in the earth will have to come out, and when Judgment commences the earth will be given a tongue so that she may tell of all, whether good or ill, that has been committed on her surface.

2. The verb *awha*, which is Mohammed's ordinary word for God-given inspiration, is used here. Normally the earth cannot speak, but at Allah's prompting she will speak.

Sura 82: page 47

1. This is usually taken to mean that in the upheaval on the Day when heaven and earth are being changed as a preliminary to Judgment, all the sweet waters will get mixed up with the salt waters, and Sura 81 says that there will be so great a churning that the seas will boil. It is not impossible, however, that this is merely meant as a parallel to the fourth verse, the sea having to give up its dead just as the earth does.

2. *din* means "judgment," but it also means "religion," and some commentators think that here the Meccans are being chidden for rejecting this new religion being preached by Mohammed.

3. These verses are generally taken to refer to the Recording Angels who keep a record of all the good and ill men do.

4. Perhaps it would have been better to translate this "fire" as in Sura 73, though here it seems rather to be a proper name, one of the names of Hell.

5. One of Mohammed's favourite ideas, repeated over and over again in the

Koran, is that no Redeemer, no Saviour, no intercessor can do anything for the individual soul at Judgment.

Sura 81: page 48

1. This is the verb used for folding up a garment to put it away.
2. It is in the tenth month of their pregnancy that the she-camels need particular attention, so their being neglected at such a time is an indication of unusual terror. The succeeding verse means that the terror will be so great that wild beasts will crowd together forgetful of their natural enmity towards one another.
3. When the bodies are raised from their graves they must be joined again by their souls so that a complete man, body plus soul, may appear for Judgment.
4. Here *Jahim* has the definite article and so is certainly a name for Hell-fire.
5. As in Sura 90 the *la* may not be a negative particle but merely a particle used to strengthen the oath.
6. *al-khunnas* is from a root meaning "to lag behind," and is said to be a general name for the five planets—Saturn, Jupiter, Mars, Venus, and Mercury—which have a retrograde as well as a direct forward motion.
7. This is generally considered to refer to the angel of revelation who was later identified with Gabriel.
8. See Sura 53, verse 7: "When He was . . . the horizon."
9. Or as we should say: "What are you going to do about it?". The verb *dhahaba* means "to go," but a *madhhab*, i.e., a place to which one goes, is the ordinary word used for the religious group one follows, so when Mohammed asks: "Where are you going?", what he means is: "What opinion are you going to adopt with regard to this new religious message?"

Sura 53: page 49

1. The commentators are unanimous in referring this to Gabriel, who, according to tradition, appeared to bring Mohammed his first revelation. The wording of the passage, however, very definitely suggests that Mohammed at first thought he had seen a theophany, so that these epithets apply to Allah, Who, in the Prophet's vision, filled the horizon and then drew near to speak with him.
2. Pious imagination has pictured this sidra-tree (or lote-tree) as a celestial tree of enormous proportions marking the boundary beyond which creatures may not pass. It is more likely, however, that the Prophet is telling of the locality near Mecca where he had seen the vision. It was by a boundary tree quite near to a certain garden pleasaunce, and the season of the year was that in which the sidra-tree was covered with blossoms. The next verses mean that he looked right at the figure in his vision, not looking to one side of it, nor looking beyond it.
3. *al-Lat* is the feminine form of Allah, and *al-Uzza* is the feminine of *al-A'azz*, so these two names mean "the goddess" and "the most beloved." *Manat* is most probably connected with the root for good fortune. All three names occur in pre-Islamic texts, and all are possibly but epithets of the ancient Mother Goddess formerly worshipped at Mecca. In Mohammed's time, however, the Koreish would seem to have considered them as three daughters of Allah (see Sura 37, ref. 22), which is the reason for the jibe in the next line. The verse beginning two lines after is, on the face of it, a later insertion.
4. This may, of course, be a quite general reference applicable to many Meccans, but it may also refer to some particular person, though the statements in the commentaries as to the identity of this person must not be taken too seriously.
5. See Sura 87, last verse. The reference here is doubtless to Abraham's willingness to offer up Isaac in sacrifice. The verb *waffa* means "to fulfil an engagement," and another form of the same verb occurs four verses later, where it is Allah who will fulfil His engagement to give due recompense.

6. As He produced each individual from the drop of semen at conception, so it is His affair to produce the bodies from the earth again at the resurrection.

7. *ash-Shi'ra* is said to be the Arabic name for Sirius, the Dog Star, which was apparently worshipped by the ancient Arabs as a rain-maker.

8. The people of Ad, like those of Thamud, were an ancient Arabian people, whose legend Mohammed makes use of in the Koran to provide another example of a people who were destroyed because they rejected Allah's messenger when he came to them.

Sura 84: page 52

1. The purpose of this creation of a new heaven and a new earth is that they may be in fit and worthy state for the great scene of Judgment.

2. *Sa'ir*, "blaze," is one of the names for Hell-fire.

3. Again this particle *la* may not be negative but merely a particle to strengthen the oath.

4. This is an example of Mohammed's irony; *bashshara* is the technical word for good tidings, and the verbal-noun from it is used in Christian Arabic for the Gospel, i.e., the good news.

Sura 100: page 53

1. This takes the *jam'an* as referring to those who ride forth in the morning, and who keep together as a band partially concealed by their cloud of dust. Others take the *jam'an* as referring not to the raiders but to the raided, and if that is so we should translate: "and therein plunge into the midst of a host."

2. I.e., on that Day all that the earth has concealed will be brought forth, and all that has been hidden in the hearts of men will be made manifest, so the Judge will have all the evidence before Him.

Sura 79: page 53

1. When this is referred to the angels who come at death, the meaning is that wicked souls are dragged forth violently but the souls of the good are eased out gently. The succeeding verses are then taken to refer to the carrying up of the soul to where decision is made as to where it is to abide till the Day of Resurrection.

2. The two words *rajifa*, "that which causes violent trembling," and *radifa*, "that which follows," are commonly taken to mean the two blasts on the Trump of Doom, the one which shatters everything in heaven and on earth, and the following one which raises the dead and ushers in the Judgment. Later in this passage the trumpet blast is called a *zajra*, literally "a shout."

3. The verb *sahira* means "to be watchful," and there are passages in the Koran which speak of the newly risen on the Day looking around watching expectantly for what will come next. The common opinion, however, is that *as-Sahira* here is a proper noun, the name of that wide open plain on which men will be assembled for Judgment, in which case one should translate: "there they are at as-Sahira."

4. This vale of *Tuwa*, the place where Moses received his call, is mentioned again in Sura 20, but no satisfactory explanation of the name has yet been found.

5. *at-Tamma* is one of the names of the Last Day, apparently indicating that it is a day of overthrowing or overwhelming. It occurs only here in the Koran.

6. The meaning is said to be that when the dead are raised it will seem to them that they have been in the grave no longer than a night.

Sura 77: page 55

1. At Judgment each of the messengers sent forth from Allah will have an appointed time at which he will give an accounting of how he fulfilled his mission, and how he was received by the community to which he was sent.

2. *fasala* is "to separate into parts," so the Day of Severance, or Day of Distinction, is the day of the separating

out the sheep from the goats, the severing of many an ancient tie, and the distinguishing of things evil from things good.

3. *furat* is sweet water as distinguished from salt water. It is also the Arabic name for the Euphrates.

4. The sulphurous smoke from Hell-fire, tawny in colour, and emitting huge sparks, is said to divide into three branches as it rises, looking like a shadow but giving no shade.

5. *hani'an* means "in good health." It is used also in the fourth verse of Sura 4, from which passage one gathers that it is used to mean: "eat without fear of digestive troubles."

Sura 78: page 57

1. *awtad* are the pegs used to fasten down the nomad's tent. The idea is that when the earth was spread out flat on the primaeval waters the mountains were set on it to keep it firm.

2. These are not the seven Ptolemaic heavenly spheres, but seven domes one above the other, set like convex bowls over the disc-like earth and the circumambient ocean which they hold in place.

3. Here the word is *Sur*, the more commonly used word for the Trump that will sound the note of doom. See note 2 to Sura 74.

4. *hamim* and *ghassaq*, the former of which is derived from a root meaning "hot," but the latter is apparently a word invented by Mohammed, so that it is only a guess of the exegetes that it means liquid pus.

5. Various heavenly books are mentioned in the Koran, viz., the celestial archetype of Scripture, the records of good and evil deeds, the Book of Decrees, and a certain Register or inventory of all things in heaven and on earth. Here the reference seems to be to the Record Book.

6. It is still quite uncertain what Mohammed meant by this Spirit *(Ruh)*, who seems always to be associated with the angels and yet is mightier than they are. By orthodox piety he has been identified with Gabriel, but one suspects that there may perhaps be a reference to the Biblical Spirit of God, or the Rabbinic Metatron, of whom Mohammed may have heard from Jews or Christians but only vaguely understood. The passage about the Spirit toward the end of Sura 17 is revealing, for there the Prophet is obviously trying to answer those who questioned him about the Spirit but is unable to do more than take refuge in the statement that this is a mystery.

Sura 88: page 59

1. *dari* is said to be a thorny desert shrub extremely bitter to the taste, and so is used here to illustrate the kind of food the wicked may expect in Hell.

2. *ibil*, like the Akkadian *i-bi-lu*, is an ordinary Semitic word for "camel," but as the next verse speaks about the sky, many commentators say that here it means the clouds, whose massed formations are at times not unlike camels with their humps.

Sura 89: page 60

1. Later exegesis insists that these are the first ten nights of Dhu'l-Hijja, the last month of the Moslem year, and the days during which annually the Greater Pilgrimage takes place. This obviously could not have been the original reference, and what was really meant by this and the next verse is still obscure.

2. Iram is taken to be the name of the chief city of the ancient people of Ad, already mentioned in note 8 to Sura 53.

3. What is meant by this is unknown. *awtad* are stakes or tent-pegs, and since the mention of Ad and Thamud is followed by a reference to their dwellings, something to do with the dwelling-places of Pharaoh would seem to be indicated, but what the reference is escapes us.

4. Paradise.

Sura 75: page 62

1. Again the *la* may not be a negative particle but merely a particle to strengthen the oath.

2. It was commonly believed in the ancient Near East that sun and moon were originally one but were separated as the creation days moved on. Since eschatology is a recapitulation of cosmology, they must be reunited once more during the events of the Last Day.

3. *wazar,* which occurs only here in the Koran, is said to mean an accessible mountain, and so a place to which to flee for refuge.

4. This word refers to the piercing of the noses of animals that they may hold the wooden ring to which the leading-strap will be attached.

5. This addition is merely an attempt to link these two out-of-place verses with what goes before and what comes after.

Middle Meccan Suras

Sura 54: page 66

1. The Summoner is doubtless Allah, though in later times, when Israfel was the angel assigned to the blowing of the Trump of Doom, the Summoner was identified with him. Others seem to have considered that the Summoner was Gabriel.

2. It is not necessarily an anachronism for Mohammed to have described Noah's contemporaries as calling him "jinn-possessed." The word *majnun* may have been so commonly used in the Prophet's day in the sense of "crazy" that he was using it with as little thought of the jinn as we are of the moon when we use the word "lunatic."

3. The "it" here is feminine and so may refer rather to the story of Noah than to the ark. Yet, since *fulk,* the word used elsewhere in the Koran for Noah's ark, is grammatically feminine, it could possibly be a reference to the widely believed story that there were remains of Noah's ark still resting on Mount Ararat.

4. In the Thamud story in Suras 7 and 11 the name of the messenger sent by

Allah to this people is Salih. For the allusion to their drinking water by turn see Sura 26, Note 9.

5. *az-zubur* here, as 11 lines below, seems to mean the Record Books, or possibly the Book of Decrees.

6. As in Sura 74, Saqar is a name for Hell-fire.

7. *bi qadarin* may, however, mean no more than "by measure" or "with a limit."

8. In all probability the reference is to the communities of Noah, Ad, Thamud, Lot, and Pharaoh in the body of the Sura, who were held up as warning examples to the Meccans.

Sura 37: page 69

1. If the opening verses are taken to refer to angelic groups, then they will be (1) those who arrange the ranks of the angels for their celestial duties (or those who dress the ranks of men for Judgment), (2) those who scare away the jinn when they try to listen in at the heavenly Council (or those who chide men for their evil ways), (3) those who recite warnings from the Heavenly Book.

2. Some think that this refers to the sun, whose actual point of rising shifts along the eastern horizon with the progress of the seasons.

3. Four orders of created beings are mentioned in the Koran: (1) angels, (2) jinn, (3) men, (4) animals. The satans are one class of jinn, for in Sura 18 Satan himself, there called Iblis, is said to belong to the jinn. It is likely, however, that this distinction of classes among the jinn is a later idea and that for Mohammed satans, demons, jinn were but different names for the same creatures.

4. This is said to refer to the shooting stars, which are popularly thought of as being cast at the satans who seek to listen in at what goes on in the heavenly Council. See the third section of Sura 15.

5. The "them" would seem to be the unbelieving Meccans.

6. One of the names of Hell; see Sura 73,

Note 3. For the Day of Severance see Sura 77, Note 2.

7. The reference in the next 14 verses is to the false gods men used to worship but who on the Day prove their worthlessness.

8. The right hand was the side of good omen.

9. *al-mursalun*, "those who have been sent," i.e., the messengers from Allah to mankind. The meaning is that the reaction of the Meccans to Mohammed's preaching was that he was a "crazy poet," one "jinn-possessed" *(majnun)* as their local poets and soothsayers were; but the reply to them is that since his message confirms the things about which former prophets preached, he must be in the prophetic succession.

10. This is Bell's translation of the word used in the refrain to these stories. *mukhlas* means one who is utterly sincere and devoted in his religion, or as we should say, one who serves God with single-heartedness.

11. This is the tree of the infernal regions. See also Sura 73, Note 4.

12. *tal'* is the word used for the spathe of the palm-tree, but here it would seem to mean the fruit of the tree Zaqqum.

13. This is the *hamim* referred to in Sura 78, Note 4.

14. I.e., those who responded to Noah's preaching.

15. The story of how Abraham examined the heavenly bodies to see if any of them were really worthy of worship such as men paid them is given more fully elsewhere in the Koran. The story doubtless derives from a misunderstanding of Genesis XV, 5.

16. The word used here for "blaze" is *jahim*, the same word we have seen used for the blazing fires of Hell. Doubtless the choice of word was intentional.

17. The remainder of this passage is a Medinan addition to the Sura.

18. This seems to mean when the son had passed out of the irresponsible stage of childhood and was old enough to begin sharing in the family responsibilities. Since the word *sa'y* is also the word used for the running between Safa and Marwa during the pilgrimage ceremonies at Mecca, and this is a Medinan passage from the time when Mohammed was busy associating the pilgrimage ceremonies with the Abraham story, Bell thinks that there may be an underlying reference to that here.

19. The caravan route to the north passed by ruins which, it is suggested here, were the ruins of the settlement to which Lot was sent as messenger.

20. I.e., he drew the counter that condemned him to be the victim. The word used here for "fish" is *hut*, which is the word for Pisces in the zodiac, but is also commonly used for "whale."

21. This is merely a guess at the meaning of *yaqtin*, a word which occurs only here in the Koran.

22. This is a separate passage, perhaps earlier in date than what precedes. It is the Meccans whom Mohammed is bidden to consult. For their notion that Allah has daughters see Sura 53, ref. 3.

23. These lines are spoken by the angels to men.

24. Cf. the opening verse of the Sura.

Sura 26: page 75

1. Here is another example of the mysterious letters which stand at the head of certain Suras (see Sura 68, Note 1). The matter is discussed in Nöldeke-Schwally, *Geschichte des Qorans*, II, (Leipzig, 1919), pp. 68-78.

2. There is perhaps a particular point in the use of the word *izza* here, for it is a word especially associated with Allah, who at the end of Sura 37 is called "Lord of greatness," while Sura 35 says: "If anyone desires greatness, why all greatness belongs to Allah." The use of this word here might thus be meant to suggest that the Egyptian sorcerers recognized Pharaoh's claim to be divine.

3. This takes the pronoun to refer to the "Lord of mankind" in whom they have confessed their belief, and who Pharaoh now says is but the chief sorcerer from whom they have learned their art of sorcery. Others, however, take the pronoun as referring to Moses.

4. Some take this to mean a good reputation, in that he will always be spoken highly of by those of later generations. Others think that it means, "put words on my tongue that will be firmly believed by later peoples." In Sura 19, Ref. 8, the "tongue of truth" is said to have been given to Isaac and Jacob.

5. *Iblis*, a name derived from the Greek *diabolos*, is commonly used in the Koran as the name of Satan.

6. This demand for obedience which occurs constantly in the Prophet stories given in the Koran arises from Mohammed's idea that a messenger sent from Allah was not only a preacher but also a legislator sent to lay down a rule of life that was to be obeyed.

7. Their objection is that the only impression made by the preaching of Noah had been on the disreputable section of the community. Noah replies that whether they were disreputable or not was a matter for Allah to decide; his own prophetic task was to warn and to accept as followers any who would believe.

8. This is generally taken to mean "give a clear decision," but it may be his prayer to Allah to open the heavens, since the next verse speaks of the ark and the drowning of the unbelievers.

9. The legend is that this miraculous she-camel drank so much they had to appoint alternate days at their well, the camel watering one day and the people of Thamud the next. See Sura 54, Ref. 4.

10. Since the people of the Grove to whom Shu'aib was sent were the Midianites, as we learn from other passages in the Koran, there have been those who equated Shu'aib with the Biblical Jethro. It seems more likely, however, that like Hud and Salih this is just a name given as a prophet-name to fit an ancient Arab legend into Mohammed's list of warning examples from the past.

11. *tanzil* is literally "a sending down," i.e., something sent from Allah. The "faithful spirit" in the next verse is regarded as a name for Gabriel, since Mohammed later associated him with the bringing of revelation. It is very possible, however, that at first it referred to the Holy Spirit.

12. *ulama*, the "learned," particularly those learned in theological matters, and so in our language "the Divines" as Doctors of Divinity.

Sura 20: page 84

1. *ath-thara* means earth which is moist after rains. In later thought, however, there had to be a lowest depth to correspond to the highest height of heaven, and so "beneath the *thara*" was taken to mean "below the lowest depths."

2. The ninety-nine beads of a Moslem rosary are meant to represent these "most beautiful names" which the pious pronounce one by one as they "tell" the beads with their fingers.

3. See Sura 79, Note 4.

4. See the second section of Sura 26. In Sura 28 Moses is bidden put his hand in his *jaib*, i.e., the opening of his gown at the bosom. Here he is told to put it into his *janah*, literally his "wing," meaning apparently under his arm-pit, which is confirmed by what follows in Sura 28, where he is bidden press his *janah* close without fear. See Exodus IV, 6, 7.

5. Cf. the second section of Sura 26. That Moses had difficulties with his speech is derived, of course, from Exodus IV, 10.

6. The word for "ark" here is *tabut*, the word used also for the Israelitish Ark of the Covenant. It means a wooden chest, whereas the word for Noah's ark is *fulk*, derived from the Greek *epholkion*, and is preserved in the

modern *felucca*. The word for "sea" in this passage is *yamm*, a loan-word in Arabic, as it was also in Ancient Egyptian, and is probably meant to suggest the Nile, which is often called "the sea."

7. Literally "day of adornment," i.e., a national feast day or holiday when the people, not having to go to their usual labours, would be able to assemble in the morning.

8. This is an anachronism, for the punishment of crucifixion was unknown in ancient Egypt.

9. This is the Aramaic word for "mountain" and is a common name for Mt. Sinai. The words for manna and quail are those used in the Hebrew Bible (Exodus XVI, 13, 15).

10. These are said to be the Seventy Elders of Exodus XVIII, 25, and it is these seventy whom Moses upbraids for not having kept the appointment, and who, ten lines below, complain that they had to bear the people's ornaments.

11. In this account of the episode of the golden calf there is, as Horovitz pointed out, a curious confusion with the story in II Chronicles XIII, 6 ff. of how Jeroboam set up calf-worship in Samaria. The Samaritan schism is doubtless what is referred to later in this section.

12. What we have here is a confused reminiscence of Exodus XXXII, 21-24.

13. The plural of the word for "blue" occurs only here in the Koran. Some suggest that it merely means "blind" (see towards the end of the next section); but to the people who heard these words, blueness was an inauspicious thing.

14. In other religions also we find this idea that the resurrected will imagine they have been but a short time in the grave.

15. The point here is that the pagan idols had to have sacrifices and offerings as daily provision from their worshippers, whereas Allah demands no such offerings, for He is the One who provides for mankind. Thus what finally will count, the ultimate issue, will not depend on the richness of the offerings man has made at altars, but on the piety he has shown towards Allah.

16. The "it" here seems to mean the message of Mohammed, which, as he often says, is in substance the same as had been revealed in previous Scriptures.

Sura 15: page 92

1. A known writing *(kitab)*, i.e., it was only destroyed when that fate was already written down in the Book of Decrees. This Book is referred to again in Sura 17 in connection with the destruction of towns.

2. *buruj* as in the opening verse of Sura 85.

3. See Sura 37, Note 4, for the jinn who try to listen in at the heavenly Councils being driven away by shooting stars.

4. This is the Alpha and Omega idea. As Allah was the sole possessor in the beginning, and has bestowed on men everything that they possess, so ultimately all will return to Him, and thus He will be the final inheritor of all.

5. The *samum* is the burning desert wind, called also in English the "simoom."

6. In Sura 26 it was only "an old woman," but here as in Genesis XIX it is Lot's wife. It will be noticed from many details in this passage how the Prophet's acquaintance with Biblical material improves as his mission advances.

7. This would seem to be a reminiscence of the Rabbinic notion we find recorded in *Genesis Rabba* L, 7, that the men of Sodom considered Abraham, by accepting these strangers in his home, to have violated the decree they had laid down about strangers.

8. In the Koran the word *saiha*, "shout," appears frequently in connection with the destruction of former peoples, e.g., those destroyed in Noah's day by the deluge (Sura 23), and Korah

and his group (Sura 29). It invariably precedes the act of destruction, and is a mighty sound from heaven, which will also precede the final act of destruction on the Last Day (Sura 36, Ref. 9). Its Biblical antecedents are the "great noise" of II Pet. III, 10, the "shout" of I Thess. IV, 16, and the voice of God which in the teaching of the Rabbis will usher in the resurrection. In Moslem legend it was such a *saiha* which caused the house to fall in on Job's children.

9. Literally, "We made the top part its bottom part." The "hardened clay" is but a guess. The word *sijjil* occurs in Sura 105 for the pellets the birds dropped to destroy the Abyssinian army, and in the parallel Lot story in Sura 11, where the pellets are said to have been marked, presumably each with the name of the sinner it was to smite. They represent the "brimstone" of the Biblical story. The next verse but one means that the caravan route to the north still used to pass the ruins as it formerly passed the city when it was inhabited.

10. Since ruins in Midian were also passed by caravans taking the route to the north, the meaning seems to be that both Sodom and Midian were destroyed, and that their tale was to be found in Scripture as a warning example.

11. Hegra was a Nabataean city in the northern Hejaz, and on the ground of the second verse preceding, some have thought that the people of Thamud are meant here. It may, however, be a memory of the rock-hewn city of Petra, whose ruins were well known, in which case this verse would refer to their great commercial enterprises.

12. *Mathani* is a word about which there has been much discussion. It derives from a root meaning "to repeat," i.e., to do a thing a second time, and there is much in favour of the suggestion that it refers to the oft-repeated stories of Ad, Thamud, etc., which were quoted as warning examples to the Meccans.

13. These four verses are an interpolation from an old piece of material which apparently refers to the Jewish and Christian practice of cutting up Scripture lessons.

Sura 18: page 97

1. *Sa'id* is a word commonly used for the place where the Final Judgment will be held, an expanse of earth on which all hills and valleys have been flattened out, and where there are no trees or other excrescences behind which a man could hide. *juruz* in this verse means bare of all herbage. See Note 1 to Sura 99.

2. The commentators present a great variety of guesses as to the meaning of ar-Raqim. The best solution so far offered is Torrey's suggestion that it arises from a misreading by Mohammed's informants of the name Decius in the Story of the Seven Sleepers of Ephesus, who suffered during the Decian persecution, though the source was more likely to have been Syriac than the Hebrew source he posits. For the story itself see the assemblage of material by Ignazio Guidi in *Testi orientali inediti sopra i Setti Dormienti di Efeso*, 1884.

3. This may refer forward to the seventh verse following, and mean that when they awoke and wondered how long they had been in the cave, there were two opinions about it. Or it may be that there were two opinions among Mohammed's informants as to the length of stay in the cave. See Note 5.

4. The Church of the Seven Sleepers at Ephesus was quite a famous monument.

5. The three hundred and nine years must be due to faulty memory. In the legend they fled during the persecution of Decius (201-251) and were discovered during the reign of Theodosius II (401-450). There is an excellent account of the legend in Gibbon's *Decline and Fall of the Roman Empire*, Chapter XXXII.

6. The two seas, one of sweet water and one of salt water, are mentioned again in four other Suras, and various

attempts have been made to locate this confluence at the point where the sweet waters mingle with the salt in the Persian Gulf or elsewhere. It seems certain, however, that the conception is a mythological one.

This and the next four verses really belong to the legend of Alexander the Great, for it was he who had gone wandering to find the fountain of immortality, and it was his servant who let the salted fish fall into the water where it came to life and swam away, and although Alexander retraced his steps to try to find that spot again they never did find it. It was al-Khidr who found it and became immortal. On all this, see I. Friedländer, *Die Chadirlegende und der Alexander-roman*, Berlin, 1913. Wensinck has pointed out that here in this Sura the Jewish legends of Elijah and Rabbi Joshua ben Levi have become mixed up with the al-Khidr and Alexander story.

7. *saraban* could possibly mean "freely," but a *sarab* is a water conduit, and since two verses later the fish is said to have made its way "wondrously" to the sea, the likelihood is that these are both references to an element in the legend which says that the fish made its way by an underground channel from the Fountain of Life to its natural habitat in the sea.

8. This is the famous al-Khidr, who is still regarded by members of the Dervish Orders as the *Qutb* (pole) of the hierarchy of Saints. His name comes from the root for "green" and he corresponds to the Elias (Elijah) of Syrian mythology, an incarnation of the ever-living spirit of vegetation.

9. "Lord of the two horns," i.e., Alexander the Great, who on some of his coins is pictured with two ram's horns attached to his head. His legendary "Life" was widely known throughout the Near East in Mohammed's day, and the form of it which appears in the Koran is closest to that known to us through the Syriac writings of Jacob of Sarugh, who died in 521.

10. In the original legend this apparently meant that he had got to a place beyond the area where Greek was understood. The place between the mountains is apparently the Pass of Derbend. See A. R. Anderson, *Alexander's Gate, Gog and Magog and the Enclosed Nations*, 1932.

11. *Firdaus* is derived, through Aramaic, from the Greek *paradeisos* = Paradise.

12. See Sura 31, Ref. 5.

Sura 36: page 107

1. This is doubtless the Record Book that is to be opened at Judgment.

2. The town is said to be Antioch. The Commentaries tell of two disciples of Jesus being sent to preach to that city, and of their being presently joined by a third.

3. The verb used here suggests auguries being taken from birds.

4. Tradition names him Habib the carpenter. The verse at Reference 5 suggests that he was martyred, and in later times his supposed tomb at Antioch became a place of visitation.

5. The assumption is that the people of Antioch were polytheists to whom the envoys preached the One God, and when Habib the carpenter believed, and was martyred for his believing, he was taken to Paradise.

6. Lit. "servants," but it seems to mean humans who are all servants of Allah.

7. The meaning is that there are male and female elements in nature, among mankind, and also in other areas of which man is ignorant, but in each case the "pairs" are the source of new life.

8. *dhuriyya* normally means "progeny," but seems here to refer to their progenitors who were in the ark with Noah.

9. See Sura 15, Note 8.

10. I.e., he will go back to a second childhood, becoming more childlike the older he grows.

Sura 71: page 111

1. The commentators say that Wadd was an idol in the form of a beautiful youth, Suwa an idol in the form of a

woman, Yaghuth in the form of a lion, Ya'uq in the form of a horse, and Nasr in the form of an eagle. It is at least curious that the Babylonian goddess Ishtar had as paramours Tammuz, a beautiful youth, a lion, a horse, and a great bird. Wadd, Yaghuth, and Nasr have been found as god-names in the South Arabian inscriptions.

2. This seems to mean that they were judged and condemned to the Fire immediately after death and did not have to wait for the Final Judgment.

Sura 17: page 113

1. Since early Islamic times these two shrines have been identified as the Temple in Mecca and the Temple at Jerusalem. Legend has luxuriated around this Night Journey that Mohammed made, on a winged steed named Buraq, in company with Gabriel, from Mecca to Jerusalem, where he led the assembled prophets in prayer, and during which he was given his vision of heaven and hell. One particular account of this Night Journey has had no little influence on the structure of parts of Dante's *Divina Commedia*. There is every reason to believe, however, that the "further sanctuary" was only a place of worship some little distance from the city, and which Mohammed used at times to frequent, and so the original reference in this verse was to a perfectly prosaic terrestrial event.

2. This would seem to refer to two periods of great religious decline, and two periods of great religious exaltation, but what these were in Mohammed's mind is a matter about which we can only conjecture. The two violations of the sanctuary by the enemy might suggest the armies of Antiochus in 170 B.C. and of Titus in 70 A.D., or perhaps the two violations by the Babylonians in 597 and 586 B.C.

3. From very ancient days in the Near East the idea has been widespread among the common folk that a man's

fate, as decreed by the gods, appears in bird form.

4. An expression of contempt. In Sura 21 Abraham uses it to his idolatrous contemporaries, and in Sura 46 there is reference to an unbelieving son who used the expression to his believing parents.

5. The injunction is against being too niggardly on the one hand and extravagantly liberal on the other.

6. *nafs* could be translated "person," but it is the common word for "soul," and the idea here is that man has no right to take the *nafs* of another save under certain justifiable circumstances. If a man has been killed without there being such justification, his next-of-kin *(waliy)* has the right of blood-revenge, a life for a life, but he is warned against making extravagant use of this right, for after all it was Allah who aided him by granting him this right.

7. This is usually taken to mean that at Judgment one will be questioned as to one's faithfulness in the matter of covenants one has made. It could mean, however, that covenants are matters that may come up for questioning in human community life, although the second verse following tips the balance in favour of thinking that Mohammed had the Judgment Day in mind.

8. *Zabur* may mean merely "Book," but it is probably meant to represent the Hebrew *mizmor*, "psalm." The superiority of some prophets over others is said to mean that some were sent merely to preach, whereas others were given a Book of Scripture in which Allah's message to mankind was recorded.

9. Those Commentators who regard the Night Journey of the opening verse as a vision, consider that that is the vision referred to here; but it is much more likely to refer to the vision whereby he was called to his prophetic mission. What the reference to the Lord being round about His people is we do not know, but the accursed tree is generally taken

to refer to the tree Zaqqum (Sura 37, Note 11).

10. This word *imam* is often translated "leaders," but it is singular not plural, and seems rather to mean the Codex in which the record of men's deeds is to be found.

11. A *fatil* is the thread of fibre in the cleft of a date-stone, and so is used to suggest a thing so small and valueless as to be insignificant, as we might say: "They will not be wronged a fly-speck."

12. This and what follows seem certainly to be a reference to the matter contained in Sura 53, Section 2.

13. This must refer to Meccan attempts to oust the Prophet. Other ancient peoples, he says, had tried to do the same thing, and it was immediately after their rejection of their messenger that they were destroyed.

14. Suras 78, Note 6; 32, Note 1; 16, Note 1.

15. This threat of causing the sky to fall in pieces on them is made in Sura 34.

16. *Sa'ir* is one of the names of Hell, but here it may be merely a common noun and mean: "We shall make Gehenna a fiercer blaze for them."

17. Lit., "magnify Him a magnifying" (*takbir*), which has come to mean making use of the phrase *Allahu akbar*, "Allah is very great," which is thus a very brief Islamic magnificat.

Late Meccan Suras

Sura 32: page 124

1. *amr* means "matter," "affair," but also means "command." In Sura 17, Ref. 14, we read that the mysterious Spirit belongs to the *amr* of Allah, and Sura 70 speaks of the angels and the Spirit mounting up to Allah in a day whose length is fifty thousand years, so it seems almost certain that the *amr* here, like the Rabbinic *memra*, is concerned with the Spirit of God.

2. A common euphemism for the male semen.

3. The commentators say that a particular individual, al-Walid b. Uqba, is pointed to in this verse, but this identification is doubtless only a later invention.

4. *Imams*, the reference being to the Elders of whom we read in Numbers XI, 16 ff., as appointed to help Moses, though some think that the reference is to the judges who judged Israel before Saul became the first Israelitish king.

5. *fath* is from the root meaning "to open," and since it is a name of the Last Day it may mean the opening up of all matters preliminary to Judgment. *fath* also, however, came to be a word technically used for conquest, and is so used in particular for the conquest of Mecca in the year 8 A.H., so it is possible that this is a reference to the day when Mohammed will take Mecca, and the sudden change from unbelief to belief on that day will not avail those who have all the time disbelieved.

Sura 16: page 126

1. Here the Spirit concerned with Allah's *amr* is definitely connected with the sending of Allah's messengers, which the Moslem divines take as confirmation of their identification of the Spirit with Gabriel. In the Old Testament, however, it is the Spirit of God who is associated with the sending of the Prophets. Thus the Spirit of God came on Saul and he prophesied (I Samuel X, 10), and Isaiah says that the Lord God and His Spirit had sent him (Isaiah XLVIII, 16).

2. *sakhkhara* means to make a thing subject so that it may serve. The idea is that Allah has made these things serve man usefully.

3. This passage seems to be addressed to the People of the Book.

4. This is in contradiction with the oft-repeated statement that no burdened soul will bear the burden of another. But that statement seems meant to exclude hope in a Redeemer who will take on himself the guilt of others, whereas here the meaning is that some of the guilt of those led

astray will be placed on those who have led them astray.

5. These two verses are clearly Medinan and are intended to encourage more of the Prophet's followers to emigrate from Mecca to Medina.

6. I.e., the Jews and Christians who have Scriptures. "Reminder" here, as in many other passages, is but another name for Scripture, one of whose main functions is to remind men of their Lord. In the next verse Mohammed's revelation is also called the "Reminder."

7. This is sometimes taken to be a warning against Zoroastrian dualism, but that is extremely unlikely.

8. I.e., they have the sons they always desire but give Allah only daughters. Cf. Sura 53, Section 2.

9. Viz., daughters.

10. Margoliouth has suggested that this is a reference to the story of Penelope.

11. This is the basis for the custom, followed universally in Islam, of always saying: "I take refuge with Allah from Satan the stoned" before commencing any reading or recitation of the Koran. The epithet "stoned" doubtless derives from an ancient ritual of lapidation, but is commonly said to be a reminiscence of how Abraham drove Satan away with stones when he tried to tempt him not to sacrifice his son.

12. This is one of the three famous verses in the Koran which support the doctrine of Abrogation, the doctrine, namely, that certain verses of the Koran abrogate others. This doctrine has had considerable importance in Moslem jurisprudence, and has given rise to a whole section of the Moslem Massora on "the Abrogating and the Abrogated" *(an-Nasikh wa'l-Mansukh)*.

13. It is clear that the Prophet's opponents knew that there was some non-Arab in the community with whom Mohammed was in contact and from whom they suspected he was getting his Biblical stories. The Commentaries give a number of names in this connection. The Prophet's answer to the charge is a very curious one, for what foreigner could have lived in that community without being able to speak Arabic? The Spirit of Holiness in the previous verse has, of course, been identified with Gabriel, though it is an accurate translation of the Syriac for "Holy Spirit" in the Biblical sense.

14. It is commonly thought that the reference here is to Mecca, so the punishment would be its capture by Mohammed in the year 7 A.H.

15. This is the same problem as that of the meat offered to idols with which St. Paul deals in I Corinthians, X, 18 ff. The verb *ahalla* used here is the cognate of that in Hebrew which is familiar to us from the word *Hallelujah*. As an animal was sacrificed the name of a deity was pronounced as a *Hallel,* and Mohammed's followers are here warned against accepting meat over which any name other than that of Allah has been pronounced.

16. The Jewish dietary restrictions are given in the passage now included in Sura 6.

17. *umma* is a community of people, and doubtless Abraham is here called an *umma* because of the promise in Genesis XXII, 17, 18. The word *hanif* has always been a puzzle. It is derived from the Syriac *hanpe,* "heathen," but was apparently used by Mohammed to mean a monotheist.

18. *milla,* from the Syriac *meltha,* "word," is used to mean religion in the sense of a formulated set of religious principles. The word is familiar to us from the fact that under the Ottoman Empire the non-Moslem elements in the population of the Caliph's dominions were governed each as a separate *milla.* The word is used by Joseph in Sura 12 and occurs also in Sura 2 (Ref. 9).

19. The probabilities are that this refers to local disputing over the Jewish and the Christian Sabbath.

20. The commentators say that this verse refers to the desire of the Mos-

lems to exact vengeance for the death of Hamza, the Prophet's uncle, who was slain at the battle of Uhud in the year 3 A.H.

Sura 30: page 138

1. It is commonly held that this refers to one of the many conflicts in North Arabia between the Byzantines and their Arab allies and the Sassanians and their Arab allies. As spelled in the *textus receptus* it mentions a Byzantine defeat and predicts their coming victory. According to the spelling in a variant reading of early date, however, it refers to a Byzantine victory and a prediction of their coming defeat. We have no means of deciding to what event the passage refers, and the suggestions of the commentators are but guesses. The mention of "the nearer part of the land," however, shows that it was a conflict on Arabian territory.

2. These two verses are said to indicate four times for prayer daily, whereas in earlier passages in the Koran only morning and evening prayer are mentioned, with perhaps a suggestion of a third prayer period.

3. Two different words for "creation" are used here, first *fitra* and then *khalq*. The verse is saying that the Hanif religion is the natural inborn religion of every man, with which he was created, just as he was created with an inborn impulse to eat and drink. Since Islam is identified with this inborn religion the claim is being made that it is the natural religion for mankind.

4. See Sura 17, Section 4.

5. This obviously follows on the second verse preceding, so there is a transposition here, and the preceding verse probably belongs with the next section.

6. This verse possibly should follow the last section but one, finishing off the signs-passage.

7. The meaning seems to be that in this life they were so involved in false conceptions that it was quite natural they should similarly be involved in falsity at the Resurrection.

Sura 31: page 144

1. The commentators say that this is a reference to one an-Nadr b. al-Harith who drew the people away from Mohammed's preaching by reciting to them the Persian histories of Rustum and Alexander the Great. Those threatened with punishment are those who make mock of Mohammed's message.

2. Hirschfeld has suggested that the name Luqman derives from Mohammed's informant misreading the name Solomon, in which case Luqman's instructions to his son would be a vague remembrance of the opening of the Book of Proverbs. In a text written in Syriac the name Solomon might possibly be misread as Luqman, but not in a Hebrew text.

3. These two Medinan verses break in on Luqman's advice to his son, which continues in the next passage. Perhaps these verses belong at the end of the next passage.

4. One of the names of Hell-fire. See Note 2 to Sura 84.

5. See Sura 18, last verse but one.

6. *al-gahrur* is one of the names of Satan.

7. These characteristic examples of things which are beyond man's power to know, but which Allah well knows, are indications that He will also know all about when the Hour is to arrive. Some have suggested that we have a reminiscence of those "words of Agur" contained in Proverbs XXX, 18, 19.

Sura 12: page 147

1. See Genesis XXXVII, 9, where, however, this is the second of Joseph's dreams. The first dream may not have been told to Mohammed by his informant, or he may have omitted it in telling the story. The commentators, of course, know the names of all the eleven stars.

2. A *jubb* is a large catchment cistern for water, such as are to be found along

the caravan trails. The unidentified speaker was Reuben. Mohammed was always chary of using proper names so that it does not necessarily follow that he had forgotten the name. It will be noted that Benjamin is always "his brother" and is never mentioned by name.

3. The suggestion is that it was the rough camel-men who seized Joseph and concealed him amidst the baggage from the eyes of the leaders of the caravan. For this reason they had to sell him off cheaply on their arrival in Egypt before they were found out. In Genesis XXVII, 28, it is his brothers who sell him to the Ishmaelites (=Midianites) and the Ishmaelites who sell him in Egypt.

4. Others take this to refer not to Allah but to his Egyptian master, whom he might quite naturally call his lord, as he does later.

5. The commentators know the Rabbinic legend of how he was saved from sinning by seeing an apparition of his old father.

6. This, we are told, was a babe that was lying in its cradle, and this is said to be one of the four cases where infants in the cradle have spoken.

7. The reference of the pronoun is ambiguous in the original. Some translate it: "So Satan caused him (i.e., Joseph) to forget the remembrance of his Lord (i.e., Allah), so he remained in prison some years" longer for the sin of putting his trust in man instead of in Allah. The original story, however, had it that the released servant forgot to mention Joseph to Pharaoh till the incident of the dream reminded him of the dream-interpretations he had heard in prison.

8. There is a hint of impatience as though the courtiers feel they are there for consultation on important matters of State, and are somewhat put out at being expected to explain tangled confusions of the ruler's dreams.

9. *suwa* means an elegant goblet of gold or silver. Two verses back the word was *siqaya*, which might have been used for any kind of drinking vessel. *suwa* occurs only in this passage, and some think that it was not a drinking vessel, but the prince's divining cup.

10. This charge that Joseph also in his youth had been guilty of theft is explained by the commentators in a way that absolves Joseph of any guilt. It may, however, be a reflection of a Midrashic legend, or it may be a confusion with the story of Rachel's stealing the teraphim, in which case the brothers are saying: "Well, it could be that he is a thief, for his mother was a thief." In this verse Joseph suggests that they are trying to get out of their plight by raking up an old scandal.

11. Judah. See Genesis XLIV.

12. I.e., the excessive weeping had caused him to go blind, and this blindness was cured by Joseph's miraculous shirt. It is still believed in the Orient that prolonged weeping causes a white integument to form over the eyes.

13. Both Jewish and Moslem legend have made much of this miraculous shirt of Joseph. There is little doubt that it derives from the "coat of many colours" of Genesis XXXVII, 3, but legend makes it a shirt that Adam brought with him from Paradise and which came down to the Patriarchs.

14. Joseph's mother, of course, had long since passed away (Genesis XXXV, 19), but apparently that had not been made clear in the tale as Mohammed received it from his informants. Some have suggested that the reference is to Bilhah, but the Rabbinic legend which makes her appear before Joseph in Egypt is late.

There is a time interval between the events of this verse, in which he has his parents with him in private, and the next verse where they appear before him as he sits in his official seat of authority, where all who enter his presence must do obeisance. The verse does not mean that he took them in to see Pharaoh.

15. "Their story" must mean the story of Joseph and his brethren and refer back to the first verse of this section ("This is one of . . ."). As such it is said to be a confirmation of the Scripture account of Joseph in the hands of the People of the Book.

Sura 19: page 158

1. In spite of the insistence of the commentators that the Lord whom Zachariah addresses in the following verses is Allah, as in the preceding verses, it must be Gabriel (cf. Luke I, 19) who speaks here and in the second and third verses following. This ought to be clear from the fact that he tells Zachariah what his Lord has said about the matter. In the parallel account in Sura 3 it is angels who announce the good tidings of John, and there again it must be Gabriel who is addressed and who replies.

2. This clearly represents the family objection to the introduction of a new name, as recorded in Luke I, 61. It could not be, as many Moslems assert, a reference to the fact that Yahya, as it is pointed in the *textus receptus*, was a name for John the Baptist unknown earlier than the Koran.

3. This may refer to his mastery of the Old Testament Scriptures, or it may mean that in Mohammed's thought John was one of those messengers who had a Book. There is but small likelihood that it is a reference to the Mandaean *Book of John*.

4. This is a clear indication that the Prophet was now working up his revelation material into a Book form, which would be a Scripture for his community such as the Jews and the Christians had. The sentence is thus almost certainly from the Medinan period when the Prophet was busy at such a project.

5. In the *Protevangelium Jacobi*, X there is an account of how Mary worked at the making of a curtain for the temple of the Lord; and as it is specifically said that she did the work on this in her home, this curtain has here been interpreted to be a curtain to veil herself off from her people.

The commentators, of course, take "Our Spirit" to mean Gabriel, for he was the one who appeared before Mary in human form; but there is clearly a confusion here between Gabriel who made the announcement, and the Holy Spirit who in the Gospel story (Luke I, 35) was to come to her. In Sura 21 it is "Our Spirit" of which Allah breathes into Mary's womb to produce Jesus, and there the reference to the Holy Spirit of the Gospels is clear.

In the next verse, the last word is *taqiy* in Arabic, meaning "a pious person," "one who is God-fearing." The use of the word in this passage is a well-known problem of interpretation. But *Taqiy* is also used as a personal name. Some think that it is so used here, and that Mary thought that Gabriel, when he suddenly appeared, was a local "lady-killer" named Taqiy, from whom she sought refuge with Allah. Others think that "if" here means "unless." The usual interpretation, however, is that she meant: "I take refuge with Allah from you, *and* if you are really a pious person *you will respect my betaking myself to Him.*"

6. The commentators are divided as to whether it was Gabriel, standing somewhat lower down, who called to her, or the newly born babe.

7. That is, Mohammed has confused Mary (=Maryam) the mother of Jesus, with Miriam (=Maryam) the sister of Moses and Aaron. This is confirmed by the last verse of Sura 66, where Mary is called the daughter of Amram; for in Exodus VI, 20, Amram is the father of Moses and Aaron.

8. As in Sura 26, Ref. 4, it may here also mean "a high reputation."

9. Or "the mountain," as in Sura 20, Ref. 9.

10. Idris is usually taken to be the Biblical Enoch. This identification fits well enough, though there is reason to believe that he really represents Andreas, the pious cook of Alexander the Great.

11. Here and in Sura 3, Israel is the name

of an individual, and is doubtless Jacob who, as the ancestor of the Children of Israel, is called Israel in Genesis XXXII, 28.

12. The two parties here seem to be the Koreish who ruled over pagan Mecca, and the Moslems who were now beginning to be a recognizable body in the community, but a body made up of only the humbler folk whom the Koreish leaders despised. *Nadiy* might almost have been translated "Senate." It was the ruling Council or Assembly that directed the city affairs.

13. The commentators, of course, know who this individual is, but their statements have little claim to be taken as historically valid.

14. There is a contrast here between *wafd* in the preceding verse, which means an official delegation coming in orderly manner and received with due honour, and *wird*, which means a disorderly herd of cattle being driven down to a watering place.

Medinan Suras

Sura 98: page 166

1. These purified sheets are commonly taken to be a reference to the heavenly archetype of Scripture, but elsewhere that is called a *tablet*, not *sheets*. The probability is that while in Medina Mohammed had begun to write out the material for his Book, and so the reference here is to these "sheets," which he claims have on them Scripture material as truly as the sheets which make up the Books of the Jews and the Christians.

Sura 48: page 169

1. Bell, in a note on Sura 32, shows that this word *fath* comes to be used by the Prophet not only for military victories, such as that at Badr, but for Allah's clearing away difficulties and opening up the path for the success of his mission.

2. *sakina* might here mean nothing more than "repose," but as there is evidence in Sura 2 that Mohammed in this Medinan period had learned about the Jewish *shekinah*, it is probable that that has influenced its meaning in this Sura and in Sura 9, so perhaps it had best be translated "spirit of tranquillity."

3. Since the pronoun with the verb "give glory" must refer to Allah, some take the other two pronouns as also referring to Allah, and so translate: "aid Him, and honour Him, and give glory to Him." It seems more likely, however, that the two former refer to the Prophet.

4. Lit., "blaze," one of the names of Hell-fire.

5. I.e., there had already been a "revelation" from Allah as to who was and who was not to take part in the expedition against Khaibar.

6. This was at Hudaibiyya.

7. I.e., there was no interference with their taking the booty.

8. This verse seems to have been written after Mecca had been taken (opened) in the year 8 A.H.

9. The construction of the verse is very clumsy, but it means that when the Meccans were preventing the Moslems from approaching the Kaaba with their sacrifices, Allah could have let the Moslems attack and gain a victory, but this would have meant that many believers in Mecca, who were unknown to the Moslems coming from Medina, might have suffered in the strife, and Moslems would thereby have become guilty of killing other Moslems. Had these Meccan Moslems been separated out, Allah might have allowed the unbelieving Meccans to be punished; but as it was, He laid down the command of restraint.

10. The Gospel reference would be to Mark IV, 28. The Torah reference is more difficult to identify, though some have suggested Deuteronomy VI, 8; XI, 18.

Sura 66: page 173

1. The story is that Hafsa found the Prophet with his concubine Mary the Copt after he had sworn to have

nothing more to do with the girl. Hafsa promised to say nothing about it, but presently told Ayesha, who made trouble over the matter and apparently combined with Hafsa against the Prophet. The next two verses urge these two to repent, and the passage holds out a threat of divorce against the outraged harem.

2. The pronoun here is plural, not dual, and so must refer to the whole harem.

3. The stones are said to mean the sacred stones which were so commonly taken as sacred objects in ancient Arabia that Clement of Alexandria could conclude that the worship of the ancient Arabs was a litholatry.

4. In these Medinan passages the word *munafiqun* (hypocrites) has become practically a technical term for that group in the Medinan community who made a show of being on the side of the Moslems though in their hearts they had no belief in the Prophet or in his mission. See Sura 48, sixth verse.

5. The story of Lot's wife is told in the Koran in a number of other Suras. The reference to Noah's wife must go back to some tale of her quarrelling with her husband over the ark, or maybe Mohammed has confused her with some other woman.

6. In Sura 28 it is Pharaoh's wife who takes Moses in and protects him.

7. See Sura 19, Note 7. This is the oft-quoted verse from the Koran which supports the Christian doctrine of the Virgin Birth of Jesus.

Sura 2: page 175

1. This is usually taken to mean the leaders of their community, and if this passage is directed against the Jews, then their religious leaders.

2. This discussion with the angels before creation is Mohammed's version of a Rabbinic legend based on the "Let Us make man" of Genesis I, 26, but which the use of the name Iblis shows must have come to him from Christian sources.

3. The verb means "to pronounce the word *quddus*," i.e., we are those who sing: "Holy! Holy! Holy! to Thee." For this reason Rodwell translates "extoll Thy holiness."

4. Since the pronoun is plural, not dual, the command is taken to mean that Adam and Eve and Satan are to make their exit, and the enmity is not between man and wife but between humans and Satan.

5. Though Adam was cast out of Paradise he was not left without guidance, and since he had now to live a life on earth Allah gave him some instructions as a Rule of Life. That is why Adam is regarded as the first in that line of prophets who had a message from Allah for human guidance.

6. This is another reference to the doctrine of Abrogation mentioned in Sura 16, Ref. 12.

7. As a few verses earlier, "those who have no knowledge" means the pagans as contrasted with the People of the Book. Constantly in the Koran we find "knowledge" used in the particular sense of religious knowledge (cf. the second verse following), and at times it is practically the equivalent of "Scripture." So here it is the pagans who have no Scripture who are contrasted with the People of the Book who have.

8. *Jahim*, as already noticed, is a name for Hell-fire, and the point here is that on the Day Mohammed will not be responsible for those to whom he has preached who prove to be among the Damned condemned to Hell-fire.

9. *milla;* see Sura 16, Note 18.

10. See Sura 16, Note 17.

11. The verb means "to dye a cloth a deep colour," so this noun seems to mean that true religion steeps a man, as it were, in Allah, much as a cloth is steeped in a dye-vat, so that he is dyed with Allah's dye. Rodwell translates it "baptism."

12. This and the following verses refer to the change in the kiblah, or direction to which one turns in prayer during worship, a change which took

place in the second year of the Hegira. Before that time Mohammed had been accustomed to face Jerusalem in his daily public prayers with his followers, but after his breach with the Jews he had them turn in prayers to face the shrine in his own city, Mecca, i.e., the Kaaba, which is still the kiblah to which all Moslems turn in prayer.

13. Some say that this refers to the false gods, the "substitutes" (andad) of the previous verse, but others think that it refers to the leaders of the religious sects.

14. Anything that is found already dead and that has not been properly killed for food according to the ritual prescriptions.

15. See Sura 16, Note 15.

16. Ramadan is the ninth month of the Moslem year. In the old Arabian solar year it would seem to have been one of the summer months, but in the Moslem lunar year it now moves gradually through all the seasons.

17. Furqan is the Syriac perqana, "salvation," and would seem here (as in Suras 3 and 25) to be another name for the Koran, though elsewhere in this Sura (as in Sura 21) it was something given to Moses and Aaron.

18. The hajj is the greater pilgrimage which comes annually at the pilgrimage season, and by the performance of which a Moslem becomes a Hajji. The umra is the lesser pilgrimage, or visitation of the sacred Shrine. In pre-Islamic times the umra was concerned particularly with the sacred spots in Mecca itself, and the hajj more particularly with those beyond the city limits. In Islam, however, there has come about a combination of the two, though the lesser pilgrimage may be performed independently at any time of the year. The hady is the name for the victim set apart for sacrifice as part of the pilgrimage ceremonial.

19. Arafat is a hill, some little distance to the east of Mecca, standing on which is an integral part of the full pilgrimage ceremonial. The pilgrims hear a sermon there, slaughter their victims, and then at great speed hasten towards Muzdalifa where stands the "sacred monument" at which other ceremonies must be observed. On all this see Burton's Pilgrimage to al-Madinah and Meccah, 2 vols. London, 1919, a detailed account by the most famous of all the Christian pilgrims who have made the journey to Mecca in disguise.

20. This is the Throne Verse, as popular among Moslem children as "Now I lay me down to sleep" has been with Christian children.

21. This apparently means that some were disturbed by the law forbidding usury, because they had money out on which they had still to collect, and so such are here bidden to cut their loss.

Sura 102: page 191

1. Al-Jahim, "the hot place," has already been noted as one of the names of Hell.

2. This refers to the questioning at Judgment, when each soul will be examined on the record of its earthly life before being adjudged to Paradise or Hell.

Sura 4: page 193

1. Lit., "blaze," one of the names of Hell-fire.

2. qintar is the Latin centenarium, which came into Arabic from Byzantine Greek through Syriac.

3. I.e., such unions contracted before a man became a Moslem need not be dissolved, but no one as a Moslem may contract such a union. In pre-Islamic Arabia apparently it was not regarded as incestuous to marry wives left by one's father other than one's own mother.

4. A Moslem is forbidden to enter into wedlock with a married woman who already has a husband, save in the case of women taken as captives, in which case their capture is considered to dissolve automatically the previous

marriage. "What your right hands possess" is a euphemism for slaves.

5. Here, as in a section of Sura 2, the Children of Israel tell Moses that they will not believe till they have seen Allah openly and so He destroyed them by the thunderbolt. This seems to derive from a misunderstanding of the account in Exodus XIX, 14-25. The raising of the mountain over them, which is mentioned also in Sura 2, seems to be a deformation of some Jewish legend about the giving of the Law at Sinai.

6. This killing of the prophets is a New Testament charge against the Jews (see Matthew XXIII, 37), and as the next verse goes on to speak of the calumny against Mary, one would suspect that Mohammed had been listening to what his Christian informants had to say about the Jews. However, since the passage goes on to state that it was not Jesus who was crucified, but someone else in his likeness, it is clear that his contact in this case must have been with Gnostics, perhaps Manichaeans, who denied the crucifixion of Jesus and whose anti-Jewish feelings were notorious.

7. Since Jesus did not die in this life, Islamic orthodoxy teaches that at his second coming he will die as all mortals do, but before his death all will come to believe in him, and he will be an important witness at the Judgment.

Sura 5: page 200

1. It is true that no Christians known to history ever claimed that God was the Messiah, though they did claim that the Messiah was God; but there is no other way of translating the sentence, so one must conclude that this is how Mohammed understood what he heard from his Christian informants.

2. The *fatra*, or breach in the prophetic series, seems to have been quite a problem to various religious groups, and Mohammed's claim here is that he has come to end the break and give a new message from the Lord.

3. See Numbers XIII, 31-33.

4. It is noteworthy that Mohammed considered the doctrine of Hell-fire to have been known even to the first generation of mankind.

5. Opinions differ as to what is meant here. Some think that the shameful deed done to his brother is the "shame," others that the exposed corpse of his brother was a shame, or that it was a shameful thing that his brother was no longer alive. The raven story is drawn from Rabbinic legend, though there it is Adam who is troubled about what to do with the dead body of Abel till he sees a raven bury another dead raven and thus learns how to dispose of the dead.

6. This derives from the Talmud, where in connection with the Cain and Abel story we find this statement in *Sanhedrin* IV, 5, with which may be compared *Kiddushin* I.

7. See Exodus XXI, 23-27.

8. *shir'a* means the same as *shari'a*, which is the usual word for the system of rules and regulations by which a practising Moslem should guide his daily life. The verse thus means that Jews and Christians and other religious communities all had their "rule of life" given them from above.

9. This does not mean that the Prophet is abrogating those food restrictions, modelled on those of the Jews, which he had earlier bidden his community observe (see Sura 16, Ref. 15; Sura 2, Refs. 14, 15; Sura 5, opening verses, not included here). What the Prophet has in mind here are excessive restrictions such as those practised by Christian ascetics.

10. The commentators tell us that this was a form of gambling very popular among the Arabs. The idol-stones and the arrows certainly refer to the casting of lots and making divination at shrines. Some strict Moslems have interpreted the idol-stones *(ansab)* as prohibiting the game of chess, the pieces of which are carved images.

11. This refers to those who have put themselves in sacral state for the pur-

pose of performing the rites of pilgrimage.

12. Note how the Gospel is regarded as something already in existence and taught to Jesus just as he was taught the Torah. Mohammed had quite failed to learn from his Christian informants that Jesus himself was the Gospel, or good news of salvation. His speaking from the cradle was mentioned toward the end of the first section of Sura 19, and it and the story of his giving life to clay figures that he made when a child are drawn from the Apocryphal Gospels. The holding back of the Children of Israel from him may be a reference to the incident when he preached in his home town of Nazareth as recorded in Luke IV, 28-30.

13. In this passage there is a curious confusion of the Lord's Supper with the table Peter saw in his vision in Acts X.

14. This would seem to indicate that Mariolatry was practised by the Christians known to Mohammed. As the word used here for "disciples" is the Ethiopic word *hawariyun,* this may well have been what he learned of Christianity from slaves of Abyssinian origin in the Hejaz.

The Closers

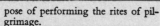

Sura 113: page 207

1. In these two Suras, as in the Opening Sura, it is man addressing Allah, and not Allah addressing man, the "Say" having been inserted to keep up the illusion that these are all words of Allah. It is not impossible to think that they were composed by the Prophet himself, but they were not included in some of the early Codices, and their present position is certainly due to the compilers.

2. Some think that this refers not to the dusk which falls each night, but to the duskiness caused by an eclipse. Others, on the ground that *ghasaqa* means "to come down like fine rain," suggest that the reference is to nocturnal emissions.

3. This is said to mean the magic practices of the "wise women" who worked spells of binding by tying knots in a string and blowing thereon. Those who see a sexual meaning in the previous verse see one also here, and think that the reference is to the "knotting" of the male that reduces him to impotence.

4. The eye of envy, the "green eye," is of course the Evil Eye, so that is the evil against which protection is here sought.

Sura 114: page 207

1. *khanasa* is "to hide oneself," and this "lurking whisperer" is usually taken to mean Satan, so that *al-Khannas* is listed as one of Satan's names.

2. *an-nas* is "men," but also "the people," as in the title of the Sura.